Jesus' BIG idea

Living in the Days of the Kingdom

Eric B. Carpenter

Illustrations by Paul Didier

Springs Community Church | Colorado Springs, Colorado | www.SpringsCommunityChurch.org

Published by: Springs Community Church, Colorado Springs, Colorado

All personal names have been changed to ensure privacy.

JESUS' BIG IDEA: LIVING IN THE DAYS OF THE KINGDOM

All Scripture is taken from the NIV unless otherwise noted.

Cover and interior design by Mike Riester

ISBN: 978-0-615-42290-9

10 9 8 7 6 5 4 3 2 11 12 13 14 15 15 16 17 18 19 20

For information, write to:
Springs Community Church, 7290 Lexington Drive, Colorado Springs, CO 80918

To order additional copies of this book, contact Springs Community Church at the address above or online at: SpringsCommunityChurch.org.

Contents

PREFACE

My first glimpses of the kingdom as Jesus' *big idea* came following a training for *The Alpha Course*. "*Alpha* is successful because it has the seeds of the Kingdom of God within it," the trainers said. Although I was a seminary-trained pastor and had been in ministry for several years, I realized that I didn't understand what the *kingdom* really was. The Spirit prompted me to study the Scriptures in depth and find out. I began in the Gospels and there it was, central to everything Jesus said and did—his *big idea.* Soon I was searching throughout the entire Bible, hungry for more of his kingdom. Though I feel the vast majority of my early discoveries of the kingdom came from my personal times in the Scriptures, I am now greatly indebted to many of the theologians and pastors that have gone before me. I would like to say a special thanks to John Wimber and George Eldon Ladd. Though they are now with our heavenly Father, I have been discipled through their excellent writings.

Living in the kingdom means living in community, in the body of Christ. Although I could try to *go it alone*, I needed to explore Jesus' big idea together with others. So special thanks go to the people at Beechwood RCA Church in Holland, MI, and especially to my small group. These were the brave folks who first ventured into studying and living in the days of the kingdom with me. I am also grateful to the people of Living Springs Community in Glenwood, IL and New Hope Church in Pueblo, CO. Both worked through the materials as church congregations before this ministry training manual was even near completion. My present congregation, Springs Community Church in Colorado Springs, CO, has walked through many personal challenges with me, as well as grappling with Jesus' big idea. I thank them for continuing to love and seek the kingdom.

I greatly appreciate my chief editor Marilyn Henne and her assistant, Sharon Hartman, whose tireless efforts, attention to detail and good humor kept this project on track. They believed in the material and its potential for transformation and renewal in people's lives. That's enough to keep any author going! I am grateful for all the others who have given wise counsel and contributed countless hours to the final product, especially Mike Riester. Mike's skills and dedication produced the final graphic design. Alice Gifford did the original graphics. Mike Kennedy and Rex Schultz served as publication consultants. Gladys Linthicum and Judy Butler (friends of the editor) reviewed the manuscript with a fine-toothed proof-reader's comb. David Henne did the final proofreading. Amazingly, the Lord provided from within the Springs Community Church family most of the expertise and willingness needed to bring this book to fruition.

Many of my pastor friends have also played a role in the development of this discipleship training manual. Bruce Bugbee often shared his practical wisdom. Tim Vink, more than any other, mentored me in thinking, praying and living in the Kingdom of God.

Eric B. Carpenter
Colorado Springs
Thanksgiving 2010

Foreword

The Gospel, the good news, is not about the Church. It's about the kingdom. It is the power of this good news of God's kingdom that creates the Church, capital "C". Gospel precedes Church. Unfortunately, today's American church has often become more about building up a particular church—its numbers and its programs—than about expanding God's kingdom. Eric Carpenter's work in *Jesus' Big Idea: Living in the Days of the Kingdom* sorts out the chaff in our church views to see more clearly the freedom and power of the kingdom that has already come in our midst but doesn't yet exist in its fullness. I applaud him calling it the *already but not yet* kingdom with all that implies about the Holy Spirit's ministry among us today.

My own life ministry has been aligning the body of Christ by getting the right people in the right places through their God-given ministry passions and spiritual gifts. This produces a vibrant, healthy body of Christ who can do the work of the kingdom. Eric lifts our eyes to see through the Church we serve to the kingdom that has called us.

Jesus' Big Idea: Living in the Days of the Kingdom is a much-needed clarifying journey for every follower of Christ and child of the kingdom. This is especially a MUST for leaders, small groups and ministry teams.

Bruce Bugbee
Regional Executive,
Reformed Church in America, Far West Region
November 11, 2010

Author: *What You Do Best in the Body of Christ: Discover Your Spiritual Gifts, Personal Style, and God-Given Passion*

Foreword

The Gospel, the good news, is not about the Church. It's about the kingdom. It is the power of this good news of God's kingdom that creates the Church, capital "C". Gospel precedes Church. Unfortunately, today's American church has often become more about building up a particular church—its numbers and its programs—than about expanding God's kingdom. Eric Carpenter's work in *Jesus' Big Idea: Living in the Days of the Kingdom* sorts out the chaff in our church views to see more clearly the freedom and power of the kingdom that has already come in our midst but doesn't yet exist in its fullness. I applaud him calling it the *already but not yet* kingdom with all that implies about the Holy Spirit's ministry among us today.

My own life ministry has been aligning the body of Christ by getting the right people in the right places through their God-given ministry passions and spiritual gifts. This produces a vibrant, healthy body of Christ who can do the work of the kingdom. Eric lifts our eyes to see through the Church we serve to the kingdom that has called us.

Jesus' Big Idea: Living in the Days of the Kingdom is a much-needed clarifying journey for every follower of Christ and child of the kingdom. This is especially a MUST for leaders, small groups and ministry teams.

Bruce Bugbee
Regional Executive,
Reformed Church in America, Far West Region
November 11, 2010

Author: *What You Do Best in the Body of Christ: Discover Your Spiritual Gifts, Personal Style, and God-Given Passion*

Introduction

Welcome to *Jesus' Big Idea: Living in the Days of the Kingdom* (*JBI*). The Lord motivated me to write this book through my personal experiences with him during these last several years. Paul encourages us in Romans 12:2, *Do not conform any longer to the pattern of this world, but be transformed by the renewing of your mind.* God birthed this study through his renewal of my mind. I feel as though I have stepped afresh into the school of the Holy Spirit. It has been a tremendous, personal experience, seeing the Bible transformed as though I were reading parts of it for the very first time. Often, I would set the Scriptures down and worship, as my spirit gave thanks for the living and redemptive Word moving through me. My deepest hope and desire is that over the course of these *kingdom days*, God will renew your mind. I long for your faith to be further rooted and grounded in Christ by seeing his words in a fresh way, thus gaining new perspectives, and even beginning some revolutionary practices.

> I long for your faith to be further rooted and grounded in Christ by seeing His words in a fresh way.

JBI has also been written from the humbling realization that for so long I have missed much of the Christian life and faith. Even though I am a practicing Christian and seminary-educated pastor, I have been amazed at my oblivion about so much of Christ's core teaching and its implications. Although I am a product of the modern western church, I am also writing from my personal conviction that much of our contemporary church has missed this core teaching as well. I believe much of the church has missed the *big idea* of Jesus' teaching, and therefore, missed out on much of the ministry and life that he calls us to live as "the church" in our world. *JBI* is not meant to be a critique of the church, but rather to help us be more biblical in our beliefs and convictions, our lives and practices. Since enrolling in the "school of the Holy Spirit," I have realized that I have ministered previously with numerous blind spots and unbiblical perspectives. Many of these, of course, were a product of my education and culture. Because of this, I want these *kingdom days* to focus us anew on Jesus' original message and ministry for the church. It is a lofty desire, one that I believe is at the center of Jesus' heart for every generation of his followers.

So, let's begin with a promise.

The Impossible Promise

> **The words I say to you are not just my own. Rather it is the Father, living in me, who is doing his work. Believe me when I say that I am in the Father and the Father is in me; or at least believe on the evidence of the miracles themselves. *I tell you the truth. Anyone who has faith in me will do what I have been doing. He will do even greater things than these, because I am going to the Father.* And I will do whatever you ask in my name, so that the Son may bring glory to the Father. You may ask me for anything in my name, and I will do it.** (emphasis added)
>
> *John 14:10b–14*

Let's focus on the promise of verse 12 (in *italics* above). Think for a moment that it is Jesus himself making this promise. Remember the things that he did while he lived on Earth—restored sight to the blind, caused weak and useless limbs to grow, drove out demons, calmed raging storms, and gave divine insight to people's lives.

Now if you include yourself in the anyone-who-has-faith-in-me category, what is your initial reaction to this promise? Do you see this promise as even a remote possibility for your life?

If you are anything like me, you may have just skipped over this promise because of its ridiculous impossibility. I mean, how in the world could a promise like this be made to a person like me? Jesus is the unique Son of God, and I'm just a guy who shops at Walmart. How could I even expect to do the things that Jesus did, let alone *even greater things*?

But because we have missed the big idea of his message, we have missed the main idea of our ministry.

I want to suggest to you that not only did Jesus mean to give this promise to regular, everyday Walmart-shopping people like us, he meant it to be the guiding principle for discipling his followers. Let me state it another way. I believe that this promise was at the heart of his disciple-making plan for us; it was the overriding strategy to transform the world, as the Father had called him to do. But because we have missed the big idea of his message, we have missed the main idea of our ministry. What Jesus meant as his guiding principle has often become for us the Impossible Promise.

We will return to this promise many times during the next 50 days, but for now I am going to ask you to MEMORIZE it.

> **I tell you the truth, anyone who has faith in me will do what I have been doing. He will do even greater things than these, because I am going to the Father.**
>
> *John 14:12*

In addition, there are three commitments I am asking you to make as you begin your journey through these Kingdom Days.

A Commitment to Read:

The format of this book is seven weeks of six days each. Some of the days' readings are longer, so you may want to split a few of them in half. I wholeheartedly believe that in order to recover the message and ministry of Jesus, we must break through a lot of unbiblical beliefs that have held us back. Some of these so-called accepted beliefs became obstacles blinding me to Jesus' message and ministry. The days are designed to build on one another. Ultimately, I hope you will reach the point where Jesus' promise above is real and active in your life.

A Commitment to Community:
At the end of each week is a study designed to be carried out in a small group. I believe life change happens best in community, which is exactly why Christ has called us into community. You will be challenged to grow in ways that can be experienced only within a community of believers, so if you work through this study individually, you will certainly miss out. You will be asked to take steps of faith in community, so it is essential to make this a shared experience.

A Commitment to Scripture:
During the course of these days, I believe you will be challenged to see things and try things that are perhaps new to you. Of course, it is always appropriate to question, challenge and test. But I want to challenge you not to rest on personal preference or on what you may be used to, but rather strive to live scripturally. Your personal experience or comfort level may not match Scripture, but I urge you to go with Scripture. Reform your thinking and strive to shape your life according to the Word of God. Don't let unbiblical conclusions or perspectives hold you back. Paul ends Romans 12:2 by saying ... *Then you will be able to test and approve what God's will is—his good, pleasing and perfect will.* God bless you as you refocus your thinking and life on the message and ministry of Jesus.

Your personal experience or comfort level may not match Scripture, but I urge you to go with Scripture.

Helpful Icons

As you work your way through this study, you will notice several icons throughout the text. These icons are designed to give pause and help you reflect on what you are learning. These icons include:

Kingdom Questions—questions that probe a little deeper into the subject matter.

Reflection—take time to meditate on what the text is saying. Ask the Holy Spirit to speak to you through these passages.

Movie Buff Moment—recollection of scenes from mainstream movies that illustrate a point in the text.

Imagination Station—imagine what life would be like if ....

Ministry Time—this is a time to put into practice what you've learned from the study.

At the end of each week, the last two days are combined, and are meant to be done as a group study and discussion.

Week One | A Promised Kingdom

"This is the meaning of the vision of the rock cut out of a mountain, but not by human hands—a rock that broke the iron, the bronze, the clay, the silver and the gold to pieces. The great God has shown the king what will take place in the future. The dream is true and the interpretation is trustworthy."

Daniel 2:45

Day 1 | Jesus' Big Idea

The Kingdom of God is near

I have come to believe wholeheartedly that he did, and still does, have a vision statement … we can read and understand … all over Scripture.

I still remember when I was in one of my first high school English classes; the teacher was desperately trying to teach us how to write acceptable papers. English was never my strong suit, so I was trying to learn any tricks or techniques that would help me get a decent grade. There was one little trick that I learned from my teacher that has served me well. She had us decide on a clear and concise thesis statement. This was supposed to be our *big idea*, the main point we were trying to express to our audience. Once we had that specific idea (we had to submit it to her for approval) we were to write it on an index card and tape that card on the wall in front of us while we worked on our papers.

This had huge value. The thesis, or big idea, was meant to be our guide for everything we wrote—every aspect of the paper, from our table of contents to the main sentences in each paragraph. Our paper was meant to be the development of, and an outflow from, that big idea. The thesis statement was also meant to be a guard; it was meant to protect us from wandering into areas that were beyond the scope of our particular paper. I remember often looking up from my paper and realizing that I was in the middle of a thought that had little or nothing to do with my thesis statement, so out came the eraser.

I have applied the principle of a thesis statement to many different areas of life. A number of years ago I began to think about it with regard to the life and ministry of Jesus. I know he didn't have index cards per se, but what about a single thesis statement? What about a big idea that encompasses his teachings and ministry? Did he have a vision statement for his life and message, and could we discover that in the pages of Scripture? As I turned to Scripture and prayer, I was hit by two very big surprises: one is that I have come to believe wholeheartedly that he did and still does have a vision statement, or proverbial index card, that we can read and understand—not just in one place but all over Scripture. The more humbling surprise is that I have missed it for so long. If his big idea were a snake, it would have bit me on the nose several times. Personally, this discovery has had a profound impact on me, not only on how I understand and see Jesus, but also on my own calling and life.

Jesus' Index Card

I believe his big idea is contained in his first public statement in ministry. Can you think what that was? Think about this for a moment: Jesus, knowing what the magnitude of his life and ministry on all humanity would be, must have chosen those words very carefully. It would be the starting point of his message, perhaps the foundation of his ministry. Not only would they be the first impression and beginning point for many who would hear and later read his words, but his first words could potentially provide a backdrop for the entirety of his message.

So what were his first words? Thankfully, they are provided for us in the first chapter of the Gospel of Mark, verse 15, surprisingly small enough to fit on a note card.

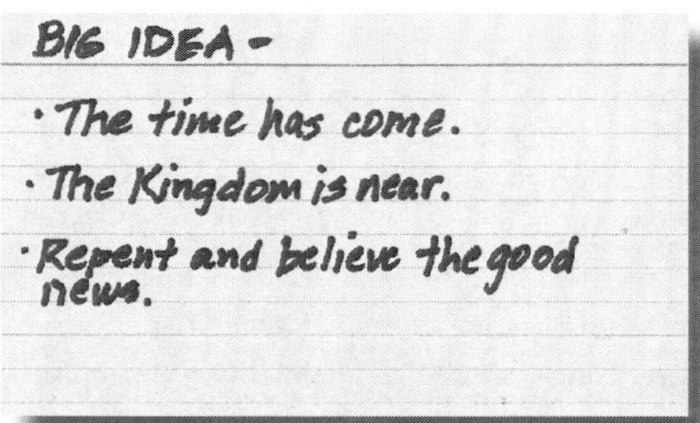

Some of these words seemed to make a lot of sense to me. *Repent*, *believe* and *good news* are all words that are a common part of our understanding of the Christian faith. But what is this business about the *Kingdom of God*? As a Christian of over 20 years, I have heard a lot on the subjects of repentance, belief and the good news, but have heard very little about this idea of the Kingdom of God. In terms of importance, the idea of the Kingdom of God hasn't seemed to rank nearly as high as some other concepts. Yet, for some reason, Jesus chose to begin his life-changing message and ministry with the idea of God's kingdom. Why?

Jesus chose to begin his life-changing message and ministry with the idea of God's kingdom.

Through the process of studying Scripture, praying, reading, and discussing with others, I have become convinced that the Kingdom of God was and is the central teaching of Christ. It is the thesis or big idea of his life, the foundation of his ministry and message. I have been astounded by the centrality of the Kingdom of God. It was not only the first sentence of his public ministry but if you begin to read the Gospels with an eye for the Kingdom of God, you begin to see the idea and discussion of the kingdom everywhere. Let me give you a little taste of what I mean.

The Kingdom Message and Others

The idea and message of the kingdom wasn't just Jesus' focus. It was the focus also of many key players before, during and after him. John the Baptist, the forerunner of Jesus, the prophet who was to prepare the way for Jesus, talked about the kingdom. In fact, John foretold the big idea before the ministry of Jesus began:

> **In those days John the Baptist came, preaching in the Desert of Judea and saying, "Repent, for the kingdom of heaven is near."**
>
> *Matthew 3:1–2*

The kingdom was not only Jesus' big idea, but he intended it to be that of his disciples as well. We will talk much more about this in later days, but I want you to see Jesus' desire to share this message now. When he sent out the Twelve to do ministry he gave them these instructions:

> **When Jesus had called the Twelve together, he gave them power and authority to drive out all demons and to cure diseases, and he sent them out to preach the Kingdom of God and to heal the sick.**
>
> *Luke 9:1–2*

Again, the Kingdom of God was the message. This was true not only for the Twelve, but later when he sent out the greater body of disciples, the Seventy-two.

Paul the Apostle, who wrote most of the letters in the New Testament, also shared the Kingdom of God as the message and big idea. He wrote to many churches addressing many specific issues, but the Kingdom of God comes up throughout his writings. At the close of Paul's life and ministry, Luke, the writer of Acts, gives us this summation:

Have you ever noticed how predominant the kingdom is?

> **Boldly and without hindrance, he preached the Kingdom of God and taught about the Lord Jesus Christ.**
>
> *Acts 28:31*

The Kingdom Message and Teaching

Think about Jesus' teaching for a moment. He was the greatest teacher to ever live, with the most astounding message and truth ever heard. The Sermon on the Mount is his most famous body of teaching. Have you ever noticed how predominant the kingdom is in that message? He starts it with this beatitude:

> **"Blessed are the poor in spirit, for theirs is the kingdom of heaven."**
>
> *Matthew 5:3*

Think for a moment about Jesus' parables. This is his most common introductory statement of a parable:

> **"The kingdom of heaven is like ..."**
>
> *Matthew 13:24; 31; 44*

OR

> **"Once again, the kingdom of heaven is like..."**
>
> *Matthew 13:47*

Even when he doesn't specifically reference the kingdom, often the parable is teaching about some aspect of the kingdom that he wants to communicate to his listeners.

The Priority of the Kingdom

In a famous request by the disciples of Jesus to teach them how to pray, again the kingdom is high priority in his teaching.

> **"This, then, is how you should pray: 'Our Father in heaven, hallowed be your name, your kingdom come, your will be done on earth as it is in heaven . . . for yours is the kingdom and the power and the glory forever. Amen.'"**
>
> *Matthew 6:9–10, 13*

In terms of Jesus' suggested focus of life and purpose, he told them not to be so focused on the material things of life like food and clothes, but to prioritize the kingdom.

> **But seek first his kingdom and his righteousness, and all these things will be given to you as well.**
>
> *Matthew 6:33*

He means for us to bring the reality of the kingdom into our lives and into the lives of others.

Even after Jesus accomplished his sacrifice for the sins of the world, the kingdom was predominant in his teaching and ministry. We are told in Scripture that after Jesus was resurrected he appeared to the disciples for forty days. Did you ever wonder what instruction Jesus was giving his disciples in his resurrected state? Luke actually tells us:

> **He appeared to them over a period of forty days and spoke about the kingdom of God.**
>
> *Acts 1:3b*

Kingdom, kingdom, kingdom—it is literally all over the place in the life of Jesus and the New Testament. Kingdom is referenced over 100 times in the Gospels alone. It is by far the subject that Jesus discussed and talked about more than any other subject. To understand Jesus' ministry and message, we have to understand the Kingdom of God.

? Kingdom Questions

Jesus not only meant to explain and teach the kingdom to his disciples of that day. He means to teach us, his present-day disciples, the same truths, the same kingdom principles. He intends for us to preach and teach others about the kingdom as we learn to live the kingdom here and now. He means for us to live in the power of the kingdom in the present day, not just hope and wait for its fulfillment in the future. He means for us to bring the reality of the kingdom into our lives and into the lives of others. He means to confer upon us the power of his kingdom and to have us do the work of the kingdom just like he did it. This is the promise at the heart of his big idea.

And that is what *Jesus' Big Idea: Living in the Days of the Kingdom* is all about—understanding and living the kingdom as Jesus has taught us. I believe that when we truly start living the kingdom we will become a kingdom community, doing the things that Jesus did, maybe even greater things! As we begin to live in these Days of the Kingdom I want you to hold some key questions in your mind.

What is the Kingdom of God? What does it look like or feel like? How do we recognize the kingdom?

What is the geography of the kingdom? What are the weapons of the kingdom and how are we supposed to advance God's kingdom?

Who is supposed to be the king of God's kingdom? What is our role as Christians in the Kingdom of God?

How do we live and/or bring the kingdom today, in our context? What difference does the kingdom make in our everyday living?

There is one command that we looked at that sums up this study we have entered into. Take a moment in prayer to commit to following this directive of Jesus:

> **"But seek first his kingdom and his righteousness, and all these things will be given to you as well."**
>
> *Matthew 6:33*

What is the Kingdom of God? What does it look like or feel like?

Day 2 Kingdom Questions

We have no king but Caesar

I recently heard a speaker at a leadership conference say, "I live for great questions." Asking questions and pursuing their answers can be an excellent source of learning and illumination. Early in my faith, as I was reading Scripture on my own, I would allow something that I didn't understand to trip me up to the point that I would stop reading altogether. But I was taught by a mentor to *carry them along* as I continued studying and reading. The idea was to face the reality of my unanswered questions but not to let them sabotage my work and faith. Sometimes the answer would be revealed in another part of Scripture. At other times I would ask friends and mentors about my questions. But I soon realized that some of these questions might never be resolved, at least not on this side of heaven.

To me this statement about swords seemed so out of character for Jesus.

In Day 1 you read about Jesus' big idea, the kingdom. Did you have questions like the ones I suggested on the last page? Well, much of my own discovery of Jesus' big idea came from carrying along these questions as I continued to study. Now I can classify some of these very questions as *Kingdom Questions*. Please carry along some of these questions with me as we seek to uncover what Jesus meant when he came to announce the nearness of the kingdom.

Question #1: What's up with the swords?

Did you ever notice that some of the disciples were carrying swords during Jesus' ministry? I remember coming across this for the very first time. Just before Jesus would face the cross, he wanted to prepare the disciples for this climactic moment. He told them that, if they didn't have swords, they should sell their cloaks and buy some. In response the disciples produced two swords and showed them to Jesus, who said, "*That is enough.*" (Luke 22:38b) To me this statement about swords seemed so out of character for Jesus.

Swords don't seem to connect with any part of Jesus' message and ministry. I wondered if Jesus was speaking metaphorically, but saw that the disciples took him literally. Why would the disciples be carrying around swords in the first place? (And how would two swords be enough for any significant event anyway?) Think about

Jesus' arrest. During the interchange, Peter pulled out his sword and whacked off the ear of the High Priest's servant. Why was Peter packing a sword? What did he think he was doing?

In college I remember bringing this to the student president of our Christian fellowship. He simply said, "Good question. I don't have the answer."

Question #2: What's the *hush-hush* about in Jesus' ministry?
When I was young in my faith and reading the Gospels for the first time, I talked with my dad about Jesus and all these discoveries I was making. I often commented on how strong and fearless Jesus was when he challenged the religious leaders of his day. It surprised me that they just didn't get who Jesus was. They were supposedly looking for the Messiah, and when he was right in front of their noses, they missed him.

Somewhat sympathetic toward the religious leaders, my father remarked, "Well, you know, Jesus never actually said, 'I am the Messiah.'" At first, I didn't believe my dad. I was sure Jesus must have said that. Wasn't it a significant part of what he came to do, to reveal his true identity to the world? Wasn't it his identity that would unlock the whole Christian faith? I guess I wasn't expecting Jesus to shout it from the rooftops, but at least I thought he would tell his closest disciples, "I am the Messiah."

Jesus never actually said, 'I am the Messiah.'

When I asked my father why he thought Jesus hadn't, he said he wasn't sure. So, here was another question, and I wanted to find out why. I started looking through the Gospels again.

As I read, I discovered that Dad was technically right. There is not a single instance when Jesus said to his disciples, or anyone else for that matter, "I am the Messiah." However, he did affirm such statements made by others at critical moments in his ministry. But why didn't he just come out and say he was the Messiah? Wasn't that central to what he had come to Earth for?

The element of secrecy about Jesus' ministry was so intriguing to me. When it came to his identity, he was all covert and clandestine. In some instances, as he talked and interacted with people, he instructed them to be hush-hush about who he was or what he had done for them. We see this hush-hush ministry throughout the Gospels.

Hushing the Demons

In the beginning of Jesus' public ministry, nobody knew who this Jesus guy was. He taught with authority and healed people left and right, and so everybody was trying to figure out who he was and where he was from.

> **"Where did this man get these things?" they asked. "What's this wisdom that has been given him that he even does miracles! Isn't this the carpenter? Isn't this Mary's son…?"**
>
> *Mark 6:2b–3*

Even the twelve disciples committed themselves to following Jesus without really knowing who he was or what he was capable of. Yet, there was one group of people who knew who he was from the beginning. As odd as it might sound, it was the demonized who knew his true identity before anyone else.

In a story of Jesus' early ministry in Capernaum, he came across a man possessed by an evil spirit, who yelled out,

> **"What do you want with us, Jesus of Nazareth? Have you come to destroy us? I know who you are—the Holy One of God!"**
>
> *Mark 1:24*

What's up with that? How is it that the least stable people of Jesus' day knew of his divine standing? And it was those who were in their right mind who didn't have a clue!

As weird as that may seem to us, it wasn't the most surprising part of the story. What amazed me was how Jesus responded to their insight into his identity. He shut them up right away and said, "*Be quiet!*" (Mark 1:25) Literally, he said, "Be muzzled." Rather than say to the people, "These demons are from the spiritual realm and they know the truth about who I am," he shut them up before they could clue the people in. I guess you could say that the demons would not be thought of as the most reliable witnesses! However, it is interesting that Jesus hushed them up, even though they were revealing truth.

As odd as it might sound, it was the demonized who knew his true identity before anyone else.

Hushing the Healed

The demons were not the only ones to whom Jesus gave the hush-hush treatment. In fact, he did this to people who would have been far more reliable witnesses about who he was and what he did. Often, throughout the Gospels, he instructed the people he healed not to give a testimony about their experience. For example, after he healed a man with leprosy, he said,

> **"...See that you don't tell anyone. But go show yourself to the priest...."**
>
> *Matthew 8:4a*

Or, think of the story where he raised a young girl from the dead. I think that would have been a great resurrection foreshadowing for the people to see, but the last sentence of the story is:

> **Her parents were astonished, but he ordered them not to tell anyone what had happened.**
>
> *Luke 8:56*

I guess you could argue for crowd control. Perhaps he wanted to prevent people from bringing dead bodies to him each day while he was teaching. Yet, Jesus taught us that part of the purpose of miracles was to reveal his identity. They are signs that point us to his special relationship with the Father. (John 14:11)

Why would Jesus suppress the sharing of these very significant signs that would have revealed his identity?

Hushing the Disciples

Even his initial twelve disciples, those who were with him day in and day out, were slow to realize his identity and purpose. But in a monumental moment they began to understand who Jesus really was. When Jesus asked the disciples specifically who the people were saying he was, they gave some ideas. Then Jesus got personal.

> **"But what about you?" he asked. "Who do you say I am?" Simon Peter answered, "You are the Christ** [Greek for the Hebrew word *Messiah*]**, the Son of the living God."**
>
> *Matthew 16:15–16*

After this Jesus bestowed an amazing blessing on Peter and the church (which we will look at later), but he also sternly admonished them. As Luke recorded:

> **Jesus strictly warned them not to tell this to anyone.**
>
> *Luke 9:21*

Where did they get this expectation that a kingdom was going to appear, and what did they think it would look like?

Again, why would Jesus do this? In the Gospel of Luke, he had just sent out the Twelve to proclaim the kingdom and heal the sick. Why wouldn't he have told them to include the proclamation of his true identity? Why wouldn't he have told them to announce that the awaited Messiah had finally come?

Question #3: Why did the people talk so much about the kingdom?
We established in our first day that Jesus' big idea was the Kingdom of God. But have you ever noticed that it was others' big idea, too? Or at least, so many of their questions and requests had to do with the kingdom. Let me just name a few:

Nathanael: Jesus told Nathanael, who later became one of his disciples,

> **"I saw you while you were still under the fig tree before Philip called you." Nathanael declared, "Rabbi, you are the Son of God; you are the King of Israel."**
>
> *John 1:48b–49*

How in the world did he get *Son of God* and *King of Israel* from the fig tree comment?

People and Parables: At one point in Jesus' teaching ministry, the people were listening to him tell some parables.

> **While they were listening to this, he went on to tell them a parable, because he was near Jerusalem and the people thought that the kingdom of God was going to appear at once.**
>
> *Luke 19:11*

What is going on here? Was the Kingdom of God one of the main motivations for people coming to listen to Jesus and his teachings? Where did they get this expectation that a kingdom was going to appear, and what did they think it would look like?

The Mother of Thunder: In what I think was one of the more humorous moments in the gospel story, James and John, nicknamed *Sons of Thunder* (Mark 3:17), were dragged before Jesus by their mom. (I can just imagine her having a vice-like grip on an ear of each of her sons, figuring if they were not men enough to ask, then she would just have to do it for them!) She came before Jesus and asked,

> **"Grant that one of these two sons of mine may sit at your right and the other at your left in your kingdom."**
>
> *Matthew 20:21b*

Not only were Jesus' close disciples anticipating a kingdom, but even their mother was. How did she put together this king and kingdom idea?

Joseph of Arimathea: Lastly, we are given a short description of a man named Joseph who would ask Pilate for permission to bury the beloved body of Jesus.

> **He came from the Judean town of Arimathea and he was waiting for the kingdom of God.**
>
> *Luke 23:51b*

How did Joseph know to wait for the Kingdom of God? What is the background that all these people share, and yet we don't know about it? The Kingdom of God may be a foreign and undefined concept to us, but not for the people of Jesus' day.

The Kingdom of God may be a foreign and undefined concept to us, but not for the people of Jesus' day.

Question #4: Was Jesus a king?

The whole motif of King Jesus always seemed so out of place to me. I had learned that Jesus was the savior, and that he died on the cross for my sin. But I never remember him sitting on a throne or leading an army into battle. I never saw him leading a rebellion like an outcast king trying to reclaim his lost throne. Jesus seemed to make all sorts of claims about himself, like being the Good Shepherd or the Bread of Life, but I don't remember him saying much about being a king. He didn't go around announcing he was king. Yet this title seems to permeate the last part of his life. Consider for a moment the major events that filled his final week on Earth, prior to the resurrection.

The Triumphal Entry

The Triumphal Entry experience of Jesus was always so confusing to me. It made sense to me that people would get excited about Jesus because of his healing and deliverance ministry. I can imagine that his amazing teaching and insight would have been intriguing to many folks, especially ordinary people. But when he entered into Jerusalem, there was something else going on. They were yelling things like,

> **"...Hosanna to the Son of David..."**
>
> *Matthew 21:9*

and

> **"Blessed is the coming kingdom of our father David!"**
>
> *Mark 11:10*

What in the world do these things mean? What were the people talking about?

And why did things change so quickly for Jesus? How could he one day be a hero entering Jerusalem, to the shouts of the people, and only a few days later be a criminal with these same people yelling for his blood? At one moment the people cried out,

> **"Blessed is the king who comes in the name of the Lord!"**
>
> *Luke 19:38a*

Then with their next breath, they screamed,

> **"Crucify him!"**
>
> *Luke 23:21b*

The Ultimate Rejection

So why did they end up killing Jesus? What was the source of the religious leaders' anger and fear of someone who did nothing but heal the sick and teach truth? Was it simply jealousy, or was there something more? Apparently, the accusations and justifications were rooted in a central theme, and that theme was the kingship of Jesus.

How could he one day be a hero entering Jerusalem, to the shouts of the people, and only a few days later be a criminal with these same people yelling for his blood?

> **"...We have found this man subverting our nation. He opposes payment of taxes to Caesar and claims to be Christ, a king."**
>
> *Luke 23:2b*

The idea of kingship was at the heart of Pilate's question,

> **..."Are you the king of the Jews?"**
>
> *Matthew 27:11b*

Because of Jesus' implied kingship, the Roman soldiers mocked him with a crown of thorns and ridiculed him by saying,

> **"Hail, king of the Jews!"**
>
> *Matthew 27:29b*

The ultimate rejection came as the crowd shouted for Jesus' crucifixion. It was the death blow to Jesus. Notice why they rejected him:

> **But they shouted, "Take him away! Take him away! Crucify him!" "Shall I crucify your king?" Pilate asked. "We have no king but Caesar," the chief priests answered. Finally Pilate handed him over to them to be crucified.**
>
> *John 19:15–16*

Think of the great irony in what was posted above Jesus' head on the cross according to Matthew 27:37:

THIS IS JESUS THE KING OF THE JEWS

Was Jesus claiming to be the King of the Jews? What kind of king was this? What kind of kingdom had Jesus thought he was bringing? Was he a failed revolutionary?

Ⓡ Reflection

Envision those final moments of Jesus' life as if you had been there. Perhaps you are an early follower of Jesus; perhaps you were healed or maybe even carried a sword. At your own personal risk you follow Jesus to Golgotha, the place of the skull. In shock and disbelief you watch as they drive the nails through his hands and feet; you watch as they hoist him upon this cross.

There are others nearby. The Roman soldiers are there with swords on their hips—they are just waiting for the death of another foolish fanatic. The religious leaders are there mocking him with taunts:

> **"He saved others," they said, "but he can't save himself! He's the King of Israel! Let him come down now from the cross, and we will believe in him."**
>
> *Matthew 27:42*

At the same time there are the two robbers hanging next to him. One is hurling insults at Jesus, chastising him in bitterness and angst. But from the other thief you hear something else, words that seem so out of place. Despite the nearness of death for both the thief and Jesus, you hear words of faith:

> **..."Jesus, remember me when you come into your kingdom."**
>
> *Luke 23:42*

Finally there is Jesus, broken and battered, struggling to breathe. In the midst of the mocking and the ridicule, you hear him cry out:

> **"Eloi, Eloi, lama sabachthani?" — which means, "My God, my God, why have you forsaken me?"**
>
> *Matthew 27:46b*

He came with such power; he healed the sick and delivered the oppressed, but now he dies broken and battered, with no one to save him.

And in that moment you begin to pray. "My God, how can this be? He was supposed to be the one. He was supposed to be your anointed, but now he is forsaken! I don't understand, God. He came with such power; he healed the sick and delivered the oppressed, but now he dies broken and battered, with no one to save him. He promised that your kingdom was near, but instead all is lost. I believed him. I committed my life to him! Now to whom shall I turn?"

Where is your kingdom, God? Where is the king?

Day 3 | Kingdom Beginnings and Ancient Callings

You will be for me a kingdom of priests

If we are going to carry along some of those questions from yesterday, we really need to carry them back into the past. Those Kingdom Questions should help us realize that there is much, in terms of the history of God's people that came before Jesus' incarnation. When Jesus broke onto the landscape announcing the nearness of the Kingdom of God, he did not do it in a vacuum. I don't think he got many blank stares from folks when he announced the kingdom. His original audience, the first century Jews, didn't look at each other in confusion thinking, "What's all this Kingdom of God stuff about?" But such a question is the response I often get today, whether from Christians or non-Christians. What may be new to our thinking today was not new with the people of Jesus' day.

It is crucial that we understand the ideas and expectations of the people that he originally ministered to.

Jesus never gave a Webster-type definition of the kingdom. Instead, he chose to teach nuances and elements of what the kingdom is. His teaching sometimes challenged and stretched the people's preconceived notions of the kingdom. Yet, we often miss these nuances because we don't understand the context in which Jesus taught. We don't understand some of the Jewish history and pre-formed ideas of what the kingdom is or at least was supposed to be in the thinking of Jesus' original audience. If we are going to make sense of Jesus' teaching on the kingdom, it is crucial that we understand the ideas and expectations of the people that he originally ministered to. It is vital that we understand the history of God's kingdom and its state at the time Jesus entered human history. I think a crucial aspect of the kingdom is related to words of promise spoken by the Old Testament prophets.

Words of Promise

Have you ever had someone who was important to you speak words of promise into your life? A young woman I once knew, named Regan, shared her testimony. She still remembered that in the sixth grade, her teacher used to do something very special. As each child came and got a drink from the drinking fountain, she would speak words of promise into their lives. She used to say things about interests, values or accomplishments. When Regan would come near for a drink, her teacher would say, "Oh, Regan, you are going to change the world." These words sank deep into her soul, continually echoing through her thoughts as she has sought her place in this world.

The Jews, as a people, have received some of the most tremendous words of promise. Spoken to them by God himself, the promises became a deep part of their identity and history. These were kingdom words that relate to what Jesus taught.

Israel's history as a people and nation really began with Abram (who would later become Abraham). Of all the people who lived on the Earth at this time, God chose to bless Abraham and make him a blessing to the world. We are not really sure why God chose this wandering and childless nomad, but he did. He spoke to Abraham and invited him into a relationship of trust. God had plans to change the world, and he began with this single individual, a simple man of the desert.

God would ask Abraham to pick up his life as he knew it, and head out to a foreign land, leaving everything familiar behind. Yet, in the midst of this sacrifice, God spoke words of promise into his life. God promised Abraham that if he listened to him and obeyed his direction, he would bless him and all his descendents. Listen to these powerful words of promise:

God had plans to change the world, and he began with this single individual.

> **"I will make you into a great nation and I will bless you; I will make your name great, and you will be a blessing. I will bless those who bless you, and whoever curses you I will curse; and all peoples on earth will be blessed through you."**
>
> *Genesis 12:2–3*

Now that is quite a promise! Notice that the words of promise that God spoke extend well beyond Abraham. They extend to the community of people that would come from Abraham, his offspring. This covenant would not only affect the Jewish people, but was a global promise involving all the peoples of the world.

Look again at the very first promise God spoke into his life. He promised Abraham that he would become a nation. God was not simply promising to preserve his family tree, but to cause his family to experience explosive growth. He would make him into a nation. Not only would Abraham change the world, but his offspring would somehow and in some way bless all the peoples of the earth.

These words of promise would become, and are to this day, foundational to the Jewish people (and now to Christians as well). Their identity would be forever intertwined with this promise. This promise or covenant would be restated in many ways throughout their history.

God would speak many words of promise to His people, but I want you to see one other covenant promise that relates to our discussion of the kingdom. When the Israelites—the Jewish people named after their ancestor Israel/Jacob in Genesis 32:28—were led out of Egypt by Moses, they experienced another huge, identity-forming promise from God. God led them to Mount Sinai and renewed his covenant with them. Listen to the beauty of God's words:

> **"'You yourselves have seen what I did to Egypt, and how I carried you on eagles' wings and brought you to myself. Now if you obey me fully and keep my covenant, then out of all nations you will be my treasured possession. Although the whole earth is mine, you will be for me a kingdom of priests and a holy nation.'..."**
>
> *Exodus 19:4–6*

God planned for the Jewish people to be his own people, his nation, and his kingdom of priests. Of all the peoples and nations of the world, God had chosen them. He would be their God and they would be his people. If they would but follow his laws and his rules, they would forever be his nation—the Lord's kingdom.

Imagine for a moment the impact of these promises on the mindset of the Jewish people. In Jesus' day (and today), they saw themselves as a covenant people, God's chosen, and rightly so. Think of how huge the Kingdom of God was to their identity as a people. Among all the nations of the world, this is what made them unique.

These words of promise were the foundation of who they were and what they were about. This was their role in the world, to be a kingdom of priests, ministering to the entire world on God's behalf. They were intended to be a nation of blessing, a kingdom of people who represented the God of the universe. God was their ruler and king, and he purposed to change the world through them.

You see, part of the uniqueness of this kingdom was its leadership.

A Broken Identity

If you read the Old Testament from this vantage point, you will see this kingdom emerge and blossom. Moses would establish the laws of God's kingdom, and it was Joshua who would bring this nation to the Promised Land (another big part of God's covenant and their identity). Under Joshua's leadership, they would become a Commonwealth of God, a nation among other nations. But wait, something went wrong!

God's promises were, and are, deeply embedded in the Israelites' identity as a people. But so also is the sad history of their breaking this covenant and turning their backs on their sacred calling. The role of the Jews was to believe the covenant promise and live according to it through obedience and love. Often, however, the people failed to keep their part of the covenant.

This distressing history of the Jewish people is told throughout the Old Testament. It is the ongoing story of God's people breaking covenant with God, again and again.

Perhaps nothing speaks more clearly of their broken identity than their desire for a king. You see, part of the uniqueness of this kingdom was its leadership. If I asked you who the first king of their nation was, you might answer, "King Saul." Technically speaking, you would be wrong. God had originally set it up so that he would be their king. God, the Lord of the Universe, intended to be their king—right from the beginning.

This unique leadership structure was meant to be a part of their identity and uniqueness as a people, but the people didn't like it. They didn't feel it was working for them and told Samuel the prophet that they wanted to abandon this unique setup. You see, they wanted to be like the other nations. They wanted a human lord that they could see and put their trust in. So, they asked for a human king.

Give Us a King

We read about the Israelites' discontent in the book of 1 Samuel. Samuel was the current leader and prophet that God had raised up, but he was growing old. It was at this point that the people of God made their fateful request:

> **So all the elders of Israel gathered together and came to Samuel at Ramah. They said to him, "You are old, and your sons do not walk in your ways; now appoint a king to lead us, such as all the other nations have." But when they said, "Give us a king to lead us," this displeased Samuel; so he prayed to the LORD. And the LORD told him: "Listen to all that the people are saying to you; it is not you they have rejected, but they have rejected me as their king. As they have done from the day I brought them up out of Egypt until this day, forsaking me and serving other gods, so they are doing to you. Now listen to them; but warn them solemnly and let them know what the king who will reign over them will do."**
>
> *1 Samuel 8:4–9*

They actually rejected a crucial aspect of their own identity.

This was a pretty amazing interchange between God and Samuel. Do you hear the Lord's sadness and disappointment in this request? It was the request that broke God's heart. It was the request that rejected him as king—the people rejected God's rule, his reign, and his words of promise. They actually rejected a crucial aspect of their own identity. It was what made them unique—a kingdom of priests.

Despite their rejection, God raised up a king for them. Unfortunately, the history of Israel's kings is pretty dismal. The king of Israel (and eventually the leader of its southern region, Judah) was meant to be God's representative, to be God's chosen and anointed leader, ruling in his stead. But the kings broke covenant as often as the people did and ended up furthering the brokenness of the relationship between God and his people. This brokenness of the kings reverberated through all the people and, as he did with the kings, God would eventually reject his people. He lamented to them,

> **"My people are destroyed from lack of knowledge. Because you have rejected knowledge, I also reject you as my priests; because you have ignored the law of your God, I also will ignore your children."**
>
> *Hosea 4:6*

The nation would be split in two, and then ultimately be conquered by foreign nations. Their identity as a nation, as a people, as a kingdom, would be shattered. All this shattered history would create a longing for the restoration of their nation. His people would be filled with a longing for the restoration of the words of promise, to make them once again his kingdom, his kingdom of priests, as originally promised in Exodus 19:6.

This ancient calling and broken identity helps us understand what state the people were in when Jesus came talking about the Kingdom of God. They believed in this calling, that it was an eternal call on their lives from God, that despite their numerous sins, God would always draw them back. They were waiting for the time when God would finally raise up a deliverer, someone to save them from the tyranny of an oppressive nation of foreigners, and restore them to their true calling, their true identity.

Despite their past sin and current state, God gave them promises and hope for the future. He promised that, in a day of his choosing (the Day of the Lord) and by a person of his choosing (the Messiah), he would restore his kingdom on Earth. They believed that the Lord would reclaim his people.

Imagination Station

Imagine yourself as a first-century Jew who, throughout your childhood, was taught about your history as a people, your ancient calling. You were not only taught your history, but you were taught the prophetic promises of your future—that someday, God would bring a new king, a Messiah, who would restore his people, his kingdom on Earth. Just as many Christians today actively look for the second coming of the Messiah, so as a first-century Jew, you would have been taught to look for his initial coming.

When he would not embrace the kind of throne that the people were longing for, they gave him a cross instead.

Now some of the questions of Day 2 begin to have answers. Why did so many people, even the mother of the Sons of Thunder, have the kingdom on their minds? It was part of their identity, part of their calling. Why were Jesus' disciples carrying swords? It was because the people were expecting a military revolution, the restoration of God's kingdom here and now. And all revolutions need weapons. Why was the triumphal entry so charged with political overtones and expectations? Because revolutions need a leader, and kingdoms need a king. We now begin to realize that when they said, *"Blessed is the king who comes in the name of the Lord… Hosanna to the Son of David!"*— these were cries of revolution. The people were longing for the fulfillment of the ancient calling, the activity of God in their lifetime.

This is what the people wanted, and yet the end result was not a throne but a cross. In an intriguing way we see a profound disconnect between the expectations of the people and the kind of king that Jesus came to be. In fact, in one instance, when the people saw the miraculous signs Jesus did, they were ready for the revolution right then and there. But Jesus was not. John tells us that the people said,

> **…"Surely this is the Prophet who is to come into the world." Jesus, knowing that they intended to come and make him king by force, withdrew again to a mountain by himself.**
>
> *John 6:14–15*

Is this profound disconnect the reason for the secrecy of Jesus' ministry? Is this why the people turned so quickly on Jesus in the last several days of his ministry? When he would not embrace the kind of throne that the people were longing for, they gave him a cross instead. And just as they had rejected God as their king so many years before, so now they rejected his Son as the king in their day.

Your Identity

Words of promise can be powerful things. For better or for worse, they can shape who we are, how we understand ourselves and our place in this world. You have been reading about the kingdom identity of the Jews, but did you realize that you were reading about your own identity? Did you know that these words of promise to them were meant to be words of promise to you as well? The Apostle Peter reminds us of our identity:

> **But you are a chosen people, a royal priesthood, a holy nation, a people belonging to God, that you may declare the praises of him who called you out of darkness into his wonderful light. Once you were not a people, but now you are the people of God; once you had not received mercy, but now you have received mercy.**
>
> *1 Peter 2:9–10*

Part of your call and identity is wrapped up in the idea of the Kingdom of God.

Have you ever realized that part of your calling as a Christian is to be part of this *royal priesthood, a holy nation*? Part of your call and identity is wrapped up in the idea of the Kingdom of God. Jesus has called you a son (or daughter) of the kingdom (Matthew 13:38), but it is hard to live like this if we don't understand what the kingdom is. This study isn't just about understanding an ancient concept, but understanding yourself—understanding a central aspect of who you are supposed to be, who you are called to be.

Ⓡ Reflection

Take some time now to reread the words of promise above. In prayer, reflect on what these statements of identity could mean to you. What does it mean to be God's treasured possession, his kingdom of priests? What does it look like to be a son or daughter of the kingdom?

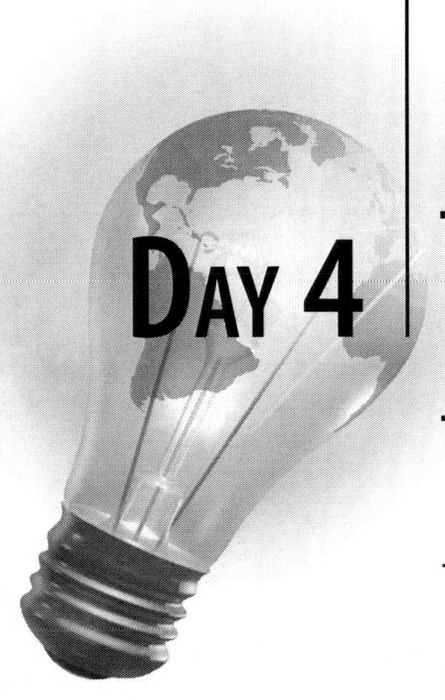

Day 4 | The Secret of the Fifth Kingdom

The secret of the kingdom of God has been given to you

Have you ever been entrusted with a secret? Sure, as kids we share all sorts of little secrets. But I am talking about a big, life-changing secret—a secret that can change lives, change families, change cultures, even change a nation. Watergate was a little like that. Key leaders were directed to keep a secret of national proportions. According to Chuck Colson, keeping this particular secret lasted only two weeks.[1] When the secret activities were revealed, it impacted an entire nation. Big secrets, of course, can be good as well as bad.

> In fact, he first entrusted this secret to his children thousands of years ago.

Movie Buff Moment

In the movie *The Fifth Element*, a sci-fi thriller with Bruce Willis, there was a secret that had universal significance. Priests on Earth were made aware of a deadly evil that had the potential to destroy all life on Earth every 5,000 years. But the priests not only knew of the evil (made known to them by the Mondoshawans), they also knew the savior. The priests were entrusted with a secret that would save all of life. That secret was called the *fifth element*. It sounds somewhat odd, but that movie has some interesting parallels to the God-sized secret he has given to his people, and wants to give to you.

Today, you are going to be entrusted with a secret as significant as the *fifth element*. It is a divine secret that has been hidden from the beginning. It is a secret that can only be understood if it is heard with a heart of faith. It is not a childlike secret or a sinful secret. It is a marvelously wonderful secret—a secret that is changing lives, that has changed nations, that is changing the world. It is a God-sized kingdom secret regarding his plans and divine activity in the world that will affect every generation until the end of time.

This is a kingdom secret that God desires to entrust to his children. In fact, he first entrusted this secret to his children thousands of years ago, but perhaps in our day

1. Charles W. Colson, *Born Again*, Grand Rapids, MI: Chosen Books, 2008.

some of us have never heard this secret, or we have forgotten it. To a certain degree, it may be that generations have not passed it on as effectively as they should have.

God told his people this secret so that it would affect and change the way they saw the world and God's role in history. As God's chosen people, it would affect how they saw armies and wars, nations and kings, and their own role in the world as a kingdom of priests.

So, would you like to know the secret?

King Nebuchadnezzar's Dream

God, the Father, chose to reveal this secret in a very unusual way, through the dreams of a pagan king and a Jewish captive. I am talking about King Nebuchadnezzar of Babylon and Daniel. It is through a series of dreams or visions and interpretations of those dreams that God revealed his sovereign plans for the world. You may be familiar with the story of Daniel, but may have missed the secret.

God, the Father, chose to reveal this secret in a very unusual way, through the dreams of a pagan king and a Jewish captive.

Daniel was one of the Jewish exiles taken to Babylon (modern-day Iraq) after Nebuchadnezzar captured Jerusalem. Daniel, along with his friends, reached a place of prominence in the king's court. At one point, while Daniel and his friends were serving in the king's court, something big happened. King Nebuchadnezzar had a disturbing dream that really riled him up. Troubled and distraught, he couldn't remember his dream or understand its meaning. Of course, none of the Babylonian wise men could tell him what he had dreamed, so he decreed that they were all to be put to death. Apparently, the king was really distraught!

On hearing this, Daniel first stepped up and pled with the king for time. Then Daniel implored God, the *revealer of mysteries*, to reveal the dream and its meaning to him. As it turned out, this dream was from God, and in it God revealed his God-sized secret. Daniel received the revelation from God and declared,

> **"The secret which the king has demanded, the wise men, the astrologers, the magicians, and the soothsayers cannot declare to the king. But there is a God in heaven who reveals secrets..."**
>
> *Daniel 2:27a–28 (NKJV)*

And then Daniel revealed the secret.

Nebuchadnezzar's disturbing vision was that of an enormous, dazzling statue with a head of gold, chest and arms of silver, belly and thighs of bronze and finally legs of iron with feet that were a mixture of clay and iron. As the king was looking at the magnificent statue, something powerful happened. Suddenly, a rock cut out of a mountain (but not by human hands) crashed into the statue and shattered all the parts into pieces. If you would like to see the whole dream and interpretation, you can read it in Daniel 2.

Daniel not only related the dream to the king, but he also gave the meaning of the dream. Within the meaning was embedded the secret. The dream was a vision of what was going to happen to the world. It was a dream of kingdoms, four successive kingdoms that would rise and fall, each in its own time. Each one would rise up in power and prominence, then be succeeded by the next kingdom. Nebuchadnezzar's Babylonian kingdom was the first of the four kingdoms, the head of gold (Daniel 2:38). But after a time, another kingdom would come to supplant his kingdom, and so on. Before we get to the God-sized secret, we need to look at two other visions that God gave directly to Daniel.

Daniel's Visions

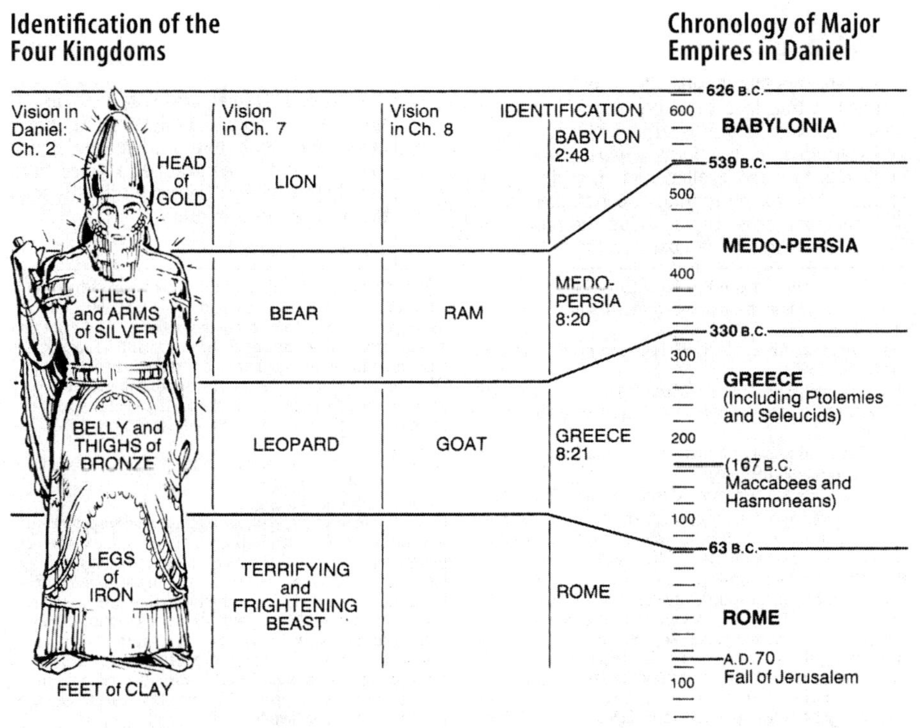

> But after a time, another kingdom would come to supplant his kingdom, and so on.

Nebuchadnezzar's dream was not the last time God spoke to Daniel about the kingdom events of history. After surviving the lions' den, Daniel would receive two more significant visions relating to King Nebuchadnezzar's original vision (chapter 2). Daniel's first vision is recorded in chapter 7. It was not of a statue but of four fearsome beasts: a winged lion, a flesh eating bear, a four-headed leopard and finally a *terrifying and frightening and very powerful* beast with iron teeth and ten horns. You can see the correlation between the four parts of the statue in chapter two and the four fearsome beasts in chapter 7. The four beasts relate to the successive kingdoms that were going to come to the Earth.

Daniel's second kingdom vision is recorded in chapter 8. There is a ram with two horns and a goat with one prominent horn. The ram and goat don't get along too well, and the goat furiously attacks the ram and tramples him. The unfriendly ram and goat correlate to two of the kingdoms of the future. Not only do the two visions relate but, significantly, God revealed the identity of the next two kingdoms that were to follow Nebuchadnezzar's kingdom. He revealed the second as the Medo-Persian kingdom (Daniel 8:20) and the third as the kingdom of Greece (Daniel 8:21). If you combine the dream of chapter 2 with Daniel's visions of chapters 7 and 8, you will get an interesting glimpse of history, unfolding right before your very eyes. To clarify it all, look at the chart on the following page, taken from the NIV Study Bible. It summarizes all three of the visions in Daniel and their interpretations.

Notice the correlation between the four parts of the statue and the animals of Daniel's visions. Also, notice how the identities of the first three are specifically revealed. Imagine for a moment that you are a Jew living in Jesus' time who has been faithfully studying your sacred Scriptures and comparing them to recent historical events. You would feel that the fulfillment of Daniel's visions was happening right in front of you. Rome is not specifically identified as the fourth kingdom, but from your perspective it seems to fit much of the ugly criteria found in its description. And the best part of the secret is yet to come. It is the prophetic revelation of the Kingdom of God that I refer to as the *fifth kingdom.*

God himself would set up the one true kingdom, making the world right again, and this kingdom would last forever.

The Fifth Kingdom

Daniel not only revealed the meaning of the statue to King Nebuchadnezzar, but also the significance and meaning of the rock. This is the cool part, not only for the Jews of Jesus' times, but for us as well. He says,

> **"In the time of those kings** [i.e., the time of the fourth kingdom that is divided], **the God of heaven will set up a kingdom that will never be destroyed, nor will it be left to another people. It will crush all those kingdoms and bring them to an end, but it will itself endure forever. This is the meaning of the vision of the rock cut out of a mountain, but not by human hands—a rock that broke the iron, the bronze, the clay, the silver and the gold to pieces. The great God has shown the king what will take place in the future. The dream is true and its interpretation is trustworthy."**
>
> *Daniel 2:44–45*

God was giving the king and all those who would read this prophetic interpretation a vision of the things to come. He was letting us know that:

> **". . . the Most High is sovereign over the kingdoms of men and gives them to anyone he wishes."**
>
> *Daniel 4:32*

This, of course, is the theme of the book of Daniel. He was not only in control of all kingdoms of the Earth, but these great kingdoms that were to come would lead up to the one-and-only God kingdom. This fifth kingdom would crush all other earthly kingdoms, demolishing them with the power and might of God. Then God himself would set up the one true kingdom, making the world right again, and this kingdom would last forever. This kingdom would change the world forever.

There is another aspect of the secret that we must know. The God-sized secret was not just about God's world-defining kingdom, but the secret also revealed something about the one who would bring this kingdom. The visions reveal the king of the fifth kingdom.

The Secret of the King

As part of the secret of the kingdom, God wanted his chosen people to know that there would be a certain person who would bring the kingdom and rule over it. It was during Daniel's vision of the four kingdoms in chapter 7 that this mysterious king is presented:

> **"In my vision at night I looked, and there before me was one like a son of man, coming with the clouds of heaven. He approached the Ancient of Days and was led into his presence. He was given authority, glory and sovereign power; all peoples, nations and men of every language worshiped him. His dominion is an everlasting dominion that will not pass away, and his kingdom is one that will never be destroyed."**
>
> *Daniel 7:13–14*

His kingdom—the *fifth kingdom*—will last forever.

Some fascinating things about this vision we need to see. First, the descriptive title given to this coming king is simply *one like a son of man*. This happens to be Jesus' favorite title when referring to himself during his earthly ministry. Later, when Daniel was in prayer, the angel Gabriel came to him and referred to this person who would bring the kingdom again. In Daniel 9 he twice called him the *Anointed One*. This, of course, is the Hebrew/Aramaic word *Messiah*. In Greek this is the word *Christ*. Interestingly enough, the kings of Israel and Judah, such as Saul and David, were always anointed to represent God-given authority to take their post.

Furthermore, not only do we hear a designation of the king who was to come, but we see the reign and rule of the fifth kingdom given to him. (Daniel 7:13-14) God, or the *Ancient of Days*, gave this *son of man* all the *authority, glory and sovereign power* of the kingdom. *His* kingdom—the *fifth kingdom*—will last forever.

Significance of the Secret

Why did God choose to reveal this world-changing secret to his children? What are his purposes behind it? Why did he choose to unfold future world events to Daniel and have them written down for people of faith to read and ponder? In what ways should this secret change our perspective of the world? How should it change our faith?

The priests in *The Fifth Element* were entrusted with their secret, because at a key time in history they were going to have to act on their knowledge of that secret. They had a crucial role to play in the world events of their time. I believe that this is true as well for us today. We are meant to be living out this secret in our daily lives.

The world still does not see or recognize this secret because it has not been revealed to them. It is a secret for believers, people of faith. Jesus said,

> **"The secret of the kingdom of God has been given to you."...**
>
> *Mark 4:11*

I believe that he has revealed this secret to us because he wants us to know his plans and purposes for the world. He also wants us to join him and cooperate with him in doing his kingdom work in this world today. He doesn't simply desire mindless servants, working unaware of the big picture. God desires co-workers, friends, who know where their labors lead to. He wants them to join him in the work of the kingdom—to join him in actually bringing the kingdom. What a privilege and honor! We can be "in the know," and serve him in the kingdom plans he has for us and the world.

Ⓡ Reflection

A Comment of Christ to Meditate Upon

> **"Greater love has no one than this, that he lay down his life for his friends. You are my friends if you do what I command. I no longer call you servants, because a servant does not know his master's business. Instead, I have called you friends, for everything that I learned from my Father I have made known to you."**
>
> *John 15:13–15*

He wants them to join him in the work of the kingdom—to join him in actually bringing the kingdom.

Day 5 | Are You the One?

Blessed is the man who does not fall away on account of me

Probably one of the most intriguing characters in the New Testament is John the Baptist. He splashes onto the pages of history as the ultimate precursor. Isaiah called him the *voice of one calling in the desert.* (Isaiah 40:3) He was preparing the people for the coming Lord, making straight paths for the coming Messiah. Apparently, John had not only received a divine calling, but also divine insight into what the Messiah would ultimately accomplish. In the Gospel of John, before Jesus had done any public ministry, John pointed him out to his disciples and declared,

> **"Look, the Lamb of God, who takes away the sin of the world!"**
> *John 1:29b*

Considering that it took Jesus' own disciples so long to figure out the significance of his sacrifice, it is pretty amazing that John understood this almost from the beginning.

Despite this divine revelation... we have the story of his [John's] struggle to know if Jesus was really *the one.*

Yet, despite this divine revelation—despite John's divine call and role—despite actually baptizing Jesus—despite watching the Holy Spirit of God descend on him in visible form, we have the story of his struggle to know if Jesus was really *the one.* John actually questioned at one point if he had somehow missed it and wrongly directed the people toward Jesus.

Later, as Jesus' ministry was unfolding in power, we learn that John the Baptist was imprisoned by Herod. At what must have been one of the lowest points in John's life, he decided to send two of his own disciples to Jesus with an astonishing question,

> **"Are you the one who was to come, or should we expect someone else?"**
> *Luke 7:19b*

How could this be? We understand that everyone has moments of doubt, but John the Baptist? I mean, he even heard the voice of God say, *This is my son whom I love.* (Matthew 3:16) How could he have questioned if Jesus was really *the one*?

The answer is rooted in what we have been talking about the last several days. It lies in John's perspective on the coming Kingdom of God. Though he had received divine revelation from God about Jesus and the things that he would accomplish, John was also a man of his time. He understood much of the coming Kingdom of God, but he also shared many of the expectations surrounding the coming king or Messiah. You can bet he was familiar with the book of Daniel, and the rest of the Old Testament as it pertained to the Kingdom of God and his Anointed. And apparently, as he witnessed for himself and heard reports about Jesus' message and ministry, they didn't all quite match up with his preconceived notions. To get a better grasp of John's kingdom expectations, let's take a moment to look at his teaching.

John's Fiery Message

The Gospels provide a snapshot of John's message. Matthew, for instance, introduces John and his big idea:

> **In those days John the Baptist came preaching in the Desert of Judea and saying, "Repent, for the kingdom of heaven is near."**
>
> *Matthew 3:1–2*

It is clear that the Kingdom of God was John's big idea.

It is clear that the Kingdom of God was John's big idea. And from that beginning, he unfolds this vision of the kingdom and what should be our appropriate response.

> **"You brood of vipers! Who warned you to flee from the coming wrath? Produce fruit in keeping with repentance....The ax is already at the root of the trees, and every tree that does not produce good fruit will be cut down and thrown into the fire."**
>
> *Matthew 3:7–8, 10*

He also gives a glimpse of who the Messiah will be and what he will do.

> **"I baptize you with water for repentance. But after me will come one who is more powerful than I, whose sandals I am not fit to carry. He will baptize you with the Holy Spirit and with fire. His winnowing fork is in his hand, and he will clear his threshing floor, gathering his wheat into the barn and burning up the chaff with unquenchable fire."**
>
> *Matthew 3:11–12*

John the Baptist didn't exactly have the most positive and uplifting message. From his key words of fire, wrath, and repentance, to his references to axes and winnowing forks, you get a frightful picture of the Kingdom of God and the Messiah. We can only assume that the people listening to his message probably expected a fierce and even frightening figure. From John's teaching we get a picture of a Messiah with an agenda of judgment and punishment for those who were disobedient and non-responsive to the Word of God.

Jesus' Intriguing Response

When we try to match this portrayal of the king and kingdom against Jesus' actual life and ministry, it is easy to understand John's perceived disconnect. Jesus' ministry in the Gospels doesn't seem to fit this fierce picture of wrath, fire and judgment. All this began to stir concerns and questions in John's heart. And that led to his surprising question.

While in prison, John had heard reports about Jesus' ministry, his miracles and teaching. These reports caused such concern that John decided to send two of his disciples to ask Jesus for clarification. Again, the surprising question that he asks is this:

> **"Are you the one who was to come, or should we expect someone else?"**
>
> *Luke 7:19b*

His disciples faithfully went to Jesus and asked him the exact question given to them by John. Note, however, that John's disciples probably had to wait to even get close to Jesus. Likely, they had to wait in line because Jesus was in the midst of a full-blown ministry—healing diseases, driving out demons and restoring sight to the blind. By the time John's men finally got to Jesus, they probably had witnessed some pretty amazing miracles. This is important, because Jesus doesn't give a direct response of denial or affirmation. Instead, he tells the disciples to look around them.

It may have caused him to reevaluate his understanding of the kingdom and the Messiah who would bring the kingdom.

> **"Go back and report to John what you have seen and heard: The blind receive sight, the lame walk, those who have leprosy are cured, the deaf hear, the dead are raised, and the good news is preached to the poor."**
>
> *Luke 7:22b*

My guess is that John's disciples returned and gave him Jesus' verbal response, but also told what they had *seen and heard*—the wondrous power of God at work in the lives of people, healing their spiritual, physical and emotional needs. And I would have to think that, though this might not have been the response that John was looking for, it may have caused him to reevaluate his understanding of the kingdom and the Messiah who would bring the kingdom. You see, many of Jesus' words (and ministry) are right from the book of Isaiah, that same book in which John's calling is foretold.

Also in Isaiah are the well-known prophecies regarding the Messiah—for instance, the *suffering servant* referred to in Isaiah 53. In that same book, numerous passages describe the new era of God that was coming, commonly referred to by theologians as the *Messianic era*. I wonder if Isaiah's words echoed in John's mind as he pondered Jesus' words and heard the stories of what his own disciples had witnessed:

Jesus said, *The blind receive sight ... the deaf hear –*

> **In that day the deaf will hear the words of the scroll, and out of gloom and darkness the eyes of the blind will see.**
>
> *Isaiah 29:18*

Jesus said, *The lame walk –*

> **Then will the eyes of the blind be opened and the ears of the deaf unstopped. Then will the lame leap like a deer, and the mute tongue shout for joy.**
>
> *Isaiah 35:5,6a*

Jesus said, *Those who have leprosy are cured . . . the dead are raised—*

> **But your dead will live; their bodies will rise. You who dwell in the dust, wake up and shout for joy. Your dew is like the dew of the morning; the earth will give birth to her dead.**
>
> *Isaiah 26:19*

Jesus said, *And the good news is preached to… the poor—*

> **The Spirit of the Sovereign Lord is on me, because the Lord has anointed me to preach good news to the poor.**
>
> *Isaiah 61:1a*

Jesus was communicating that he was exactly the Messiah that he was supposed to be.

You see, in reminding John of Isaiah, Jesus was communicating that he was exactly the Messiah that he was supposed to be. God the Father had planned and ordained his ministry from the beginning, and Jesus ushered in the new era of the kingdom, just as it was promised.

Was John wrong in his understanding of the Messiah and the kingdom? I believe the answer is "No." Wrath, fire and judgment are a significant part of the Kingdom of God, to be sure. Jesus speaks often about judgment and the fire of hell in his ministry, but he most often associates those elements with the time of his second coming when the kingdom is consummated in its fullness. We will talk more about that in later days, but what we shouldn't miss is Jesus' description of the Kingdom of God and how he understands his ministry as a fulfillment of Isaiah's prophecy. There is a profound emphasis on the healing, restoration and renewal of life as Jesus preached and demonstrated the kingdom. Jesus was not only implying a response of "Yes, I am the Messiah," but was also saying, "Look and see, this is the kingdom." The power and ministry of the kingdom in this time was the restoration and healing of the people, just like Isaiah had prophesied it would be.

In the next several days we are going to explore Jesus' explanation of the Kingdom of God, but before we do, I want to challenge you with a statement from John the Baptist's story.

A Perplexing Statement

Jesus ends his response to John with this:

> **"Blessed is the man who does not fall away on account of me."**
>
> *Luke 7:23*

We often think that people who come to trust in Jesus never stumble in their faith or take offense at him. But this seems to be exactly what John was in danger of doing—falling away—because the person and ministry of Jesus didn't quite meet his expectations.

Aren't we all in danger of doing that to a certain extent? We receive Christ and begin to live the Christian life; but something happens, and it becomes a disconnect for us. In the midst of our struggle (in John's case, a jail cell), we turn to God and say, "What's up? Why won't you do something about this? Why have you allowed this to happen, God? I never expected this to happen. You told me that I am your child, but you don't seem to be treating this child very nicely."

For me there have been key moments of questioning and struggle where the way God has set things up doesn't make a lot of sense. I think if we are honest, we all have these "John the Baptist moments."

"God, I have committed to following you and serving you, so why have you put me in such a lonely place?"

The person and ministry of Jesus didn't quite meet his expectations.

"Father, this physical ailment seems so contrary to what you are doing in my life, why are you allowing this to be such a distraction?"

"Jesus, you know how much I loved them and how critical to my life and family they were. Why would you take them now at this time?"

"God, I poured my life into these people and yet they have turned their back on me and you, why won't you pull them back in?"

"Father, I have prayed so hard for my marriage and spouse, but nothing seems to work, and I am so tired … are you listening?"

"God, you promised me that you are more powerful than the deceiver in the world, yet I can't seem to break from this cycle of sin. I am so ashamed. What must I do? Where is your Spirit?"

It was at this moment that Jesus was inviting John to accept him as the Messiah that he was (and is), even if he didn't understand everything. That last statement is an invitation to accept the ministry that Jesus brought, to accept the nature of the kingdom and how it is unfolding in human history. Jesus gives the assurance that not only has God the Father ordained it, but you will be blessed if you receive it as such.

Kingdom Questions

We have talked a lot about expectations the Jewish people of Jesus' day would have had, the expectations that they brought to Jesus' life and ministry. In many ways, Jesus didn't meet those expectations; he never intended to. But to enter the kingdom, we have to first recognize any unbiblical expectations we have placed on God or Jesus, and then be willing to let go of those expectations in order to understand God's plans and purposes not only for this world, but also for us as his church and as individuals. His call is for us to understand and enter his kingdom, and to play a role in bringing his kingdom to this world that so desperately needs it. **Are you willing to go there?**

Are you ready to accept the kingdom as Jesus explains and demonstrates it?

Are you willing to follow where Jesus leads us, despite your preconceived notions? Despite your theological ideas?

> His call is for us to understand and enter his kingdom, and to play a role in bringing his kingdom to this world that so desperately needs it.

Will you follow Jesus in this, despite past disappointments or doubts?

Will you enter in and receive in faith what Jesus has for you, because that is what Jesus instructed us to do?

John was in danger of making Jesus a stumbling block, rather than his rock, in part because of his current circumstances and theological constructions. Will you push through?

Will you accept the Christ as he has been given?

Will you become a son or daughter of the kingdom as Jesus intended?

A great way to respond to questions like these is to bring them to God in prayer!

Days 6 & 7 | Entering In

No one can see the Kingdom of God unless he is born again

Today we are going to look at a fascinating interaction between Jesus and Nicodemus, a religious leader of his time. This seems to be early in Jesus' public ministry, so the religious leaders, as well as the people, were still trying to figure out who Jesus was and exactly what he was up to. Nicodemus came to Jesus at night, indicating some hesitancy, perhaps a fear that he would be looked down on if caught fraternizing with this young teacher. Yet, to Nicodemus' credit, he did come.

The religious leaders, as well as the people, were still trying to figure out who Jesus was and exactly what he was up to.

Read John 3:1–10 together:

> **Now there was a man of the Pharisees named Nicodemus, a member of the Jewish ruling council. He came to Jesus at night and said, "Rabbi, we know you are a teacher who has come from God. For no one could perform the miraculous signs you are doing if God were not with him."**
>
> **In reply Jesus declared, "I tell you the truth, no one can see the kingdom of God unless he is born again."**
>
> **"How can a man be born when he is old?" Nicodemus asked. "Surely he cannot enter a second time into his mother's womb to be born!"**
>
> **Jesus answered, "I tell you the truth, no one can enter the kingdom of God unless he is born of water and the Spirit. Flesh gives birth to flesh, but the Spirit gives birth to spirit. You should not be surprised at my saying, 'You must be born again.' The wind blows wherever it pleases. You hear its sound, but you cannot tell where it comes from or where it is going. So it is with everyone born of the Spirit."**
>
> **"How can this be?" Nicodemus asked.**
>
> **"You are Israel's teacher," said Jesus, "and do you not understand these things?"**

Kingdom Questions

1. **Right away, Jesus began speaking to Nicodemus about the Kingdom of God. Based on your reading from the previous week and on Nicodemus' role as a first-century Jewish leader, what do you think he expected the Kingdom of God to be like?**

2. **This is the only place in Scripture that Jesus uses the phrase *born again*. What two concepts does Jesus associate with the idea of being *born again*?**

Obviously, Nicodemus did not understand what Jesus meant by the phrase *born again* or the kingdom concepts he was introducing. Perhaps we also don't understand.

I have found the following graphics tremendously helpful in understanding Jesus' words here. They are actually a depiction of you and me, of what makes up a person from a biblical perspective.

Flesh gives birth to flesh, but the Spirit gives birth to spirit.

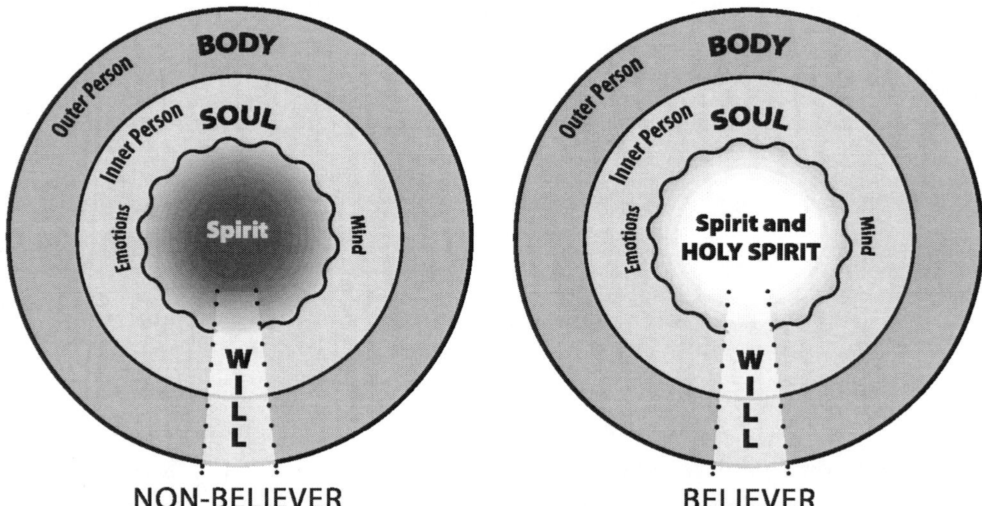

The Bible teaches that we are not just a conglomeration of matter, nor are we just an assembly of physical parts or nerve cells and molecules. We are much more than that! We are spiritual beings; we are actually souls with a body. There is an outer person to us that we can see and touch and feel, but also an inner person—a soul and spirit—made up of our conscious mind, our emotions, our will, and our personality. We can't touch and feel this part, because it is nonmaterial. But it is the soul (nonphysical) that gives life to the body or the physical.

Entering and Seeing

3. **Nicodemus was confused by the *born again* talk. If you were to use the graphic to explain the phrase *born again* to Nicodemus, what would you say? How would you connect Jesus' words *Flesh gives birth to flesh, but the Spirit gives birth to spirit* to the graphic?**

Look at the graphic on the right. This is a picture of those who are not born again. Jesus implied in John 3:5–6 that when we are born physically as babies, all of us are born spiritually dead. We need not only physical birth, but for the Holy Spirit of God to enter into our interior, and bring life to our spirit.

4. When Jesus uses the word *enter* in relation to new birth, what do you think he is talking about?

5. According to Jesus, being *born again* doesn't just change our standing before God, but it also affects what we "see" and perceive. What do you think Jesus means when he talks of seeing the kingdom? Do you think that you presently can see or recognize the Kingdom of God?

6. When the Apostle Paul talked about this born again difference, he said:

> **Therefore, from now on, we regard no one according to the flesh.... if anyone *is* in Christ, *he is* a new creation; old things have passed away; behold, all things have become new.**
>
> *2 Corinthians 5:16–17 (NKJV)*

What do you think it means to regard someone *according to the flesh*? What alternative did Paul give?

If you have entered the kingdom, then now is the time to begin praying for a kingdom perspective.

Ministry Time—Two Possible Responses

If you have not been born again, if you have not believed and received Jesus Christ as your forgiver and Lord (John 3:16), then please talk about this with the rest of your group. Consider taking this step now. If you want to really understand and live the kingdom, you must enter it.

If you have entered the kingdom, then now is the time to begin praying for a kingdom perspective. Pray that, in these next days, God would reveal his kingdom, both in and around you. Pray that he would open your eyes and reveal the secret of the kingdom. I believe he wants you to begin seeing the kingdom in Scripture, as well as in the world around us.

Suggested Prayer to Receive Christ [2]

Lord Jesus Christ,

I am sorry for the things I have done wrong in my life. [Take a few moments to ask his forgiveness for anything particular that is on your conscience.] Please forgive me. I now turn from everything that I know is wrong.

Thank you that you died on the cross for me, so that I could be forgiven and set free. Thank you that you offer me forgiveness and the gift of your Spirit. I now receive that gift. Please come into my life by your Holy Spirit to be with me forever.
Thank you, Lord Jesus. Amen.

2. Adapted from *The Alpha Course: Small Group Leader's Guide*, NY, 1996, p. 46.

Week Two | Jesus Brings the Kingdom

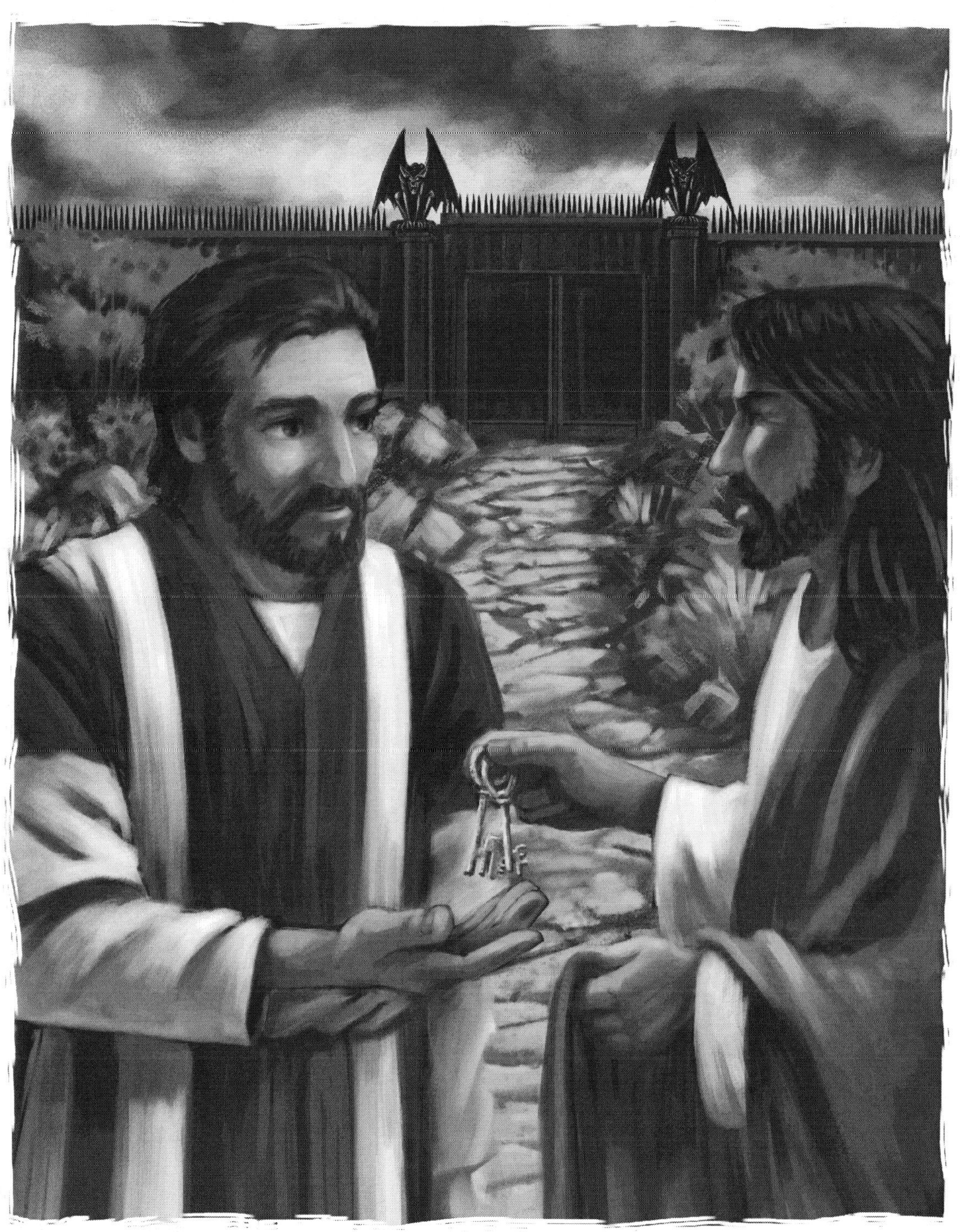

"I will give you the keys of the kingdom of heaven; whatever you bind on earth will be bound in heaven, and whatever you loose on earth will be loosed in heaven." Then he warned his disciples not to tell anyone that he was the Christ.

Matthew 16:19–20

Day 8 A Kingdom Vision

There will be no more death or mourning or crying or pain

Have you ever worked on a vision statement? I have some friends who have created personal vision statements for their life and ministry. Many companies and churches have refocused their efforts by creating new vision statements. A vision can be a powerful thing. It can bring great energy and focus; it can inspire others as they see and begin to believe in the vision. Many entrepreneurs or inventors begin with a vision, a dream. It is what sustains them in the challenges and disappointments. An inspired vision is a picture of the future. It is a dream of what could be. We are not there yet; it is not our reality yet, but it is what we long for and strive for. It is a yearning for a new and better reality.

Jesus knew exactly the reality that he longed for on the Earth, because it was the reality that he came from.

Jesus had such a vision. Unlike an inventor or entrepreneur, Jesus didn't have to just dream of what could be, or what should be. Jesus knew exactly the reality that he longed for on the Earth, because it was the reality that he came from. Jesus is not of the Earth; he is of heaven. This is an important motif in John's Gospel. Jesus often points out that part of his uniqueness is that he came from heaven. At different times he said:

> **"... I am the bread that came down from heaven."**
>
> *John 6:41*

> **"No one has ever gone into heaven except the one who came from heaven—the Son of Man."**
>
> *John 3:13*

In the beginning he was with God (John 1:1), but then he became flesh and lived (Greek *tabernacled* or *tented*) among us (John 1:14). Jesus said plainly to his disciples,

> **"I came from the Father and entered the world; now I am leaving the world and going back to the Father."**
>
> *John 16:28*

Jesus was from the reality of heaven. He was from a place where the rule and reign of God is perfect and all-encompassing. He didn't have to imagine what the kingdom would look like; he didn't have to dream of what it could be. He was there in the beginning creating the heavens and the Earth when they were all part of the Kingdom of God, perfectly submitted to the rule and reign of God.

Jesus was there in the Garden of Eden before the Fall and saw humankind living in the perfect presence of God. Jesus was there when the man and woman fell from his presence and lost the reality of his perfect governance. He was from the reality of the Kingdom of Heaven, and sought to bring it to Earth. Jesus created the kingdom reality on Earth in the beginning, and now he had come to recreate it in the world, to restore all that humankind had lost. He came to create a New Heaven and a New Earth, a place where God could reign again, fully and completely. Jesus came to change life as we know it to life where no sin or curse or enemy will be present to rob creation of all that God intended it to be. He came to give us a new reality in which to live, a new era, a new and restored life.

Jesus' Vision of a New Reality

Jesus proclaims the renewal, restoration, and healing of all things

In the book of Revelation, Jesus articulated his vision for us and the world more clearly than in any other place. He had returned to heaven and spoke to the Apostle John through a vision, a vision of a New Heaven and a New Earth—the new Kingdom of God reality.

> **Then I saw a new heaven and a new earth, for the first heaven and the first earth had passed away, and there was no longer any sea. I saw the Holy City, the new Jerusalem, coming down out of heaven from God, prepared as a bride beautifully dressed for her husband. And I heard a loud voice from the throne saying, "Now the dwelling of God is with men, and he will live with them. They will be his people, and God himself will be with them and be their God. He will wipe every tear from their eyes. There will be no more death or mourning or crying or pain, for the old order of things has passed away." He who was seated on the throne said, "I am making everything new!"**
>
> *Revelation 21:1–5a*

Do you see the vision? Do you see the picture that Jesus wants in our hearts? It is a picture of the completion of the Kingdom of God. Our first Earth, or present reality that we live in now, gives way to a new way of living, a new life in Christ, a new reality before God. It is the new reality of the Kingdom of Heaven fully realized in and among God's people. Jesus proclaims the renewal, restoration, and healing of all things—all aspects of our reality. This was Jesus' vision statement from the beginning: *I am making everything new!* He had lived that dream out in part while he walked on this Earth, and now this is a picture of it fully completed.

This is not only Jesus' vision, but as his followers, he desires it to be ours. It is not just a vision about our future in heaven, but it is meant to be a vision realized more and more in the present. He fully intended for us to share in this vision for the world, and to join him in seeing its reality spill out today, in the present. Because of that, let's take a moment to reflect on the promised new reality. The vision may not be realized in full, but as his disciples live it out, it becomes clear.

Spiritual Healing

> **Now the dwelling of God is with men, and he will live with them. They will be his people, and God himself will be with them and be their God.**
>
> *Revelation 21:3b*

What a profound picture of restored intimacy between God and his people! It points us back to the Garden of Eden where it all began. Before Adam and Eve's sin created a barrier between them and God, they enjoyed life, delighting in their intimacy with God the Father. From the breath of life that brought the first man into being (Genesis 2:7), to the intimate interaction and provision of God for his people, we know that we were originally created to experience an in-depth relationship with him. Yet, because of the Fall, we lost that cherished place; we were removed from that life-giving relationship. But in this picture of a new reality, once again our intimate friendship with God is restored and renewed. God lives with us in a new garden (or city!). We are his people and he is our God—completely and fully, as it was intended. God promised this long ago.

> **"I will rejoice over Jerusalem and take delight in my people."**
>
> *Isaiah 65:19a*

He fully intended for us to share in this vision for the world, and to join him in seeing its reality spill out today, in the present.

Suffering Separation

I think one of the most intriguing things for non-Christians is to hear Christians authentically share about a "relationship" with Christ. From my conversations with non-Christian friends, I hear how distant they feel from God. Talk of a personal relationship is usually foreign; the idea of intimacy with the living God is unfamiliar and unknown.

Yet, even as Christians, we know that this reality is only here in part. We know this from life experience; we know this from our ever-present longing for more of God. In my own spiritual life, I often struggle in a relationship that longs for, but lacks, the intimacy with God pictured here. It's in the times of listening that I can't seem to hear him speak—the times of asking when he doesn't seem to be listening—the times of longing for closeness when my heart remains in a distant place—the times of ministry when I feel so empty of his power and his presence. There is an intimacy that is restored and renewed by the tearing of the curtain, and yet there is a life and relationship with God that still feels the effects of the Fall in Eden. There is a profound struggle to reclaim the spiritual wholeness we were made for. We are restored, yet still being restored. And in the restoration process, we are called to reach out to a lost and distant world—to offer an intimacy with God that it has never known. I have found this message to be strange to the world's ears, yet captivating to its soul.

Emotional Healing

It is almost impossible to imagine that kind of reality where all the sadness and distress of life are removed from us. Think of what our relationships with others would look like if they were free of the things that cause hurt and sadness. Think of our marriages free from *crying*, our friendships free from *mourning*. Think of our emotional lives free of regrets, free from guilt and indignation. Hard to imagine, yes, but this is part of Jesus' vision—part of the promise of kingdom reality.

As a pastor, I have walked with many people and couples suffering under enormous distress and sadness. From the struggles of marriage, to the suffering of loss; from the painful words and actions of others, to the shameful mistakes of our own hands—life is hard. When we peel away the I've-got-it-all-together masks, and take a long, hard look at the painful places, we quickly realize we are not in heaven yet. We are part of the creation that groans for the new reality to come. Our souls long for a place where God dries all of our tears and heals all our wounds.

Think of what our relationships with others would look like if they were free of the things that cause hurt and sadness.

A Tearless Reality

The vision to which we hold as Christians is that of a tearless reality. It is a place where not only our intimacy with God is restored, but where the pain and hurt in our relationships with others are wiped clean. The effects of sin are removed. The reservoirs of pain and weeping are filled and healed. As Isaiah says,

> **"...the sound of weeping and of crying will be heard in it no more."**
>
> *Isaiah 65:19*

This is an inner healing that can only be accomplished by God. An amazing aspect of the Kingdom of God is that it isn't a reality that we can only long for in the future. Sometimes we find it in the present—not in whole, but in part.

It's true that this reality can seem elusive, so difficult to attain and live in. Yet, we may miss it because we don't realize it is part of the vision of Christ for us today. We may long for its reality in the future, but don't seek God's resources for the kingdom today. So often we just don't see it as a possible, present reality. We don't share the dream. Jesus came as a healer. He came to make all things new, including our hearts and our relationships. He is at work right now, today, restoring hearts, calming fears, mending wounds, renewing dreams. It was Jesus' vision in his life, and it is his vision for our lives as well.

Physical Healing

> **"'There will be no more death' or mourning or crying or pain, for the old order of things has passed away."**
>
> *Revelation 21:4b*

Just as we suffer today from broken relationships and emotional wounds, so we all suffer physically. With our fragile and aging bodies, ultimately we will all perish and die. This is the way of things, since we were removed from the garden—the garden that contained the tree of life. From the agony of birth defects to the battle with terminal diseases, we all struggle with our health and strength. Even those of us with the best health practices and good family genes ultimately succumb because of the Curse. In our time, we have made great progress in counteracting the physical effects of the Fall. Still all creation groans as the Curse of the world runs its course.

But the question is, "Do we see the vision of physical restoration as part of God's plan for us today?" I have changed my own language now because of the Kingdom of God. I never used to give assurances of healing to people when praying for them, because I never knew if it was God's will. But now I do. Now I know that this is part of Jesus' vision for us in the world. Physical healing is part of the dream. This is part of his salvation for you and me. Now I can say with confidence that our healing in all things is God's will. I just don't know if it will be in this life or the next. I don't know the causes and the course of the sickness or disease, but I do know that ultimately it will be healed.

Most of us have been raised with the idea that heaven is a completely future hope.

A Cancer-Free Heaven

Part of the promise of this new reality is that there will be no more disease or defects in heaven. The things that plague us physically will be wiped away forever in the presence of a God who heals. The cancer that destroyed a friend will itself be destroyed; the unexplainable accident that shattered a friend's life will itself be shattered. God says through the prophet Isaiah,

> **"Never again will there be in it an infant who lives but a few days."**
> *Isaiah 65:20a*

This will be the destruction of the enemy and all his work in this world and in our lives. We will be free from his ill motives and destructive work that leaves all of creation longing for the renewal. And sometimes, just as Jesus promised, when we pray for the kingdom to come in the life of a person, that sickness or pain will be removed instantly, miraculously. That is when the Kingdom of God is here, now!

The restoration, the renewal, the healing of all things—this is our glorious hope. This is what Christ has called us to. It is the vision that he wants to plant in our hearts. It is the labor he calls us to share as he makes all things new. We need to know it, believe it and live it.

The Presence of the Future

But here is the kicker for us. Most of us have been raised with the idea that heaven is a completely future hope. Our perspective has been that we merely hope for heaven as we struggle in this life with all the effects of the Fall. Sure, if modern medicine and psychiatry can help alleviate the pain, great! We will take it.

But because we have missed the vision of the reality of heaven being available today, we rarely even turn to God or ask him for healing. It was his vision for our lives, but we don't even seek that vision to be a reality today.

Yes, most of us as Christians pray when we struggle. Our prayers, however, often reflect more of a perspective of God bringing pain and suffering to us, rather than a vision of him removing that pain and suffering. Our prayers for ourselves and others often lean more in the direction of, "God, if it's your will, give me the strength to endure," or, "Lord, I ask for your comforting presence and your peace that transcends understanding." I am not suggesting that these prayers are wrong or inappropriate. They may be prayers that are very appropriate based on the present circumstances. But what I am suggesting is that our perspective of life and ministry in terms of sickness and suffering has not reflected Jesus' vision. We may believe in and hold to his vision for the future, but we have not allowed this future hope to leak into our present. Yet this is just the very thing Jesus wants us to do.

Our hope has often been merely in the future, but we haven't dared to hope in the present. I want to suggest to you that Jesus intends us to live in this tension. He desires this kingdom tension in order to influence how we live and love, how we minister and how we pray. It is a life with the vision of heaven spilling out on Earth—right here, right now!

I am suggesting that our perspective of life and ministry in terms of sickness and suffering has not reflected Jesus' vision.

? Kingdom Questions

When a church or a company has a strong vision statement, we expect that new members or employees will commit themselves to helping fulfill that vision. The vision serves as a guide for decisions to be made and priorities to be established.

If you adopted the vision statement of Revelation 21:1-5a for today, how would that change your life?

Would it affect how you interact with people—how you speak to them—pray for them—engage them?

Would it affect your time, your focus, your thinking?

Would it affect your ministry or sense of calling?

R Reflection

A prayer to think about and pray—

Our Father in heaven, hallowed be your name. Your kingdom come, your will be done, on earth as it is in heaven. Father, please bring the reality of your kingdom into my life now—spiritually, emotionally and physically. May your kingdom spill over into my life and ministry, my perspective and my dreams.

Day 9 An Ancient Promise of a New Reality

The Spirit of the Lord is on me because he has anointed me… to proclaim the year of the Lord's favor

Several years ago, I was looking for a new position as a pastor. There I was poring over many church profiles, advertisements for various openings and numerous job descriptions. My major search had been for solo or senior pastor positions, but then I received a phone call from the lay leader of a search committee. The man told me how he had approached one of my friends regarding the pastoral position they needed to fill. But, after hearing about the job, my friend suggested that the man contact me. It was a short conversation, and we decided that the next best step was for the leader to send me the job description. My wife actually read the job description first and, handing it over to me, she said, "This is you!" It was a position description of a Pastor of Evangelism and Discipleship, highlighting various activities related to these two purposes. I read it over and said to her, "I don't think I could write a better job description for myself if I tried." We were both very excited. It seemed like there was a position out there that was created with my name on it. It was a role that related directly to what I believed was my calling and giftedness. We decided to check this position out; and ultimately it was where God led us.

In Jesus' time there were a lot of confused expectations about who the Messiah, the Anointed One, would be.

We have been talking a lot about the Kingdom of God—what it is and what it isn't. In Jesus' time there were a lot of confused expectations about who the Messiah, the Anointed One, would be and what he would do when he came. Perhaps it was because of these expectations that Jesus never announced directly he was the prophesied Messiah. But what Jesus *did* say quite clearly was that he had been anointed to carry out the messianic agenda. He announced his *messianic job description* and declared that he was the fulfillment of this divine mission. If today we pay attention to his words, we will learn what Jesus came to do and accomplish. If we keep paying attention, this job description will help develop our picture of the Kingdom of God.

An Ancient Job Description

The word *Messiah* comes from the Hebrew word for *anointed*. In the Old Testament, prophets, priests and kings were anointed with oil as a sign of their divine calling. King David is a good example. Samuel anointed him king even before Saul had been moved out of the way. The anointing signaled that God the Father had chosen and called him to serve a special purpose.

Before Jesus began his public ministry, before he taught or performed a miracle in public, he received his own anointing. Luke records Jesus' baptism like this:

> **...Jesus was baptized....And as he was praying, heaven was opened and the Holy Spirit descended on him in bodily form like a dove. And a voice came from heaven: "You are my Son, whom I love; with you I am well pleased."**
>
> *Luke 3:21–22*

Immediately after that, Jesus, *full of the Holy Spirit* according to Luke 4:1, was led to the desert and tempted by the devil. Jesus returned from the desert *in the power of the Spirit* and began to teach and preach (4:14–16). Following this he went to his hometown of Nazareth and at the Sabbath day worship service he did something amazing. He claimed the job description and anointing of the Messiah.

The anointing signaled that God the Father had chosen and called him to serve a special purpose.

> **The scroll of the prophet Isaiah was handed to him. Unrolling it, he found the place where it is written: "The Spirit of the Lord is on me, because he has anointed me to preach good news to the poor. He has sent me to proclaim freedom for the prisoners and recovery of sight for the blind, to release the oppressed, to proclaim the year of the Lord's favor." Then he rolled up the scroll, gave it back to the attendant and sat down. The eyes of everyone in the synagogue were fastened on him, and he began by saying to them, "Today this scripture is fulfilled in your hearing."**
>
> *Luke 4:17–21*

Please notice some very significant things from this proclamation by Jesus. The first is that Jesus indirectly declared himself the Messiah who was to come. He read from Isaiah 61, a well-known passage, and the Jews listening to Jesus would have been very familiar with this book. Isaiah is the prophet that talks most about the Messiah or king who was to come. There are many sections of judgment against Israel and other nations, but in the midst of all the woeful passages and prophecies of destruction, a profound hope surfaces throughout the book. The hope is for the establishment of the Lord's kingdom. The book steadily moves toward a restored people, a restored heaven and a restored Earth—a new Messianic Age. The Lord would bring all this to his people and to his creation primarily through the new messianic king, or *suffering servant*, who was to come.

Isaiah 61 is the declaration of the *year of the Lord's favor* when all would be restored. God would raise up and anoint the Messiah for this special purpose. Jesus not only read this passage out loud in the synagogue, but claimed this anointing—claimed this special purpose (or job description) for himself.

> **"Today this scripture is fulfilled in your hearing."**
>
> *Luke 4:21*

What an incredible statement!

Jesus was saying, "The time is now; this is the time of the Lord's favor." This was the time of the restoration and renewal that God had promised. In other words, the Kingdom of God was there. Jesus was the fulfillment of the messianic promises.

The reason that the renewal and restoration of God is upon us today is because Jesus is the king empowered to bring it. This was and is his focus and direction, his ministry, as he fulfilled the calling of the Messiah. This was why he was anointed with the Holy Spirit at his baptism, to bring the era of God's kingdom—to bring the new age of blessing, favor and restoration.

The Focus of Jesus' Ministry

If, a number of years ago, someone had asked me to articulate Jesus' job description, I would not have turned to Luke 4. I probably would have said something like, "Jesus died on the cross for our sins, so that we might be forgiven and receive eternal life in heaven." I would have gone more to John 3:16, not Luke 4. Yet Jesus didn't talk about dying on the cross until well into his public ministry, and even then, only with his disciples in secret. But again, if someone had asked me to describe Jesus' basic message, I would have talked about his sacrifice and how he paved the way for us to live eternally with God in heaven.

The reason that the renewal and restoration of God is upon us today is because Jesus is the king empowered to bring it.

Today I answer that question differently. You see, I believe that Jesus came with a focus first and foremost to bring heaven to Earth. He came to bring heaven as a reality in our lives. He came for the restoration and healing of all creation, especially his people. Yes, part of his calling was to get *us into heaven*, but first he wanted to get *heaven into us*. Previously, I had been committed to share the good news of Jesus Christ, how he died on the cross for us. I had never even thought about the *good news of the kingdom* that Jesus was sent to proclaim. (Luke 4:43) In conversations, I used to talk about getting into heaven and enjoying the blessings of heaven. Never did I mention God's restoration today, God's Kingdom of Heaven present in a believer's life here and now.

Think how connected Jesus' Messianic call (Luke 4) is to the picture of heaven that we studied in Revelation 21 on Day 8. Both the vision and the calling are focused on restoring God's people and creation to himself. Look back to Isaiah 61, and you will see a chapter filled with blessing and favor.

> **...He has sent me to bind up the broken hearted...to comfort all who mourn, and provide for those who grieve...to bestow on them a crown of beauty instead of ashes, the oil of gladness instead of mourning, and a garment of praise instead of a spirit of despair....**
>
> *Isaiah 61:1–3*

Not only would this be the Messiah's agenda, but also the agenda of the people who would follow him.

> **They will rebuild the ancient ruins and restore the places long devastated; they will renew the ruined cities that have been devastated for generations.**
>
> *Isaiah 61:4*

Jesus the Messiah came with this great calling, he came with the divine job description to rebuild, restore and renew. He came to do this not only for the people of his time, but also for you and me. He came not only to get us to heaven, but to bring the restorative power and promise of heaven to us right here, right now. This was Jesus' special calling, his special job description. The Kingdom of God was a hope for a new reality prophesied in ancient times—a vision of the future promised from the throne room of heaven—a present reality claimed by the Messiah himself for you and me.

He came not only to get us to heaven, but to bring the restorative power and promise of heaven to us right here, right now.

Reflection

Prior to this chapter, how would you have described the focus of Jesus' ministry? Now how would you articulate his job description?

Have you ever realized that rebuilding, restoring and renewing were so close to the heart of the Christian message?

Is there a way in which you as an individual Christian share in this "Messianic job description"?

Imagination Station

Read through all of Isaiah 61. Try to imagine what these promises would look like if they were lived out today. Bring all this to God in prayer.

Day 10 | Timing Is Everything

Some who are standing here will not taste death before they see the Kingdom of God come with power

> We live in a fallen place . . . far from God's intentions.

While in college I attended a week-long leadership retreat. I still remember the pastor's messages. He had been preaching a couple of times a day, and Scripture seemed to be cutting through me in ways I never thought possible. This man seemed to lead us to the throne room of God each day, just as if we were sitting at the feet of Jesus. There was one message in particular that I don't think I will ever forget. The pastor was sharing about his brother whom he lost a number of years ago. The brother had been in an accident and was paralyzed from the neck down. A husband and father, he would soon die from complications. The pastor recalled sitting next to his brother's hospital bed and weeping. His brother was also a person of deep faith, and during those weeks in the hospital, as the devastation and loss settled into their souls, the two often wept with one voice. The pastor didn't just seek to comfort and support his brother, but they also struggled together through the mysterious *whys and wherefores*.

During the retelling of this story, the pastor shed a few tears, and as students we wept with him. Yet, we also looked to him for some truth or meaning in the face of such pain and sorrow. The truth the pastor repeated over and over again was this: "We must never forget that this place in which we live is not heaven." We live in a fallen place, a place far from God's intentions. It is a place that groans with sadness and weeps with loss—a place of birth defects and miscarriages—a place of Alzheimer's and dementia—and all that is in-between. In these things God does not delight; they make him weep for his people. It is because of such things that he has given us the hope of heaven.

The words "Never forget, this is not heaven," resonated through my soul. It didn't necessarily answer all the *whys and wherefores*, but it expressed a much needed perspective. It also gave me a new way of looking at the cross—ultimately, God's answer for suffering was revealed in the suffering of his Son. His suffering was for our suffering. His passion was the place for our sorrow and pain, but also the place for our hope.

And that is where many of us are. In the midst of pain and loss and distress, we turn our hopes to heaven, the time we all look forward to. We comfort those in distress with the hope of glory, the hope of heaven. Yet, I don't think that our future hope is all that the cross has accomplished for us. It is certainly a huge part, but in Christ we find perspective in the midst of the present. You see, my outlook has changed since studying the Kingdom of God. The hope of healing and restoration is the same, but what is different is the timing.

Timing of the Kingdom

One of the most confusing aspects of the Kingdom of God is timing. If you read over Jesus' numerous statements regarding the timing of the kingdom, you want to ask, "Well, is it here or isn't it?" Jesus talked about the nearness of the kingdom.

> **"The time has come," he said. "The kingdom of God is near. Repent and believe the good news!"**
>
> *Mark 1:15*

Is the kingdom here or isn't it?

When he sent out some of his disciples, he told them to repeat this concept of nearness:

> **"Heal the sick who are there and tell them, 'The kingdom of God is near you.'…"**
>
> *Luke 10:9*

This nearness communicates a sense that the kingdom is coming. It is close at hand, and yet, perhaps it is not completely here, not fully realized. It is near, we can say, but not *fully* here.

At other times, Jesus talked as if the Kingdom of God had come; as if it was more than just near, even was actually here. After driving out a demon and being questioned by the religious leaders, Jesus said,

> **"But if I drive out demons by the Spirit of God, then the kingdom of God has come upon you."**
>
> *Matthew 12:28*

So what's up? Is the kingdom here or isn't it?

Perhaps one of the most perplexing Scriptures is Jesus' promise to the disciples that they would see the Kingdom of God come with power. He had just made a reference to judgment day when he would come in the Father's glory and with angels. Then he said,

> **"I tell you the truth, some who are standing here will not taste death before they see the kingdom of God come with power."**
>
> *Mark 9:1*

The problem with this passage is that it seems like Jesus is promising some of his disciples that they will be alive when the final judgment day comes and God sets everything in order. Since the disciples did indeed die, some have suggested that Jesus simply got it wrong. This goes along with the idea that Jesus was a failed revolutionary because he died and never brought the kingdom that he promised.

I believe that a more accurate understanding of Jesus' statement cited above comes from a clear understanding of the timing of the kingdom. It is true that the disciples died before the final judgment day. They never saw it. But just after this statement, three of them did get a glimpse of the kingdom. In fact, all three synoptic Gospels (Matthew, Mark and Luke) record a version of this statement. Immediately following it, they tell the story of the transfiguration. Mark 9:2–4 and 7 tell part of the story.

> **After six days Jesus took Peter, James and John with him and led them up a high mountain, where they were all alone. There he was transfigured before them. His clothes became dazzling white, whiter than anyone in the world could bleach them. And there appeared before them Elijah and Moses, who were talking with Jesus.…Then a cloud appeared and enveloped them, and a voice came from the cloud: "This is my Son, whom I love. Listen to him!"**

Peter, James and John (Jesus' inner circle) caught a glimpse of Jesus' true identity, his true self as the unique Son of God. His dazzling clothes represented the glory that Jesus came from and would return to. They glimpsed a little of his true state of splendor. In the Kingdom of Heaven, Jesus is fully majestic, fully God. All of heaven surrounds and worships him, the king and Savior of all. The three disciples got a glimpse of this. They saw Jesus in his splendor as God's Messiah and as the one true king of heaven. The Father, by his words, affirmed Jesus' identity.

The classic theological expression of the Kingdom of God is the concept of *already but not yet.*

However, after the privileged three saw and experienced the transfiguration, the heavenly glory of Jesus was cloaked again in his humanity. So the question is: "Was the kingdom there?" Absolutely! They saw the kingdom in its power, or as Matthew put it,

> **"…some who are standing here will not taste death before they see the Son of Man coming in his kingdom."**
>
> *Matthew 16:28*

But then the disciples returned to a place and time that was only *near* the kingdom—not the kingdom fully realized, as it had been at the transfiguration. Yes, they saw the kingdom, they experienced the glory of God fully and caught a glimpse of the vision of the kingdom; but ultimately they returned to a place of *somewhat.*

Diagramming the Presence of the Future

The classic theological expression of the Kingdom of God is the concept of *already but not yet.* When Jesus or his disciples healed or restored a person, when they drove out demons or raised the dead; then the Kingdom of God, or the reality of the kingdom, splashed onto Earth. In those moments, the kingdom was truly there among them. In our world where sickness remains, and sin-sick souls struggle and demonic activity is still at work, the Kingdom of God has not yet fully come. It will not come fully and completely and eternally until Christ returns in all his glory.

The theologian George Ladd clearly enunciates this understanding in his book *The Presence of the Future.* [3] He explains how the church at present is living "between the times" of the *already* and the *not yet.* Two diagrams adapted from *The Alpha Course* [4] are helpful in grasping this timing of the kingdom. The first diagram shows the expectations of the Jewish people.

Keep in mind all the expectations the Jews of Jesus' time had regarding the kingdom and the Messiah. Like us, they struggled in this fallen world with loss and pain, as well as with Roman rule and subjection. Their yearning turned toward a time when God would come and heal all that, a time when the Messiah would restore justice and freedom. When the Messiah came, the Jews thought, he would judge all things and right all wrongs. The Messiah would re-establish Israel to its golden age of dominance. His coming would usher in a new age and reality. With Messiah as the new king, the Kingdom of God would be established forever; and all the other kingdoms of the world, especially Rome, would be overthrown. Diagram 1 depicts the Jewish expectations.

He brought the kingdom in part through his first coming.... Jesus also knew that the Kingdom of Heaven would not be fully realized until his second coming.

Diagram 1

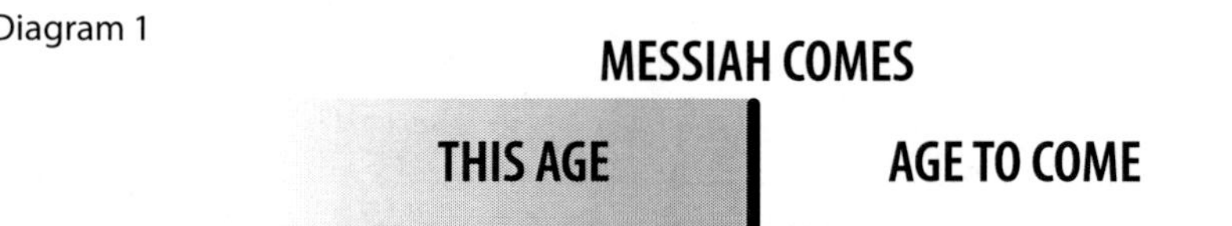

Jesus arrived and, in response to the idea presented in Diagram 1, he could have said, "Yes, *but not exactly.*" Jesus demonstrated this idea in his ministry. He brought the kingdom in part through his first coming. With every act of healing and restoration, with every new person submitting to the lordship of Christ, the kingdom splashed on the world. Yes, Jesus brought it in part, but not in fullness, like the inner three had glimpsed at the transfiguration.

In one sense, Jesus was the Messiah who brought the kingdom. That is why he began with the announcement of its nearness. It was his big idea; and he was fully aware that as he ministered to the people of God, he brought the Kingdom of God into their lives. And yet, Jesus also knew that the Kingdom of Heaven would not be fully realized until his second coming. Diagram 2 illustrates the timing of the kingdom.

Diagram 2

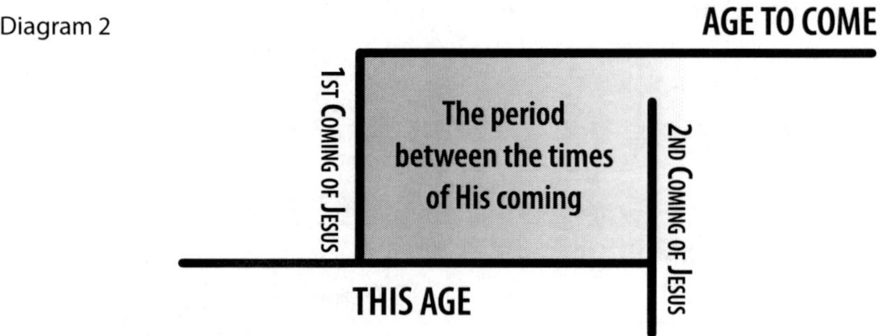

3. Ladd, George Eldon. *The Presence of the Future: The Eschatology of Biblical Realism.* Grand Rapids, MI: Wm. B. Eerdmans Publishing Company, 1974, p. 338.

4. The two charts used here are adapted from *The Alpha Course Manual,* Section 13: "Does God Heal Today?" Alpha North America, NY, 1995, p. 51.

From Diagram 2, we see that Jesus initiated the coming of the kingdom. It came in the healing and restoration of people's lives physically, emotionally and spiritually. It came when he squelched demonic activity. It came as individuals and families embraced Jesus as Lord and Messiah. Yet, at the same time, the new age of the kingdom did not come fully. The rule and reign of God, the restoration of all things, did not come completely. The new age will come when Jesus returns—not as a baby, but in his full glory as the Lord of Lords.

Another thing we realize is that we are presently living *between the times*. The kingdom has come and is coming; yet we are still living in a sin-saturated and fallen world. We still experience the pain of loss and separation; we still struggle with ailments and diseases. And yet, Jesus is at work bringing the Kingdom of God into our world and reality. The huge challenge of kingdom living is persevering in this tension, the *already but not yet* tension. Furthermore, as we will see in the next several days, Jesus envisioned his disciples as those who would continue to bring the kingdom. Jesus envisioned a church that would be focused on bringing the fullness of the kingdom in greater and greater degrees within the fallen world.

The huge challenge of kingdom living is persevering in this tension.

Reflecting on a Parable

One of my favorite parables about the kingdom is about the mustard seed. It is simple and straightforward. Read the parables of the mustard seed and the one about yeast in the Scripture passage below, and reflect on what Jesus wanted to communicate about the kingdom.

> **He told them another parable: "The kingdom of heaven is like a mustard seed, which a man took and planted in his field. Though it is the smallest of all your seeds, yet when it grows, it is the largest of garden plants and becomes a tree, so that the birds of the air come and perch in its branches." He told them still another parable: "The kingdom of heaven is like yeast that a woman took and mixed into a large amount of flour until it worked all through the dough."**
>
> *Matthew 13:31–33*

Kingdom Questions

Who might the man/woman represent in the parable?

What might the *field* and the *dough* represent?

Is there significance to the words *planted* (first parable) and *mixed* (second parable)?

What do you think the significance of the smallness and largeness is in the first parable?

What do you think the significance of the phrase *worked all through* is in the second parable?

How have these parables enlarged your understanding of the kingdom?

Day 11 Enemies of the Kingdom

How then can his kingdom stand?

Jose and Lupe were a Latino couple, relatively new to the church. They were both very nice and gentle folks, and that made their story all the more surprising.

> An expression on their faces said, "Please don't think we're crazy."

They looked at me with an expression on their faces that said, "Please don't think we're crazy," and began to share the strange things happening in their house. It was spooky, supernatural stuff, and they didn't have a clue how to deal with it. They talked about how they often felt an evil presence in some of the upstairs rooms of their house. In the office, the computer would turn off and on randomly. Jose had tried a number of things, but there wasn't a logical solution as far as he could tell. He was scared to enter the room at certain times in the evening because of the feeling of that evil presence.

On a couple of occasions, Jose and Lupe and their children were awakened in the middle of the night by what they said sounded like someone in the kitchen pulling all of the dishes out of the cupboards and shattering them on the floor. When Jose and Lupe would rush downstairs to the kitchen, there would be nothing and no one to be found. This would tend to dissuade you from sneaking down to the kitchen for a late night snack, wouldn't it!

Probably the scariest and most disconcerting thing Jose and Lupe told me was that their son would not sleep in his room. He was afraid of what he called the Shadow Lady. Numerous times in the middle of the night, he had been awakened by the Shadow Lady crying in the corner of his room. So now he was sleeping in his sister's room. Can you blame him? When Jose and Lupe asked what the Shadow Lady looked like, their son said that the one time she turned her face toward him, it was the face of his mom. Very scary stuff!

Jose and Lupe asked what I thought about all this. I assured them that I didn't think they were crazy. More importantly, they asked if I could do anything about it. Now, I will ask you the same two questions: What do you make of events like these? Could you help this couple in any way?

In just a moment we will look at a biblical story similar in nature to Jose and Lupe's. But before we do, let's address a common blind spot that many western Christians have when it comes to stories of the supernatural.

The Blind Spot of Rationalism

Rationalism is the theory that the exercise of reason—rather than experience, authority, or spiritual revelation—provides the primary basis for knowledge. When I refer to the blind spot of rationalism, I am not suggesting that the exercise of reason is bad. God has certainly given us our reasoning faculties and wants us to use them. But rationalism becomes a blind spot when we exclude all other possible elements of life and reality that are beyond our reason. In our Western mindset, we have been trained to disbelieve, to devalue, or to give no credence to anything beyond reason. Anything unexplainable or outside the laws of nature or the natural order is not valid.

We have been trained to disbelieve, to devalue, or to give no credence to, anything beyond reason.

We have marinated in this Western mindset for so long that we automatically filter out any supernatural activity from our understanding of reality. We have actually removed the whole category of the supernatural or spiritual realm from our perspective of reality. The missiologist Paul Hiebert[5] points out that this perspective is unique to the Western culture. He comments that almost every society or culture in the world has a category in their belief system for supernatural activity through divine intervention, angels, demons, and the like—every society or culture, that is, except ours!

Not only is this an unbiblical perspective but it creates a blind spot. It too narrowly defines truth and limits the search for it. When we come to a story such as Jose and Lupe's, as well as many found in Scripture, we may have already predetermined that the supernatural elements are fiction. We disallow spiritual elements from informing our worldview.

Jesus was very rational in his teaching. Yet, as most cultures do, he fully embraced the reality and presence of the supernatural. He taught about this reality and informed us of both the good and the evil aspects of this realm. One of the reasons we have missed the kingdom and many other aspects of God is because of this blind spot. We must recognize it and allow the Word of God to inform and reform our thinking. As we do that, we learn more about the kingdom and its enemies. To understand and address Jose and Lupe's situation, we have to understand our adversary from a biblical perspective. Scripture teaches that the Kingdom of God has an enemy, and we must contend with him.

The Kingdom of Darkness

In the Old Testament we get some glimpses of our enemy, Satan, and his desire to tempt and inflict evil upon humankind. But it is in the New Testament, especially in the life and ministry of Jesus, that we get a fuller picture of the enemy and the evil he has brought into the world. What is important for our study of the Kingdom of God is that the New Testament often uses kingdom language to describe and help us understand Satan.

5. *The Missiological Implications of Epistemological Shifts: Affirming Truth in a Modern/Postmodern World.* Paul G. Hiebert. Harrisburg, PA: Trinity Press International, 1999.

Somewhere in the history of heaven and the world, Satan fell away from all that is good. Rather than destroy him, God chose to banish him to the Earth. Jesus told his disciples,

> **..."I saw Satan fall like lightning from heaven."**
>
> *Luke 10:18b*

This may have been a reference to the event recorded in Isaiah that many ascribe to Satan:

> **How you have fallen from heaven, O morning star, son of the dawn! You have been cast down to the earth ....**
>
> *Isaiah 14:12*

And though the Earth was created good, evil entered. When Adam and Eve fell, all of creation fell with them. Life for all humankind was now lived out of the garden, separated from the perfect dominion and presence of God.

Because of Adam and Eve's fall, as well as Satan's, our world has become Satan's domain. It is sobering to look at Satan's power and authority from a biblical perspective. Jesus referred to Satan as the *prince of this world* (John 12:31; 16:11). Satan is also called *the god of this age* (2 Corinthians 4:4) and *the ruler of the kingdom of the air* (Ephesians 2:2). We learn from Satan's temptation of Jesus in the desert how profound his rule is over the world.

Jesus resisted the tempter, but did not challenge his claim of authority and rule.

> **The devil led him up to a high place and showed him in an instant all the kingdoms of the world. And he said to him, "I will give you all their authority and splendor, for it has been given to me, and I can give it to anyone I want to. So if you worship me, it will all be yours."**
>
> *Luke 4:5–7*

Jesus resisted the tempter, but did not challenge his claim of authority and rule. Jesus came knowing full well Satan's end game, because it was the complete opposite of his own.

> **The thief comes only to steal and kill and destroy; I have come that they may have life, and have it to the full.**
>
> *John 10:10*

The apostles taught that the evil one is still alive and active in this world. Peter tells us to

> **Be self-controlled and alert. Your enemy the devil prowls around like a roaring lion looking for someone to devour.**
>
> *1 Peter 5:8*

Satan is not a toothless lion, but is busy scheming and plotting our demise (Ephesians 6:11). His purpose is clear—our destruction.

What a frightful picture—an evil presence in the world that has the desire and the power to attack and bring down human beings. He is by no means equal in any way to God, for he is a part of the created order. But he still has power and authority over this world, fighting to remain its prince.

A Clash of Kingdoms

One of the most important aspects of understanding Jesus is to realize that his mission was in direct conflict with Satan. As he brought the restoration and healing of heaven, he was undoing and fighting back the kingdom of darkness. Jesus understood that his ministry was a clash of kingdoms. Jesus explains this in Matthew 12.

> **Then they brought him a demon-possessed man who was blind and mute, and Jesus healed him, so that he could both talk and see. All the people were astonished and said, "Could this be the Son of David?" But when the Pharisees heard this, they said, "It is only by Beelzebub, the prince of demons, that this fellow drives out demons." Jesus knew their thoughts and said to them, "Every kingdom divided against itself will be ruined, and every city or household divided against itself will not stand. If Satan drives out Satan, he is divided against himself. How then can his kingdom stand? And if I drive out demons by Beelzebub, by whom do your people drive them out? So then, they will be your judges. But if I drive out demons by the Spirit of God, then the kingdom of God has come upon you."**
>
> *Matthew 12:22–28*

He is by no means equal in any way to God, for he is a part of the created order.

These verses have huge implications for how we see the Kingdom of God. The religious leaders accused Jesus of working on behalf of Satan—that is, having Satan as his power source. Jesus responded by saying, "Let's think about this rationally." Okay, so he didn't actually say that! But he did respond with a very logical argument. He said that whether it is a kingdom, city or household, if it is divided, it will not stand. Jesus was saying that it doesn't make sense that he would drive out Satan by the power of Satan. He explained what is really going on. As Jesus healed the man, he was fighting against the kingdom of darkness. This was a clash of powers and authorities—a clash of kingdoms. It's the Kingdom of God against the kingdom of Satan. Jesus didn't come to play nice. He came to fight—fight for every life and every aspect of life that Satan had afflicted. He came to destroy the work of the enemy in the lives of God's people.

For too long we have missed the existence of this opposing kingdom. I think that many of us have been guilty of doing the opposite of what the religious leaders in Jesus' time were doing. Because we have missed or denied the existence of the prince of this world, we have viewed his work as God's work. We have looked at God as the one causing sickness and disease, loss and brokenness. We are in danger of seeing Satan's work as God's work and attaching unhealthy purpose and meaning to works, which are in fact, works of the enemy. Jesus demonstrated something that we miss so easily today. This man's muteness and blindness were not works of God, but works of the enemy. God's work, his kingdom work, is restoring the goodness of life that the thief has taken from us. Satan's work is sickness, destruction and division. God's work is healing, restoration and wholeness.

Robbing the House

Jesus ended his defense with a very short parable.

> **"Or again, how can anyone enter a strong man's house and carry off his possessions unless he first ties up the strong man? Then he can rob his house."**
>
> *Matthew 12:29*

To understand a parable, you have to discern what the different aspects of the parable represent. So think for a moment about what we have just learned concerning the clash of kingdoms. Then, answer these questions:

Who is the strong man? ______________________________

Tying him up and carrying off his possessions is doing what? ______________________________

Don't continue reading until you have written your answers.

No, the strong man in this parable is not Jesus, but Satan. He had taken the afflicted man's possessions (his ability to speak and see) and was holding them captive. But a stronger man came along—the Messiah. He tied up the strong man and took back what God intended the afflicted man to have. He brought healing and wholeness to his life.

And Satan wasn't really after a couple of bedrooms and the kitchen; he was after their marriage and lives.

Let's apply this to Jose and Lupe's story by asking some more questions.

What kingdom was at work in Jose and Lupe's home? ____________________

What had the strong man stolen from their family? ____________________

How do you think Jesus wanted me, as the pastor, to help Jose and Lupe and their family? ______________________________

It seems obvious now, doesn't it? The kingdom of darkness was at work in their home. And Satan wasn't really after a couple of bedrooms and the kitchen; he was after their marriage and lives. He was robbing them of peace and security in their own home. The evil one was hard at work in their son, driving fear and insecurity into his heart. It seemed obvious that Jesus wanted me to enter that house, tie up the strong man and take back what God intended for Jose and Lupe.

Ⓡ Reflection

I am going to finish the Jose and Lupe story in Day 12 of our study, but right now, I want to ask you a very important question. Please take some time to write your answer. Here's the question:

What is the evil one robbing you of right now? ______________________

This could be something physical, spiritual, emotional, or relational. Is there any area in your life that the strong man has influenced—an area in which he has a foothold? Is there a place he has taken and said, "That is mine," or "This is my territory"? Is he actively fighting for an area of your life that you are not sure how to hold onto? Is it something in your marriage like trust, hope, health, or security? Maybe it's something from you personally—your identity or sense of self worth? Is there something physical—a disease or ailment that is keeping you from being all God intended you to be? Please take time to write down your personal answers, and then respond in prayer.

Is he actively fighting for an area of your life that you are not sure how to hold onto?

Day 12 | Hell Is a Gated Community

And the gates of Hades shall not prevail

Something about Jose and Lupe's story stuck with me. Perhaps the most haunting statement of their story was that the face of the Shadow Lady was Lupe's. The Lord seemed to impress on my heart that I should pursue that.

> I felt it was time to bring the power of God against the strong man in their home.

The following week I came to their house, and we sat in their living room talking about their family. As it turned out, they had been struggling mightily in their marriage for some time. Jose had always been extremely jealous of Lupe. He would call her several times a day to check on her while she was at work. He constantly needed to know where she was, yet seemed unaware how his jealousy came across as lack of trust. Lupe felt smothered under his scrutiny and lack of trust. You could see the sadness in her face as they talked about Jose's jealousy.

I had a strong sense that we needed to deal with their marital strife before we dealt with the issues going on in their physical house. I was honest with Jose. I didn't think Lupe would last much longer in their marriage if he didn't change. He wanted to change; he wanted his marriage and house healthy and whole. We identified some of the lies of the enemy that had consumed Jose. Then I spoke truth in place of those lies and prayed. I gave Jose some pretty stringent guidelines for his behavior toward Lupe. We talked about some spiritual disciplines to practice when the feelings of anxiety arose within him.

The next week when we talked in their living room, Jose and Lupe each had a completely different countenance. Jose had fought hard, and trusted strongly in the Lord. He was experiencing some freedom from his feelings of anxiety. Lupe was enjoying a relationship with some trust and freedom. I felt it was time to bring the power of God against the strong man in their home.

I talked with Jose and Lupe about the fact that Jesus Christ has given us authority as Christians to defeat and drive out any evil presence in our lives and homes. I brought out my little bottle of anointing oil and talked about it being a symbol of the presence and power of the Holy Spirit. In the name and power of Jesus, it was our right to take back what evil had taken away. This was good news to them, to be sure. We prayed together. I prayed for them and anointed them with oil. I prayed for their marriage and the trust that God wanted to seal in them. We prayed for their children and their sense of security, and for their protection. We prayed through all the rooms of their home, even anointing the walls with oil. In the authority of Christ, we bound an evil presence in their home and claimed their home as a dwelling place of the Lord. We loosed or released peace, security and trust.

There was really no overwhelming supernatural manifestation as we prayed, but there was a sense of God working in their home. There was a sense that the calming presence of the Kingdom of God was now there. After that day, they had no more evil, weird stuff in their home. Through the weeks I watched as their marriage grew and flourished under the new freedom of trust. I saw the kingdom come into their lives.

We began Jose and Lupe's story by looking at Matthew 12. To conclude their story let's look at Matthew 16 in order to understand another aspect of the kingdom—its territory.

We prayed through all the rooms of their home… and claimed their home as a dwelling place of the Lord.… I saw the kingdom come into their lives.

Keys of the Kingdom

> **When Jesus came to the region of Caesarea Philippi, he asked his disciples, "Who do people say the Son of Man is?" They replied, "Some say John the Baptist; others say Elijah; and still others, Jeremiah or one of the prophets." "But what about you?" he asked. "Who do you say I am?" Simon Peter answered, "You are the Christ, the Son of the living God."**
>
> **Jesus replied, "Blessed are you, Simon son of Jonah, for this was not revealed to you by man, but by my Father in heaven. And I tell you that you are Peter, and on this rock I will build my church, and the gates of Hades will not overcome it. I will give you the keys of the kingdom of heaven; whatever you bind on earth will be bound in heaven, and whatever you loose on earth will be loosed in heaven." Then he warned his disciples not to tell anyone that he was the Christ.**
>
> *Matthew 16:13–20*

This famous confession by Peter apparently occurred deep into the ministry of Jesus and the disciples. Jesus had waited patiently for this truth to be revealed to them. He had worked toward this confession, waited for this confession. In this climactic moment, Jesus affirmed his true identity, but he also spoke of power and authority. Based on this confession, Peter and the church would be given the power of God over and against all the adversarial forces they would face while proclaiming the Kingdom of God. Jesus revealed that the *keys of the kingdom* are given to all those in the church who face the forces of Hell.

How significant is this authority that is given to the church? Significant enough that the things we bind on Earth will be bound in heaven. If we come against the strong man and his work, it is done in heaven. Whatever Satan's work—oppression and possession, sickness and infirmity, emotional turmoil and depression—Jesus has given us authority to tie up the enemy and to take back everything he has robbed us of and of those we love.

Loose and *loosed* always seemed odd to me. Yet, I understand it more now from a kingdom perspective. By the grace of God we can bind Satan and *loose* whatever he has robbed. Just as Jesus brought us the healing and restoration of heaven, so now we can loosen and free the healing power of God in the lives of his people. As the grace of heaven is released on Earth, our lives and the lives of others will be restored. What a privilege, what an honor, what a responsibility!

Hell Is a Gated Community

There has been much theological discussion about the Matthew 16 passage above. There are two questions crucial to understanding what Jesus said here.

What exactly are the *keys of heaven* and how are we supposed to use them?

What exactly are the *gates of Hades* (Hell) and how can gates *overcome*?

As the grace of heaven is released on Earth, our lives and the lives of others will be restored.

Let's start with the second question first. Think for a moment—how do gates prevail? Let's say you live in a gated community. What is the purpose of the gates of a gated community? The answer, of course, is to keep the unwanted people out, to keep the riff-raff outside of the community. The gates do their job if they keep the unwanted people out.

Yet these gates that Jesus talked about are not the pearly gates of heaven. They are the gates of hell! They have closed around people's lives, or at least around some aspects of their lives. And the riff-raff that the enemy wants to keep out are Christians—you and me. He doesn't want the likes of us Christians, who have been given the power and authority of heaven, to break into his community and start taking things back.

The gates prevail if they keep us out. And these gates are not only closed, but they are locked. The only way to get them open would be if we had the right keys. Ah ha! This leads us to the first question.

It seems so obvious now, doesn't it, when we think about this from a kingdom perspective. Jesus gave the authority to fight and defeat the kingdom of darkness. He came proclaiming the presence of the Kingdom of Heaven and demonstrated its presence by healing and taking back all that had been wounded, broken and stolen away. When Jesus revealed the Kingdom of God, it was in direct conflict with the kingdom of darkness. Now, based on Peter's foundational confession, he charged his disciples and the nascent church to continue his work and ministry—to bring the Kingdom of God.

Notice that the ministry of the church is not meant to be defensive, but offensive. Gates are defensive. Hell has possession of much in this world and is trying to keep the territory it has. Jesus has sent us on the offensive, to unlock the gates and storm the gates of hell with the power and authority of heaven. In one sense, Jesus is sending us into the territory of hell to do battle. Why would we want to go into the gated community of hell? Because that was Christ's mission, and now it is the mission of the church.

We Are the New "Promised Land"

It is important to realize that from a Kingdom of God perspective, there is a new territory. The territory that God is concerned about is not physical land. It is the lives of people. Jesus tried to communicate this to the religious leaders who were so focused on Israel and the Promised Land.

The ministry of the church is not meant to be defensive, but offensive.

Jesus' ministry was not about raising a military force to take back the Promised Land and rule it as the anointed king. His ministry was to take back people, to restore lives and remove the authority and influence of evil. His desire then and now is to rule within people as king, to be the Lord of life. People are what is important to God, not land. The ministry of the church is not about land or buildings or programs, but about people. We should only be involved in all those things as far as they relate to the lives of people. The keys of the kingdom and the gates of hell have to do with you and me. There is a cosmic battle going on between good and evil, and you and I are the prize. Satan has attacked God the Father and the kingdom by bringing down the pinnacle of creation, human beings. Now Jesus Christ and the church are taking it back.

Remember Jose and Lupe? God was far more concerned about their marriage and family life than the physical rooms of their home. We focused on the rooms only as far as it impacted their personal lives. Now they are free from the powers of the strong man. We used the keys of the kingdom to unlock the gates of hell that had been set up in their lives. Jesus won. Now Jose and Lupe live in his kingdom.

Ⓡ Reflection—Prayers of Authority

In Day 11, I asked you the question: What has the strong man taken from you? Self-awareness may be one thing, but an openness to receive healing and restoration is probably another. In our culture of psychoanalysis and counseling, we are pretty good at diagnosing problems. Yet, because much of counseling is done independently of the power of God, we are not brought through to the most important step—healing and restoration. Today, I would like us to begin learning how to pray the verses mentioned before in Matthew 16:13-20, thus releasing the power of the kingdom into our lives. We all need to learn how to pray in the authority and language that Jesus has given us in this passage. Here are the questions for today:

Kingdom Questions

What evil work in your life needs to be bound? What little gates has the enemy set up in your life that are locked and shut tight?

What aspect of heaven needs to be loosed into your life? What *keys of heaven* do you need to pull out, insert and turn, to open the locked gates of hell?

As an example, I will tell you about my friend named Mike. He and I had been meeting for a few weeks. His marriage had recently fallen apart, and for the first time in his life, he was truly seeking God. Mike recommitted his life to Christ and was trying to live and pray as Christ would have him do. One example of how we prayed relates to unforgiveness. He and his wife were steeped in it. Here is a sample of the kind of prayer we used.

"Father, by the power and authority given to us by your Son Jesus Christ, I bind unforgiveness from the lives of Mike and his wife. Help them to see that the spirit of unforgiveness is not from you, but from the enemy. We ask that you would bind and remove this stronghold of the enemy. We know that in your kingdom we are called to forgive one another just as you have forgiven us, so please bring forgiveness and grace to Mike's marriage. We want to release or loosen the forgiveness of heaven into their marriage. May they bring humble hearts and attitudes to one another in a spirit of grace."

We used the keys of the kingdom to unlock the gates of hell that had been set up in their lives. Jesus won.

Now it is your turn.

What do you need to bind and loose in your life?

Days 13 & 14

Opening Gates and Loosening Heaven

I will give you the keys of the kingdom of heaven

We have covered a lot of kingdom material during the past five days. In this small group session, let's take time to discuss all that has been covered, and also begin stepping out into kingdom ministry toward one another.

Jesus' teaching of the Kingdom of God was still emerging in their thinking.

The Nation of Israel vs. the Kingdom of God

Luke (as inspired by the Holy Spirit) tells us about the time when the resurrected Jesus appeared to the disciples.

> **He appeared to them over a period of forty days and spoke about the kingdom of God … So when they met together, they asked him, "Lord, are you at this time going to restore the kingdom to Israel?" He said to them: "It is not for you to know the times or dates the Father has set by his own authority."**
>
> *Acts 1:3b, 6–7*

The disciples still hadn't gotten it completely. They (like the rest of the Jewish people) were still focused on the earthly nation of Israel. Jesus' teaching of the Kingdom of God was still emerging in their thinking, as it probably is in ours. So let's take a moment to look at a comparison between the nation of Israel and the Kingdom of God. Please look at the chart on the following page to help clarify some of the ground we have covered.

Nation of Israel (Acts 1:6)	The Kingdom of God (Acts 1:3)
Ancient History: God told Abraham, "Leave your country, your people and your father's household and go to the land I will show you. I will make you into a great nation and I will bless you…." (Genesis 12:1-2a)	**Ancient History:** Same as nation of Israel, but in 605 B.C. Nebuchadnezzar, King of Babylon, conquered Judah. Then, through visions God revealed a redefined kingdom of God, the 5th kingdom. (Daniel 2:44-45)
Recent History: Following World War II, the British withdrew from their mandate of Palestine, and the UN partitioned the area into Arab and Jewish states, an arrangement celebrated by the Jews and rejected by the Arabs.	**Recent History:** With the coming of the Christ, the Kingdom of God has been planted and is growing throughout the world. (The Mustard Seed and the Yeast, Matthew 13:31-33)
Leader: Israel's Prime Minister.	**Leader:** Jesus of Nazareth was the Messiah, the king of the Jews, who announced the kingdom. (Matthew 27:11)
Geography: Middle East, bordering the Mediterranean Sea, between Egypt and Lebanon (slightly smaller than New Jersey).	**Geography:** The lives of God's people are the territory of the Kingdom of God. "The kingdom of God is within you." (Luke 17:21)
Population: 7,590,000 [6] Jews: 76.2% Arabs: 19.5% Others: 4.3%	**Population:** This is unknown but includes all who have been born again since the history of the church as well as the Old Testament "believers". "I tell you the truth, no one can enter the kingdom of God unless he is born [born again] of water and the Spirit." (John 3:5)
Primary Enemy: The Israelis defeated the Arabs in a series of defensive wars after they refused to accept the UN partition agreement and acknowledge Israel's right to exist.	**Primary Enemy:** Satan and his kingdom of darkness. Though ultimately defeated on the cross, Satan is still the prince of this world. (John 16:11)
Nationality: Israeli, Jerusalem as official capitol.	**Nationality:** Sojourners on earth, our citizenship is in heaven. (Philippians 3:20)
Language: Hebrew (official), Arabic used officially for Arab minority, English most commonly used foreign language.	**Language:** Every tribe and language, including some languages of angels unknown by humans. (Revelation 7:9)
Government: Parliamentary democracy.	**Government:** Benevolent autocracy. "For to us a child is born, to us a son is given, and the government will be on his shoulders. And he will be called Wonderful Counselor, Mighty God, Everlasting Father, Prince of Peace." (Isaiah 9:6)
Military: Israel Defense Forces (IDF): Ground Corps, Navy, Air and Space Force (including Air Defense Forces); historically there have been no separate Israeli military services.	**Military:** Each Christian has been given the authority and power to defeat and drive out any enemy forces they face. (Matthew 16:18-19)

6. "Israel" (2010). *U.S. Department of State*. Web. <http://www.state.gov/r/pa/ei/bgn/3581.htm#profile>.

Kingdom Questions

Do you have any questions about the chart comparing the nation of Israel with the Kingdom of God?

Since you began to study Jesus' big idea, what key observations have you made about the Kingdom of God?

What are some of your remaining questions about the kingdom?

During the last two days we have focused on the Kingdom of God in conflict with the kingdom of darkness. We saw that Christ has given us authority to bring the healing of heaven into the dark places of hell. My hope is that you have begun to pray the kingdom into your own life. Now let's do that together in our small group.

Kingdom Ministry

This is how we bring the kingdom into our lives—by recognizing the darkness and then praying against it.

There is power in the community of faith in a way that is not present in us individually. Christ promised,

> **"Again, I tell you that if two of you on earth agree about anything you ask for, it will be done for you by my Father in heaven. For where two or three come together in my name, there am I with them."**
>
> *Matthew 18:19–20*

In Scripture we are told to practice many things with *one another*. We often neglect this, so here are three scriptural *one another's* to do now with each other:

> ***Carry* each other's burdens, and in this way you will fulfill the law of Christ.** (emphasis added)
>
> *Galatians 6:2*

> **Therefore *confess* your sins to each other and *pray* for each other so that you may be healed….** (emphasis added)
>
> *James 5:16*

It can be uncomfortable to share a burden or struggle. It can be especially difficult to share a sin that we are struggling with, but this is supposed to be foundational for us as Christians. This is how we bring the kingdom into our lives—by recognizing the darkness and then praying against it.

But recognition is the first step. Jesus said,

> **"Blessed are the poor in spirit** [those who recognize and acknowledge their spiritual poverty] **for theirs is the kingdom of heaven."**
>
> *Matthew 5:3*

So let's take some steps of faith. In Day 11, the question was: What has the strong man been robbing you of? In Day 12, we learned some ways of praying into those places. So let's do this together as a small group.

 **Ministry Time—**Praying the Kingdom Together

Suggested Opening Prayer (use this or something similar):

Father, we have gathered in the name of your son Jesus Christ, so we invite your presence here by your Holy Spirit. Please come and fill us, Holy Spirit; be present to bring the kingdom into our lives.

Sharing Burdens and Confession

As led by the Spirit, begin to share the challenges you are facing. Ask for a volunteer to begin. Remember, we share for the purpose of praying the kingdom into needy places in our lives, so don't spend all your time talking.

So let's take some steps of faith.... What has the strong man been robbing you of?

Praying the Kingdom

If people are comfortable with being touched, gather around and lay hands on them. Take turns praying kingdom prayers for them. Remember to use the language of the Scriptures we have been looking at.

Sample Prayers:

In the name and authority of Jesus, we bind ____________(e.g. fear, bitterness, pride, unforgiveness, etc.) *If this has been a foothold of the enemy we ask that you would remove it.*

We recognize this thought as a lie from the pit of hell. In your name, Jesus, we silence that lie and now we pray-in this biblical truth: ______________________
(e.g. forgiveness, peace, humility, faith, joy, etc.).

We loosen the ____________ (e.g. forgiveness, healing, grace, etc.) *of heaven into this circumstance; we ask that by the power of your Spirit, you would bring* _________ *in the place of this darkness.*

Once you have taken turns praying for one person in your small group, allow another to share a burden and then repeat that ministry to one another.

Suggested Closing Prayer

Lord Jesus, thank you for the work that you have done in our lives tonight. We ask that you would seal this work in your name. Help us to live in the kingdom reality that we have prayed for tonight.

Week Three We Bring the Kingdom by the Spirit of the King

All of them were filled with the Holy Spirit and began to speak in other tongues as the Spirit enabled them.

Acts 2:4

Day 15 Conferring on Us a Kingdom

And I confer on you a kingdom

We look to God to work, but can miss the role he has called us to play.

My seminary conducted a survey in order to look at various aspects of the students' spiritual lives. They asked questions about spiritual disciplines and divided the results based on denominations. The results gave a general profile of the various students from the different denominations. It revealed some of the strengths and weaknesses of those students and the denominations that had raised them. In the published findings one item particularly bothered me. Of all the denominations represented at Fuller (and Fuller is one of the largest inter-denominational seminaries in the world) apparently the Reformed Church in America students reported praying the least. For a first-year Reformed student, this finding was very discouraging. I asked myself why and came to a conclusion that might be considered debatable, but requires some pondering.

One of the greatest strengths of the Reformed theological tradition is the emphasis on God's sovereignty—God is in control, he is orchestrating history and our lives, and by his providence all things happen according to his plans. I think this biblical perspective is shared in many church contexts. You can hear it in phrases such as, "It's not about you," or "It's a God thing," or "Just let go and let God," or "Remember, it is the Spirit that does the work, not you." This is a great biblical emphasis. It *is* important to continually reflect a belief that *God is in control.*

However, there is a flip side. Perhaps some of us are guilty of emphasizing the sovereignty of God to such a degree that we adopt a theology of inaction. If God's providence is not brought into tension with the idea that God has given us a role to play, then we can fall into a kind of prayerless passivity. God has called us to join in his work and teaches us that our prayers and actions can and do make a very real difference in this world. If we lose sight of this truth, we become uninvolved and inactive. We look to God to work, but can miss the role he has called us to play. Hence the lack of prayer by the Reformed students. I believe this disappoints our Father in heaven, who calls us to live and work on his behalf.

Before we get lost in a theological debate regarding free will and the sovereignty of God, let's take a look at the role God calls us to play in the kingdom. If you haven't noticed by now, it is very clear that the saints (that would be you and me) have a role to play in this idea of *bringing the kingdom.*

Daniel's Promise

Remember Daniel and the vision of the five kingdoms? (Day 4) We looked at the promise of the kingdom, and a little about the promise of the king. But what we haven't looked at is our role as subjects of the kingdom.

After Daniel's first vision (chapter 7), he felt troubled in his spirit and asked for an interpretation. He was told of the four kingdoms and how the saints would struggle against their rulers. It was during the fourth kingdom in particular that evil rulers would speak against God and oppress his saints, but God would rescue them.

As his representatives, we are called to share in his kingly rule.

Read Daniel's words in chapter 7:

> **As I watched, this horn was waging war against the saints and defeating them, until the Ancient of Days came and pronounced judgment in favor of the saints of the Most High, and the time came when they *possessed the kingdom.*** (emphasis added) *(vs. 21-22)*
> **Then the sovereignty, power and greatness of the kingdoms under the whole heaven *will be handed over to the saints,* the people of the Most High. His kingdom will be an everlasting kingdom, and all rulers will worship and obey him.** (emphasis added) *(vs. 27)*
> **But the saints of the Most High will *receive the kingdom and will possess it forever*—yes, for ever and ever.** (emphasis added) *(vs. 18)*

Wow! It is clear that we, as God's saints, have a significant role to play in the kingdom. We are told that God will hand it over to us, and we will possess it forever. In some way we will serve as the rulers, princes and princesses. We will reign on behalf of God. This language is similar to how Adam and Eve were called to *fill the earth and subdue it.* (Genesis 1:28) He designed and called us to *rule over* all of creation. As his representatives, we are called to share in his kingly rule. Though much of this capacity for and vision of dominion was lost in the Fall, it remains part of God's desire for us. We are not only called to *possess* or *receive* the kingdom in the future, but to bring it and rule in it today.

Jesus' Discipleship Plan

Jesus shared the Father's plan for us to play this significant role in the kingdom. It is clear in his teaching that the kingdom was for us to possess and rule. He said to his disciples,

> **"Do not be afraid, little flock, for your Father has been pleased to give you the kingdom."**
>
> *Luke 12:32*

This giving over of the kingdom was not only the Father's plan, but also his delight. This is the Father's big idea for us, his calling. We become so focused on and stressed about possessing all the small stuff of life, that we miss the big calling—possessing the kingdom.

Jesus also said,

> **"And I confer on you a kingdom, just as my Father conferred one on me."**
>
> *Luke 22:29*

How amazing is that statement? The Father granted or bestowed his kingdom upon Jesus, and Jesus modeled for us how to live the kingdom. Jesus has conferred on us that same kingdom. And he calls us to model it—just as he did. Jesus came bringing the kingdom. Now he desires us to bring it—just as he did.

From this perspective, Jesus' discipleship plan becomes so evident in Scripture. His plan included these four elements for us: **call—model—equip—send**. Think about this for a moment. He extended an invitation to his disciples to follow him—**calling**. So they went with Jesus everywhere, watching and learning how he lived a life of bringing the kingdom—**modeling**. He proclaimed the kingdom and demonstrated it through miraculous signs. Then, right in the middle of his ministry, Jesus decided to send the Twelve.

Then he gave them their marching orders. In essence, he said to do two things: Preach the kingdom and bring the kingdom.

> **When Jesus had called the Twelve together, he gave them power and authority to drive out all demons and to cure diseases, and he sent them out to preach the kingdom of God and to heal the sick.**
>
> *Luke 9:1–2*

Jesus endowed the disciples with power and authority to do the things they had seen him do—**equipping**. Then he gave them their marching orders. In essence, he said to do two things: Preach the kingdom and bring the kingdom. Proclaim that the Kingdom of God is near and then heal the sick. Afterwards, much like a mother bird launches her chicks out of the nest to fly, so Jesus launched his fledgling disciples out into the world—**sending**. And the cool thing about this story is that the Twelve actually did it. Just like Jesus. They saw Jesus "do the stuff," as John Wimber would say, and now they were "doing the stuff."

Yet this wasn't just for the Twelve. Apparently, Jesus meant this kingdom ministry to keep expanding. At the beginning of the following chapter in Luke, Jesus extended the circle.

> **After this the Lord appointed seventy-two others and sent them two by two ahead of him to every town and place where he was about to go.**
>
> *Luke 10:1*

Guess what their marching orders were.

> **"When you enter a town and are welcomed, eat what is set before you. Heal the sick who are there and tell them, 'The kingdom of God is near you.'"**
>
> *Luke 10:8-9*

Hmm…seems to be a trend here! They were called to preach the kingdom and bring the kingdom. Again, the notable thing is that the Seventy-Two did the stuff just like the Twelve. The Seventy-Two returned all pumped up and reported, *Lord, even the demons submit to us in your name* (Luke 10:17). Jesus shared in their joy and shared in the Father's pleasure of revealing the *things* of the kingdom (Luke 10:21).

Ask the Father what role he is calling you to play in the kingdom today.

Ⓡ Reflection

I realize that the temptation is to say, "Well, yes, that was for the close disciples of Jesus' time, but not for us." Let me suggest that you ask the Father what role he is calling you to play in the kingdom today. Begin that request with this Scripture and a few questions. This is the commission at the end of the Gospel of Mark:

> **He said to them, "Go into all the world and preach the good news to all creation. Whoever believes and is baptized will be saved, but whoever does not believe will be condemned. *And these signs will accompany those who believe:* In my name they will drive out demons; they will speak in new tongues; they will pick up snakes with their hands; and when they drink deadly poison, it will not hurt them at all; they will place their hands on sick people, and they will get well."** (emphasis added)
>
> *Mark 16:15-18*

? Kingdom Questions

Do you include yourself in the designation of *those who believe*?

If you answered, "Yes," might the signs listed in Mark 16:15–18 be a part of your life and ministry?

Take time to pray about bringing the kingdom.

Day 16 You Have an Anointing

You have an anointing from the Holy One

Daniel was a very intelligent and well-spoken doctoral student. Serving on InterVarsity Christian Fellowship staff, he worked primarily with graduate students. He was somewhat older and many of the younger staff looked at him as a mentor figure. We learned a lot from Daniel and he was someone we looked up to.

Where did Jesus get his power to do the things he did?

Daniel was also a prickly individual. He was not as gracious as he might have been about other perspectives, or other expressions of the faith. In particular, most things Pentecostal or charismatic in nature always seemed to rub him the wrong way. I think it stemmed from his brother and sister-in-law attending a different kind of church. I remember Daniel telling us of a conflict he had with his sister-in-law. She told him she had been praying for him and felt as though the Lord had impressed upon her something vital related to Daniel's calling—to live in the anointing of Luke 4. In Day 9, we called this passage Jesus' job description, preaching the good news, restoring sight to the blind, proclaiming freedom, and so much more.

I think Daniel's sister-in-law had hoped that this word would be an affirmation to him as a campus pastor. It did not have the desired effect. In fact, Daniel responded very negatively. He pointed out to his sister-in-law that Luke 4 was Jesus' calling and his calling alone. He went as far as to say that she was blasphemous for even suggesting that anyone but Christ could share in the calling of the Messiah.

I can't imagine that Daniel's response went over very well with his sister-in-law or the rest of the family. But even though Daniel's argument was communicated in a less than gracious way, it seemed to make sense to me. In my theological constructs, I had always regarded the calling or job description in Luke 4 as solely that of the Messiah. Yet, since that time I have changed my perspective.

Theological Blind Spot

Let me ask you a question for reflection: **Where did Jesus get his power to do the things he did?** Think about this for a moment. How did Jesus receive the power to drive out demons, heal the blind, walk on water, etc.? In the past, my answer has always been, "Well, he was divine. He could do all those things because he was God incarnate, and God can do all those things." Most Christians I ask that question of today give me that same, or similar, answer. At face value, it seems to be a good answer. But there is a problem—that isn't how the New Testament answers the question. Now let's try to look at this question from a New Testament perspective.

The Apostle Paul, in the classic Philippians passage, reflects on the incarnation of Christ. Through Paul, the Holy Spirit says this of Jesus:

> **Who, being in very nature God, did not consider equality with God something to be grasped, but made himself nothing, taking the very nature of a servant, being made in human likeness.**
>
> *Philippians 2:6-7*

Some significant theological perspectives emerge from this passage.

- **First** is that the words affirm Jesus' divinity. You can't grasp or hold onto something that you don't have. So Christ, prior to coming to the Earth, was equal with God.

- **Second**, though Jesus was and is God, in some way (which we will never fully understand on this side of heaven) he gave up aspects of that equality. The literal Greek word is *kenosis* and is translated "emptied." So, in some mysterious way, he "emptied himself" when he came to the Earth.

- **Third**, as he emptied himself of that divine equality, Jesus fully and completely embraced the nature of our humanity. He became human, just like you and me.

Jesus fully and completely embraced the nature of our humanity.

Theologians have tried to articulate this mystery in a number of different ways. In his book, *How to Have a Healing Ministry Without Making Your Church Sick*, Peter Wagner refers to the agreement that Jesus must have had with the Father regarding his incarnation. Wagner suggests that Jesus must have agreed to suspend the use of his divine attributes for the duration of his earthly ministry. Notice, I am not suggesting he ever ceased to possess his divine attributes. But even though he had them, Jesus voluntarily agreed not to use them.

If this is an accurate description of the truth that Paul proclaimed, then it has significant ramifications for how we see Jesus' power and ministry. It would mean that the answer to the question is—it was not because he was God that Jesus was able to do all the miraculous things he did. He had emptied himself of that divine equality and became like you and me. So, how *did* Jesus do the things he did if he was living with the same human limitations we have?

Jesus' Power Source

The New Testament answers this question very specifically and it is consistent with our conclusions from Philippians. Jesus was anointed with, and empowered by, the Holy Spirit to do the things he did. Though he was living as a mere man, with all of our limitations and fragility, Jesus was anointed by the Holy Spirit of God to accomplish the will of the Father.

We see this in Jesus' life and ministry. In fact, we don't even read of him doing a single miraculous thing until after the important event of his baptism. Remember, Jesus received the anointing of the Holy Spirit *before* he began his public ministry. It is only after this anointing that Jesus began the ministry of the miraculous. It is only after the Holy Spirit came to rest on Jesus that he began to proclaim the kingdom and heal the sick.

Jesus also taught us about his power source. Remember the first line from his job description in Luke 4?

> **"The Spirit of the Lord is on me, because he has anointed me to..."**
> *Luke 4:18*

In other words, though Jesus was a man, he was an anointed man. The living Spirit of God anointed him to live and minister just like God the Father had called him to do.

He would never have trained his disciples in empowered ministry if the source of his power had been unavailable to them as mere men.

It is clear that the apostles and the early church recognized the reality of this anointing. In their prayers, they recognized Jesus as the Anointed One against whom the *kings of the earth take their stand* (Acts 4:26). In those days, crucifixion was an accepted means used by the rulers to *conspire against [the Father's] holy servant Jesus, whom [he had] anointed* (Acts 4:27). Just as David had been anointed by God long before to be king, so Jesus was anointed to be the Messiah and king. When Peter first preached to a non-Jewish audience, he referenced Jesus' ministry like this:

> **"You know what has happened throughout Judea, beginning in Galilee after the baptism that John preached—how *God anointed Jesus* of Nazareth *with the Holy Spirit and power*, and how he went around doing good and healing all who were under the power of the devil, because God was with him."** (emphasis added)
> *Acts 10:37–38*

Jesus came as the *God-man*, but lived as a man anointed by the Spirit of God to do the work of the kingdom. He was anointed and empowered with the same Spirit that now anoints and empowers us.

Our Anointing

Think back to Jesus' promise that we started with in the Introduction. Jesus would never have promised for us to do the things that he was doing, let alone even greater things, if he had done those things because of his divine nature. If he had done them as God, he would never have sent his disciples out to preach the kingdom and heal the sick just as he did. He would never have invited Peter out for a walk on the water. He would never have trained his disciples in empowered ministry if the source of his power had been unavailable to them as mere men. But Jesus did.

He did all things because his divinity was *not* the source of his power. The Spirit of God was the source of his power, the same Spirit who is upon and within us today. His power source is not inaccessible to us. In fact, Jesus promises to give us the source of his power, so that we might participate in his job description and share in his empowered work.

The apostles and early church not only understood Jesus' anointing, they also realized that all his followers were to share in it. They understood that Jesus had promised to anoint all believers with the same power and person of the Holy Spirit. Read the Apostle John's reminder to us that we are anointed people and need to stay true to that anointing.

> **But you have an anointing from the Holy One, and all of you know the truth.... As for you, the anointing you received from him remains in you, and you do not need anyone to teach you. But as his anointing teaches you about all things and as that anointing is real, not counterfeit — just as it has taught you, remain in him.**
>
> *1 John 2:20, 27*

Jesus promises to give us the source of his power so that we might participate in his job description.

The relationship between the Spirit of God and kingdom ministry is huge. Yet, I have discovered that many Christians, even mature Christians, understand very little about the Holy Spirit. This is unfortunate, because if we are ever going to do kingdom ministry in the way Jesus tells us to, we must do it in the power and the anointing of the Holy Spirit. There is really no other way. For this reason, during the next few days in this kingdom study, we will discover the promise, work, and gifts of the Holy Spirit. We will learn about how he desires to work in us and through us.

Kingdom Questions

Do you see yourself as someone who is called to share in the ministry of Christ?

Do you see yourself as a person anointed with the Holy Spirit?

Ask the Lord to help you understand and live in the anointing that he has given you.

Day 17 | The Promise Poured Out

You will receive the promise of the Father

Promises can be very powerful things, depending on who makes them.

Promises can be very powerful things, depending on who makes them. Promises can be sources of comfort and security, something to cling to in times of uncertainty. But promises can also be sources of pain and sadness when they are broken and unrealized. As a father, I think long and hard before I make promises to my son or daughter, because I know the power of promises kept and promises broken.

If you read Scripture very much at all, you know that God is a Father who makes promises. He made many promises to his people throughout the Bible. Today, we will look at one of the most significant promises in all of God's Word. The fulfillment of this promise is a large part of what made Jesus' New Covenant new. The initial fulfillment of this promise was what began the New Testament church and now enables it to spread far and wide. Ultimately, this promise is what will enable us to live the Kingdom of Heaven right here on Earth. It is a promise of a gift, a gift from our heavenly Father to each one of us—the gift of the Holy Spirit.

The Holy Spirit is often referred to as the least known person of the Trinity. This has certainly been my experience. I remember receiving very little teaching about the Holy Spirit in any church or parachurch organization. After studying the Holy Spirit personally, I began teaching about him in *The Alpha Course*[7]. During one course, after a night of teaching about the Spirit, a leader said to me, "I feel ripped off!" I asked him what he meant, and he replied, "I have grown up in Reformed churches and have never been taught about the Holy Spirit." I have found this to be true of many Christians today, from many denominational backgrounds, so we will take some time to understand this most important, promised gift of the Father. We will learn how to live in the Spirit as Scripture teaches. In order to receive all the Father intended for us, we need to survey a lot of Scripture and make some key observations.

7. At an *Alpha Course* people explore the Christian faith in a relaxed setting. The course features ten thought-provoking weekly sessions, and a day or weekend away. www.AlphaUSA.org

God's Empowered Leaders

Despite popular misconceptions, the Holy Spirit does not first show up in the New Testament. As it turns out, he is very present and active in the Old Testament. In fact, we find the Holy Spirit in the first two verses of the Bible.

> **In the beginning God created the heavens and the earth. Now the earth was formless and empty, darkness was over the surface of the deep, and the Spirit of God was hovering over the waters.**
>
> *Genesis 1:1–2*

From the very beginning, we see the Holy Spirit creating life—bringing life out of nothingness—and shining light into the darkness. In Genesis 2:7 we see his Spirit as the breath of God, intimately involved in the creation of man. In this most tender moment, God the Creator breathed life into the first human being.

From these life-giving and intimate beginnings, a theme emerges in the Old Testament regarding the work of the Holy Spirit.

From these life-giving and intimate beginnings, a theme emerges in the Old Testament regarding the work of the Holy Spirit.

At different points in God's story, we see his Spirit coming upon people and empowering them for a particular role or task in his kingdom. Following are a few examples:

Judges, Gideon and Samson

> **Then the Spirit of the Lord came upon Gideon, and he blew a trumpet, summoning the Abiezrites to follow him.**
>
> *Judges 6:34*

> **The Spirit of the Lord came upon him [Samson] in power.... Finding a fresh jawbone of a donkey, he grabbed it and struck down a thousand men.**
>
> *Judges 15:14b–15*

Kings, Saul and David

> **"The Spirit of the Lord will come upon you [Saul] in power... and you will be changed into a different person."**
>
> *1 Samuel 10:6*

> **So Samuel took the horn of oil and anointed him in the presence of his brothers, and from that day on the Spirit of the Lord came upon David in power....**
>
> *1 Samuel 16:13*

Moses and the Elders

> **Then the Lord came down in the cloud and spoke with him [Moses], and he took of the Spirit that was on him and put the Spirit on the seventy elders. When the Spirit rested on them, they prophesied....**
>
> *Numbers 11:25*

There are a few important things to notice about the Spirit's work. First, look at the language used in these stories. There is the aspect of the Spirit *coming upon*, or *resting on*. Along with this, there is usually the element of *empowerment*. Another important principle was that the Spirit in the Old Testament generally came upon people chosen by God as *leaders*. They were judges, prophets, kings and elders. God intended for them to lead with his Spirit upon them, empowering them for ministry.

To recap, in the Old Testament, we find the Spirit *coming upon* different leaders in various circumstances, at particular times, for particular reasons.

A Prophetic Wish and a Promise

In the story of Moses and the elders, Joshua became a little jealous of some of the elders who weren't with the main group when the Spirit came upon them; yet they were filled and prophesied like the others. Moses said to Joshua,

> **"Are you jealous for my sake? I wish that all the Lord's people were prophets and that the Lord would put his Spirit on them."**
>
> *Numbers 11:29*

We find the Spirit coming upon different leaders in various circumstances, at particular times, for particular reasons.

This statement by Moses is like a prophetic wish regarding the Spirit. In the midst of God coming upon leaders of his people with his Spirit, he began to speak of a new day coming. Through different prophets, in different generations, God spoke of a covenant promise that would bring significant change to his people—change from the inside out. He would change their hearts and their minds, and then change how they lived. This new covenant promise would also change their relationship with him, bringing an intimacy previously known only by a few.

Read what God said through Jeremiah, the prophet.

> **"The time is coming," declares the Lord, "when I will make a new covenant with the house of Israel and with the house of Judah. It will not be like the covenant I made with their forefathers … I will put my law in their minds and write it on their hearts. I will be their God, and they will be my people. No longer will a man teach his neighbor or a man his brother, saying, 'Know the Lord,' because they will all know me, from the least of them to the greatest."…**
>
> *Jeremiah 31:31–34*

When the Lord spoke of each and every one *knowing* him, he didn't mean merely academically; within a biblical context, the phrase *knowing him* also includes experientially, relationally. He promised a new kind of intimacy, a relationship that would begin in the hearts and minds of all his people.

The prophet Ezekiel picked up this new covenant language and pointed us to the source of this change.

> **"I will give you a new heart and put a new spirit in you; I will remove from you your heart of stone and give you a heart of flesh. And I will put my Spirit in you and move you to follow my decrees and be careful to keep my laws."**
>
> *Ezekiel 36:26–27*

The Spirit would bring a softness to the heart of God's people in a new and fresh way. The Spirit would be *in* the people, leading to obedience to his word. In addition to this intimacy and obedience, the Lord also spoke of empowerment. In perhaps the most significant prophecy regarding the gift of the Father, Joel made an awesome statement in which God proclaimed,

> **"...I will pour out my Spirit on all people. Your sons and daughters will prophesy, your old men will dream dreams, your young men will see visions. Even on my servants, both men and women, I will pour out my Spirit in those days."**
>
> *Joel 2:28–29*

His Spirit would not only bring greater intimacy as he dwelt within them, but also empower them for ministry.

It's clear that the Lord had great plans for his people. His Spirit would not only bring greater intimacy as he dwelt within them, but also empower them for ministry. He planned this for all people—men and women, young and old. He purposed a new life for them, one filled and empowered by his Spirit.

You can imagine the anticipation these prophecies must have built among God's people. I hope that same anticipation is building within you. Yet, for the original hearers, these plans and prophecies would remain unfulfilled for over three hundred years. His people continued to wait and yearn for this new day, praying for the promise of the Father.

It is in the life of Jesus that the activity of the Spirit increases. Even before he was born, the Gospels tell us of the Holy Spirit stirring in Mary, Elizabeth, Zechariah and Simeon. In the New Testament, the people began to speak of the promise once again. John the Baptist proclaimed,

> **"...I baptize you with water. But one more powerful than I will come, the thongs of whose sandals I am not worthy to untie. He will baptize you with the Holy Spirit and with fire."**
>
> *Luke 3:16*

Think of the visual imagery of baptism. John talked about an immersion, a plunging or soaking. John said that Jesus would drench you with the Spirit. Jesus modeled a life filled and empowered by the Spirit (we will learn more about that in Day 18) but also spoke of the promise of the Father.

> **"Whoever believes in me, as the scripture has said, streams of living water will flow from within him." By this he meant the Spirit....**
>
> *John 7:38–39*

> **"And I will ask the Father, and he will give you another Counselor to be with you forever—the Spirit of truth."**
>
> *John 14:16–17a*

In his resurrected state, before he ascended to heaven, Jesus gave his disciples strict orders.

> **..."Do not leave Jerusalem, but wait for the gift my Father promised, which you have heard me speak about. For John baptized with water, but in a few days you will be baptized with the Holy Spirit...you will receive power when the Holy Spirit comes on you."**
>
> *Acts 1:4–5, 8a*

Jesus was talking about Pentecost. In a few days, as the disciples huddled together praying, the Spirit came upon each of them in power.

> **All of them were filled with the Holy Spirit and began to speak in other tongues as the Spirit enabled them.**
>
> *Acts 2:4*

As you can imagine, this activity attracted a crowd.

As you can imagine, this activity attracted a crowd. Some thought the disciples were drunk, but Peter stood and explained how people don't get drunk so early in the morning.

> **"These men are not drunk, as you suppose. It's only nine in the morning! No, this is what was spoken by the prophet Joel ...."**
>
> *Acts 2:15–16*

And guess what? Peter quoted the very passage from Joel that we read. He proclaimed that this was the day that God was fulfilling his promises of a new relationship with him, a new life empowered by the Holy Spirit.

> **"Exalted to the right hand of God, he [Jesus] has received from the Father the promised Holy Spirit and has poured out what you now see and hear."**
>
> *Acts 2:33*

Peter's audience was so taken with his explanation and message that they asked him what this meant for them—what should they do?

> **Peter replied, "Repent and be baptized, every one of you, in the name of Jesus Christ for the forgiveness of your sins.** [As good evangelicals, many of us stop there, but Peter didn't.] **AND you will receive the gift of the Holy Spirit."** (emphasis added)
>
> *Acts 2:38*

Ⓡ Reflection—A Promise for You

For some reason, many Christians have not understood this most significant promise of the Father. We have never realized how central the Spirit is in the life of the church and the individual believer. Many of us understand the "removal" aspect of God in the gospel—the taking away of our sins. But we have not understood the "bestowal" part—the giving of the promised Spirit. [8] Or, maybe we have understood some of the promise, but have assumed it was not for us. Peter would disagree with that. He said,

> **"The promise is for you and your children and for all who are far off—for all whom the Lord our God will call."**
>
> *Acts 2:39*

We have never realized how central the Spirit is in the life of the church and the individual believer.

Perhaps the best thing we can do in light of these instructions is to accept the gift—to receive the promise. Please look back over this day's study and choose a Scripture—a promise or prophecy—and meditate on it for a few moments. In prayer, embrace these prophesies as your own. You are the one whom the Lord has called.

8. Stott, John R.W. *The Spirit, the Church, and the World: The Message of Acts*. Downers Grove, IL: InterVarsity, 1990, p. 156.

Day 18 Inward and Outward Works

Now to each one a manifestation of the Spirit is given

Yesterday we laid the groundwork for understanding the promise of the Father, the Holy Spirit. I hope you saw how significant that was in the plans of God for his people. What is equally challenging is to understand how God intended his Spirit to work in and through us. There are many ways in which the Holy Spirit works with us, but let's look in two major directions—an **inward** movement and an **outward** movement. The key word for the inward work of the Holy Spirit is **intimacy**. The key word for the outward work is **power**.

Jesus is our model in all things, including the work of the Holy Spirit.

Jesus is our model in all things, including the work of the Holy Spirit. As we have learned, Jesus lived and ministered not out of his divine nature, but out of his human nature that was empowered by the Spirit. From a new covenant perspective, Jesus is our prototype as the first Spirit-filled and empowered man. In his life, we see the inward and outward works of the Spirit.

Jesus, the First Spirit-Filled Man

The wonder and the mystery of the Incarnation is that Jesus was born not of a man and woman, but born of the Spirit of God. The Gospel of Matthew describes it like this:

> **...she [Mary] was found to be with child through the Holy Spirit.**
>
> *Matthew 1:18*

And the angel explained it to Joseph in a dream in a similar way:

> **...what is conceived in her is from the Holy Spirit.**
>
> *Matthew 1:20*

So, in some incredible and amazing way, Jesus began his life on the Earth from and with the Spirit. And though we don't often think of it, Jesus as a child had to learn and grow as any other child. He would need to learn to crawl and walk, just as other children did. He would need to learn the language of his people and grow physically and intellectually.

From his childhood on, we see the work of the Holy Spirit in his growth and development. We don't have much information, but we catch a glimpse of his growth.

> **And the child grew and became strong; he was filled with wisdom, and the grace of God was upon him.... And Jesus grew in wisdom and stature and in favor with God and men.**
>
> *Luke 2:40, 52*

We can see Jesus as a boy, growing not only in stature but also in wisdom and the grace of God. This was some of the internal work of the Spirit in the life of Jesus the boy. I also don't want you to miss the relational growth within Jesus by the Holy Spirit. He grew not just in his relationship with others (as we all do as a part of life), but also in favor and in his relationship with God the Father. Even at an early age he referred to the temple as *my Father's house* (Luke 2:49)—a radical statement for anyone to make, especially in his Jewish context. At Jesus' baptism, the Father testified to the intimate relationship between them:

We understand this baptism of the Holy Spirit as one that came on or upon Jesus for power.

> **..."You are my Son, whom I love; with you I am well pleased."**
>
> *Luke 3:22*

This is a statement of their developed relationship—one that included love, obedience and intimacy.

Even though Jesus experienced the indwelling work of the Holy Spirit in his life, as we discussed in Day 16, he was not doing any miraculous works before his baptism when the Holy Spirit came *on* him.

> **As Jesus was coming up out of the water, he saw heaven being torn open and the Spirit descending *ON* him like a dove.** (emphasis added)
>
> *Mark 1:10*

We understand this baptism of the Holy Spirit as one that came on or upon Jesus for power. It was an empowerment to do the work of the Kingdom of God. Remember, Jesus' job description in Luke 4 was all about kingdom work. How was Jesus enabled to carry out his role? He himself told us,

> **"The Spirit of the Lord is *ON* me, because he has anointed me to ..."** (emphasis added)
>
> *Luke 4:18*

Jesus was conceived and growing in the Spirit and in favor or intimacy with God the Father. Yet, at his baptism, the Spirit came upon him to empower his ministry. After his baptism, then, Jesus began his power-filled healing and deliverance ministry.

Intimacy in the Spirit

What we have seen in Jesus as the first truly Spirit-born, Spirit-filled and empowered man is now meant to be lived out by us—a people born, indwelt and empowered by the same Spirit. Just as Jesus was conceived of the Spirit, so we are born of the Spirit. Remember, from Jesus' discussion with Nicodemus (John 3) we learned that the Spirit gives birth to spirit. When we believed in Christ, we were born spiritually and received the indwelling Spirit of Christ. As Paul said,

> **And if anyone does not have the Spirit of Christ, he does not belong to Christ.**
>
> *Romans 8:9b*

If you are a Christian, you belong to Christ, and you have the Spirit. You cannot enter the kingdom unless you are born of the Spirit. And when you entered the Kingdom of God and received the Spirit this began the process of the indwelling Spirit working within you. Many call this sanctification. It is a process of growth and development in a number of different ways, but all led by the Spirit.

Relationship and Intimacy with God

It wasn't enough for God to be merely *with* us, he promised to be *within* us.

Just as Christ grew in favor and intimacy with God, so we can as well. Jesus, when talking about the Holy Spirit, made this promise:

> **"...But you know him [the Spirit], for he lives with you and will be in you. I will not leave you as orphans; I will come to you."**
>
> *John 14:17–18*

We are not alone. We are no longer orphans in this world, separated from the God who loves us. But it wasn't enough for God to be merely *with* us, he promised to be *within* us. The Holy Spirit has changed how we relate to God. We are now as intimate as children with our daddy; now we are sons and daughters.

> **But you received the Spirit of sonship. And by him we cry, "Abba, Father." The Spirit himself testifies with our spirit that we are God's children.**
>
> *Romans 8:15b–16*

As people who have come alive in Christ, we are now growing in relationship and intimacy with God, just as a child grows in relationship with a parent. Paul tells us,

> **God has poured out his love into our hearts by the Holy Spirit, whom he has given us.**
>
> *Romans 5:5b*

Such intimacy and relationship grows through obedience and submission. Part of the Holy Spirit's role is to teach us all things and remind us of Jesus' words (John 14:26). The predominant name Jesus uses for the Spirit is *Counselor*. Think of how relational that word is. He is the One who walks and talks with us continually, giving insight and wisdom, helping us to see with clearer vision and make right decisions.

We no longer live as the world does, according to our needs and wants, according to our sinful nature—we live for the purposes of our kingdom. Here is how Paul described the way Christians are meant to live:

...but those who live in accordance with the Spirit have their minds set on what the Spirit desires ... the mind controlled by the Spirit is life and peace.

Romans 8:5–6

This walk and sanctification is why Paul admonished us to live in the Spirit.

Since we live by the Spirit, let us keep in step with the Spirit.

Galatians 5:25

The indwelling work of the Spirit is a process of growth, maturity and sanctification. Through a process of nature, an apple tree produces its fruit. As we grow, the Spirit produces his fruit in the same way.

But the fruit of the Spirit is love, joy, peace, patience, kindness, goodness, faithfulness, gentleness and self-control....

Galatians 5:22–23

Just as Jesus grew with the Spirit within him, he, as a man, needed to receive the empowerment of the Spirit.

The Holy Spirit grows these aspects of our character within us, as we *keep in step* with him.

As this kind of new life and indwelling work of the Spirit was true of Jesus, so it is true for us now. However, it wasn't the only work of the Spirit in the life of Jesus. There was also the aspect of empowerment, the Spirit coming upon him.

Empowerment by the Spirit

Just as Jesus grew with the Spirit within him, he, as a man, needed to receive the empowerment of the Spirit. He was baptized by John and empowered by the Spirit, and then he began to bring the kingdom. The same was true of his disciples. They had believed and received Christ as the risen Messiah, but still needed a new covenant empowerment. That was why Jesus told them to wait in Jerusalem. Listen to the empowerment language.

I am going to send you what my Father has promised; but stay in the city until you have been clothed with power from on high.

Luke 24:49

Then Pentecost came and the disciples were baptized with the Spirit. As you read the story, pay attention to the symbols used to represent the Holy Spirit.

When the day of Pentecost came, they were all together in one place. Suddenly a sound like the blowing of a *violent wind* came from heaven and filled the whole house where they were sitting. They saw what seemed to be *tongues of fire* that separated and came to rest on each of them. All of them were filled with the Holy Spirit and began to speak in other tongues as the Spirit enabled them. (emphasis added)

Acts 2:1–4

Notice how the Holy Spirit is talked about like a violent *wind* and like *fire*. In other places, he is likened to *living water* (John 7:38) as well. These images are far different from those of a Counselor. They are not personal in nature, but communicate a kind of power or force. We should never sever the power of the Spirit from the person of the Spirit, but it is important to note that these are different aspects of the Spirit and his work.

Paul encouraged his young disciple Timothy with these words:

> **For God did not give us a spirit of timidity, but a spirit of power, of love and of self-discipline.**
>
> *2 Timothy 1:7*

Paul understood that there are different aspects of the Holy Spirit that work within and upon us. We have talked of the love and discipline of the Spirit, but Paul knew there was more. He knew there was an aspect of empowerment that Timothy needed to experience and live into, in order to fulfill his calling.

The Kingdom of God is brought by the Spirit of God.

Gifts of Power from God

The common way the New Testament speaks of this empowerment is by referring to them as *gifts*. Many Christians today understand very little about the gifts of the Spirit, especially those that some call *manifestational* gifts. Yet, Paul didn't want it to be that way. He wrote:

> **Now about spiritual gifts, brothers, I do not want you to be ignorant.**
>
> *1 Corinthians 12:1*

Because of the spiritual aspects of gifts, people may push them aside with fear and doubt. But again Paul told us to do the very opposite.

> **Follow the way of love and eagerly desire spiritual gifts....**
>
> *1 Corinthians 14:1*

These gifts and empowerment of the Holy Spirit are designed to be a significant part of our lives and ministry as Christians. Paul said,

> **Now to each one the manifestation of the Spirit is given for the common good.**
>
> *1 Corinthians 12:7*

We will talk a lot more about the gifts of the Spirit later, but for now I want you to understand a few key points.

> **First**, this is a different operation of the Holy Spirit. This is an empowerment for ministry for the profit of all. The Kingdom of God is brought by the Spirit of God. We are empowered with gifts, and those gifts are manifested through us to bring the kingdom.

Secondly, this empowerment works in a slightly different way than does the relational and character work of the Spirit. The Spirit *within* is likened to a tree that produces fruit. The Spirit *upon* us is more like a Christmas tree, where gifts are given and then opened.[9] There are, as well, manifestations of the power of God such as in healing, deliverance, and tongues, which are more episodic or occasional in nature.

By way of comparison, we should never stop growing in the relational fruit of kindness, for example. This is meant to be an ever-increasing fruit of the Spirit in our lives. However, if we are given a gift of empowerment such as *the word of knowledge*, this gift is meant to be used in specific contexts at specific times.

We see that Jesus and the disciples used these gifts at different times and on different occasions, as the Spirit determined. For example, a sick woman in a crowd who had the faith to be healed of her bleeding touched Jesus' cloak as he went by.

> **At once Jesus realized that power had gone out from him.**
>
> *Mark 5:30a*

If we are going to bring the Kingdom of God as Jesus did, we must learn…to be empowered by the Spirit for ministry.

Jesus was using the *gifts of healings* (1 Corinthians 12:9 NKJV) as manifested by the Spirit. In the same way, when Peter healed the crippled beggar on the way to the temple he used those same gifts (Acts 3:6).

When Paul talked about his ministry, he reminded his readers that it was not just words. It wasn't about human effort and skilled oratory.

> **…our gospel came to you not simply with words, but also with power, with the Holy Spirit and with deep conviction.…**
>
> *1 Thessalonians 1:5*

If we are going to bring the Kingdom of God as Jesus did, we must learn not only to *keep in step* with the Spirit's work within us, but also to be empowered by the Spirit for ministry.

? Kingdom Questions

Do you feel as though you are growing in intimacy with God?

Are there any fruits of the Spirit or character issues that you need to focus on in your spiritual growth?

How do you feel about the idea of God giving us supernatural gifts?

Have you ever experienced the Spirit's power or a particular manifestation of his gifts?

Ask yourself if there are any of these issues that you need to speak with the Lord about.

9. I am indebted to Zeb Bradford Long, executive director of Presbyterian-Reformed Ministries International, for the idea of the Christmas tree as presented in *The Dunamis Course: Experiencing the Person and Work of the Holy Spirit* (PRMI, 2002).

Day 19 The Prominence of the Promise

All of them were filled with the Holy Spirit

I had a good friend named Jennifer who attended a Christian music festival on a college campus in Illinois. Many popular up-and-coming Christian bands had gathered together, and the concert lasted a couple of days—like a Christian Woodstock.

The night she was supposed to be returning from the concert, I received a late night phone call. It was Jennifer, and she was a little freaked out. Yes, she was safely home, but she had experienced something the last night of the festival that she was still trying to sort out.

On the last night, one of the bands had moved into a time of worship with all the students. Jennifer really enjoyed this time. There she was with her friends, lifting her heart and hands to God, when something unexpected happened. She began to sing and speak in a different language. When this happened Jennifer closed her mouth and looked around. Thankfully, the music was so loud that none of her friends had heard. Unsure of what to do next, she decided to return to worship. As she did this, the different language continued to come out. Since she could carry on without being noticed by her friends, Jennifer continued in this new language, a language that was not known or recognizable to her, worshiping as she felt led.

On the way home, she decided not to tell her friends. After all, she didn't want them to think she was weird. Instead, when she got home around midnight, Jennifer gave me a call. Her question—"What in the world is going on?" You see, Jennifer had received almost no teaching about the Holy Spirit and his gifts, and she had had even less experience with him.

Of course, I told Jennifer that she must be some kind of freak and really questioned whether she was actually a Christian—no, no, no, I am just kidding! Actually, I told her to get her Bible. We turned to 1 Corinthians 12-14. There we were, engaged in a late-night Bible study, working through those chapters. Jennifer discovered that this strange language was a gift from the Spirit, a gift of love that he had decided to bless her with.

Jennifer discovered that this strange language was a gift from the Spirit, a gift of love that he had decided to bless her with.

After a long discussion, we prayed together. Then I asked her how she felt. "Well," she said, "I feel like I am supposed to pray in this new language." I replied, "Then that is what you better do. I am going to hang up now and go back to bed." Later, Jennifer told me that she had stayed up most of the night praying in her new language.

What do you make of this story? There are many intriguing aspects, but one angle has always bothered me. Here was a committed and growing Christian who displayed much fruit of the Spirit in her life. In a beautiful way, the Spirit blessed her with a new gift. Yet, this strong Christian had received so little instruction about the Spirit and his gifts that she barely recognized her experience as a gift. What kind of statement does that make regarding the church? Have we, as a church, allowed a central aspect of the New Covenant to go unrealized in the lives of our people?

The good news is…also about the giving of the Spirit for new life and the empowerment to live that new life.

Prominence of the Promise

We have discovered how prominent the promise of the Holy Spirit was in the Old Testament as the prophets pointed people to a New Covenant. (Joel 2:28–29) We have seen John the Baptist highlight a baptism that would change the world. (John 1:32–34) Jesus talked about the promise as *streams of living water* that run in and through believers' lives. (John 7:38–39) He spoke of a new day when people would be *clothed with power*. (Luke 24:49) The early church leaders clearly understood how central the Spirit was to be in the lives of the disciples. Let's take a moment to see how prominent the Spirit was in the early church.

Prominence in the Message

The first time Peter preached the gospel, he not only shared the story of Jesus the Messiah, but he also included the Holy Spirit in his invitation to those listening.

> **"…And you will receive the gift of the Holy Spirit. The promise is for you and your children and for all who are far off – for all whom the Lord our God will call."**
>
> *Acts 2:38–39*

For many congregations today, this aspect of the good news is neglected or simply not taught. The good news is a message about the removal of sin for salvation. But it is also about the giving of the Spirit for new life and the empowerment to live that new life.

The apostles faced much persecution from the religious leaders of the day. As they defended themselves, they summarized their ministry like this:

> **"We are witnesses of these things, and so is the Holy Spirit, whom God has given to those who obey him."**
>
> *Acts 5:32*

Prominence in Leadership

As the church grew, the demands of leadership became too great to be handled only by the apostles. They directed the church to pick additional leaders for different aspects of ministry. Listen to the characteristics they were to look for:

> **"... choose seven men from among you who are known to be full of the Spirit and wisdom. We will turn this responsibility over to them."**
>
> *Acts 6:3*

Notice how being *full of the Spirit* was the primary characteristic they desired in future leaders of the church.

God was in the process of raising up Saul (Paul) to be a leader in his church. Part of his transformation from a persecutor of the church to a leader of the church was the filling of the Spirit.

> **Then Ananias went to the house and entered it. Placing his hands on Saul, he said, "Brother Saul, the Lord Jesus, who appeared to you on the road as you were coming here, has sent me so that you may see again and be filled with the Holy Spirit."**
>
> *Acts 9:17*

This early disciple had an amazing ministry that included miraculous signs, healings and deliverance.

Paul then understood the truth and was filled and enabled to proclaim it in the power of the Holy Spirit.

Prominence in Congregations

The gospel spread to Samaria, and there unfolds a fascinating story about Philip. This early disciple had an amazing ministry that included miraculous signs, healings and deliverance.

The apostles in Jerusalem got wind of this exciting ministry, so they sent Peter and John to check things out. Peter and John noticed there was something absent, even from this powerful kingdom ministry.

> **...he [Philip] preached the good news of the kingdom of God and the name of Jesus Christ....Simon himself believed...astonished by the great signs and miracles....**
>
> *Acts 8:12–13*

> **When they [Peter and John] arrived, they prayed for them [Samaritans] that they might receive the Holy Spirit, because the Holy Spirit had not yet come upon any of them; they had simply been baptized into the name of the Lord Jesus. Then Peter and John placed their hands on them, and they received the Holy Spirit.**
>
> *Acts 8:15–17*

Think for a moment about the correction that the apostles were bringing to the ministry in Samaria. It is not that Philip was preaching something wrong. Obviously, God was blessing his message and ministry. It is just that he had not included a central aspect of new covenant faith—the empowerment of the Holy Spirit for all people. The followers obviously had the Spirit, because they could not have been born again without the Spirit. But they had not yet been *clothed with power*. The apostles made every effort to keep the Spirit *upon* emphasis as a central aspect of the message and ministry of the church.

The story of the Samaritans in Acts 8 is similar to the story of Paul when he encountered some disciples in Ephesus.

> **...Paul took the road through the interior and arrived at Ephesus. There he found some disciples and asked them, "Did you receive the Holy Spirit when you believed?" They answered, "No, we have not even heard that there is a Holy Spirit." So Paul asked, "Then what baptism did you receive?" "John's baptism," they replied. Paul said, "John's baptism was a baptism of repentance. He told the people to believe in the one coming after him, that is, in Jesus." On hearing this, they were baptized into the name of the Lord Jesus. When Paul placed his hands on them, the Holy Spirit came on them, and they spoke in tongues and prophesied. There were about twelve men in all.**
>
> *Acts 19:1–7*

...[we] are woefully under-taught and ignorant when it comes to the works of the Spirit.

Notice how diligent the early apostles were in bringing the whole message of the New Covenant. The Samaritans in Acts 8 did not quite have a complete picture of Jesus or the Holy Spirit so Peter and John explained the message more fully. I think the group of Ephesians was similar to Jennifer and many of us regarding the Holy Spirit. *No, we have not even heard that there is a Holy Spirit.* Okay, most of us have heard of the Holy Spirit but are woefully under-taught and ignorant when it comes to the works of the Spirit.

Experiencing the Promise

Despite our ignorance or fears, the Holy Spirit often breaks into our life experiences. That was certainly true for Jennifer. She knew very little of the Spirit and of his gifts, yet she received his gift of tongues anyway. We will have an opportunity to receive the filling of the Holy Spirit when we gather in our next small group in Days 20–21. But, before we do, let's explore what some people have experienced.

In the stories of the New Testament, as well as today, people can usually recognize the filling of the Holy Spirit within them and within others. Oftentimes, there is an outward sign or response that people can see. We have noticed a few in the stories we have read. (Acts 8:15–17; 19:1–7)

Praise and Worship

We are often told that when people are filled with the Spirit they are released in praise. In Day 18 we talked about how the inward work of the Spirit in our lives produces more intimacy with Christ. As our relationship grows with God through the Spirit, it makes sense that we would be drawn more into worship and praise. This was true of many in the early church. Peter and the other Jews were astonished by the folks in Cornelius' house, because…

> **…the Holy Spirit had been poured out even on the Gentiles. For they heard them speaking in tongues and praising God.**
>
> *Acts 10:45–46*

This is true for me personally. The times I feel the closest and most intimate with God are during times of worship. Sometimes this is in corporate worship as part of a people united together in giving praise to God. Or sometimes it is just me and my guitar, humbly approaching my Father's presence. I believe that is why revival movements throughout history are almost always associated with fresh songs of worship. The Spirit inspires love and intimacy and, therefore, worship.

Part of the gracious working of the Spirit is that he often deals with us in ways that fit with our personality and background.

Outward Manifestations

Did you notice that the Gentiles in Cornelius' home not only praised God in response to the Spirit, but also began speaking in tongues? The Spirit's filling has almost always been recognized by some manifestation in people's lives. Sometimes it was tongues, sometimes prophecy and sometimes praise, but other times we don't know what it was; we just know the people recognized his work.

An outward sign of the Spirit's work isn't always present; but because it often is, I have learned to pray with my eyes open. I have come to realize that the outward expressions of the Spirit are often a reflection of what is happening on the inside. Sometimes, a person will shed some tears while being prayed for, and this can be a beautiful response to his filling.

In one small group, we were discussing spiritual gifts. It was obvious that some folks were nervous about being prayed for, because they didn't want to be embarrassed by any unusual manifestation. My counsel to those who were fretting was to trust. We, too, need to trust that our Father is a good God and desires only the best for us. Part of the gracious working of the Spirit is that he often deals with us in ways that fit with our personality and background. At the time, my encouragement seemed to give a little peace to the folks with anxious reservations. I really didn't think the Father was going to lead these conservative and quiet people to be loud, boisterous and embarrassing as they experienced the filling of the Holy Spirit. God is gracious to us, his children. To give you some comfort with a potentially uncomfortable topic, I want you to use your imagination for a moment.

Imagination Station

Imagine for a moment that I had some unique qualities as a person. One was that I was invisible. No one could see me, but if I touched someone they could feel me. Also imagine that I had the ability to speak to you in a very quiet, small voice that sometimes only you could hear.

Now picture us talking to each other. You begin to share some very personal things, ways in which you had been hurt in the past. I speak words of comfort, but only you can hear my voice. At one point you begin to cry as you share your heart. I reassure you. Then, at one point, I decide to give you a hug to encourage and support you. You lift your arms up and wrap them around me, and hold on tight.

Now imagine that someone had been watching you during all this time. Remember, no one could see me or hear me, so when you began to cry and talk (seemingly to yourself) it looked a little weird—especially when you hugged me (they thought it was all air). They thought you were really far-out. Yet to you, it all made perfect sense because, although you couldn't see me, you believed in me and were responding to my comforting presence in your life.

As Christians, we shouldn't be "weirded out" by people's individual responses to the Spirit.

Isn't that really a picture of the Holy Spirit? If there really is a Spirit of God—someone who pours love into our hearts, gives us a sense of God's presence, gives gifts for us to use and respond to—then doesn't it make perfect sense that we are going to respond to the Spirit in various ways?

As Christians, we shouldn't be "weirded out" by people's individual responses to the Spirit. It should be an acceptable and normal part of our faith. If we really believe that the Spirit works in the way Scripture tells us he does, then couldn't manifestations of the Spirit be important and valuable parts of our Christian faith?

I am not suggesting that we accept every weird thing people do in the name of the Holy Spirit. What I am saying is that we stop stiff-arming all Spirit-related work in our lives and the lives of others. Rather than label them as weird, let's move in him and his gifts as the New Testament promises we can.

Reflection

> **"So I say to you: Ask and it will be given to you; seek and you will find; knock and the door will be opened to you. For everyone who asks receives; he who seeks finds; and to him who knocks, the door will be opened. Which of you fathers if your son asks for a fish, will give him a snake instead? Or if he asks for an egg, will give him a scorpion? If you then, though you are evil, know how to give good gifts to your children, how much more will your Father in heaven give the Holy Spirit to those who ask him!"**
>
> *Luke 11:9–13*

Days 20 & 21 | Filled and Filled Again

Instead, be filled with the Holy Spirit

Paul wrote to the church in Ephesus, admonishing them not to live as they had before they met Christ. He encouraged them to continue putting off their old self, and begin putting on their new self. (Ephesians 4:22-24) He gave many practical suggestions on how to accomplish this feat. The following example is particularly relevant to our study.

> **Do not get drunk on wine, which leads to debauchery. Instead, be filled with the Spirit.**
>
> *Ephesians 5:18*

He [Paul] encouraged the church in Ephesus to continue putting off their old self, and begin putting on their new self.

The word for *be filled* in Greek is in a special command form.[10] It gives the idea of continuing to be filled, i.e. "keep on being filled with the Spirit." When we received Christ and were born again, that was a one-time experience. But in terms of the empowerment and filling of the Holy Spirit, that is meant to be a repeated experience throughout our Christian life.

We see this repeated filling even in some of the leaders in the Old Testament. Samson, for example, was empowered by the Spirit in fresh ways for different occasions in his life, especially in serving the Lord. (Judges 13–16)

This filling was evident in Jesus' life, as well as in the early disciples. Take a moment to trace the filling that happened to Peter and the early disciples starting at Pentecost.

> **All of them** [including Peter] **were *filled with the Holy Spirit* and began to speak in other tongues as the Spirit enabled them.** (emphasis added)
>
> *Acts 2:4*

While Peter was speaking to the religious leaders, they challenged him:

> **..."By what power or what name did you do this?" Then Peter, *filled with the Holy Spirit*, said to them....** (emphasis added)
>
> *Acts 4:7–8*

10. Present passive imperative

While praying in response to threats, the believers prayed,

> **"Now, Lord, consider their threats and enable your servants to speak your word with great boldness. Stretch out your hand to heal and perform miraculous signs and wonders through the name of your holy servant Jesus." After they prayed, the place where they were meeting was shaken. And they were all *filled with the Holy Spirit* and spoke the word of God boldly.** (emphasis added)
>
> *Acts 4:29–31*

Kingdom Questions

Have you ever understood the filling work of the Holy Spirit to be regular and ongoing?

Have you ever asked to be filled with the Holy Spirit?

Have you ever had a group of believers lay hands on you and pray for you to be filled with the Holy Spirit?

Are there any questions, concerns or doubts that you have about the work of the Holy Spirit that would prevent you from asking to be filled right now?

For everyone who asks receives; he who seeks finds; and to him who knocks, the door will be opened.

Ministry Time

Begin with a Promise

> **"So I say to you: Ask and it will be given to you; seek and you will find; knock and the door will be opened to you. For everyone who asks receives; he who seeks finds; and to him who knocks, the door will be opened. Which of you fathers, if your son asks for a fish, will give him a snake instead? Or if he asks for an egg, will give him a scorpion? If you then, though you are evil, know how to give good gifts to your children, how much more will your Father in heaven give the Holy Spirit to those who ask him!"**
>
> *Luke 11:9–13*

Enter God's Presence through Worship

- A Song of Worship
- One-sentence prayers to our Father
- The reading of some Scripture

Listen for Direction

- What should we pray?
- What does the person want or need?
  - —To be filled with the Spirit as the Father promised.
  - —To experience more of his love and presence (Romans 5:5).
  - —To be empowered by the Spirit to face a particular issue, e.g., a relational issue, problem with a job, a bad habit.
  - —To be empowered for a particular ministry or kingdom work.

Pray as the Spirit Directs

- Gather around an individual and pray according to the need.
- Use anointing oil as a symbol of the Holy Spirit's filling.

What should we pray?
What does the person want or need?

Week Four | A Kingdom Community

Day 22 A Broken Community

Day 23 A Gifted Community

Day 24 A Listening Community

Day 25 A Discerning Community

Day 26 A Worshiping Community

Days 27 & 28 A Kingdom Community

The LORD came and stood there, calling as at the other times, "Samuel! Samuel!" Then Samuel said, "Speak, for your servant is listening."

1 Samuel 3:10

DAY 22 | A BROKEN COMMUNITY

Blessed are the poor in Spirit

It's taken me a while to get it. Get what? Let me explain. In the beginning of my faith journey, I was disconnected from meaningful Christian community. Yes, we attended church sometimes, but I wasn't really part of a community of faith.

> His desire for us is to live and serve and pray in community, not just as individuals.

Another reason it took me a while to get it was that in our American culture, we are pretty individualistic. We value independence and self-direction to such a degree that we often overlook any biblical instruction related to community.

What I personally had missed for such a long time was Christ's call to community. Of course, it was very significant when I realized that Christ calls each one of us to follow him, to be his disciple, to live in a personal relationship. But it wasn't until much later that I realized his call to follow him included a call to be in community with others. Jesus came to call people to follow him, but he also came to create a new community, a new people of God.

Much of what Jesus said and commanded was meant to be understood from a shared perspective. He came to establish his church, a community of people who would be the Kingdom of God, who would bring the kingdom to others. His vision was a kingdom community.

The concept of community is one reason I have urged you to work through this material in a small group. His desire for us is to live and serve and pray in community, not just as individuals. Because of this, for the next few days we will talk about some significant aspects of a *kingdom community*. We will begin with a surprising one—exactly where Christ himself began.

The Sermon on the Mount is Jesus' most famous body of teaching (see Matthew 5-7). Even those who are not followers of Jesus may be familiar with this famous discourse. It occurred toward the beginning of Jesus' ministry, like an inaugural address. King Jesus described the kind of life and community he envisioned for members, or subjects, of this new kingdom. His opening line has intrigued people for centuries:

"Blessed are the poor in spirit, for theirs is the kingdom of heaven."
Matthew 5:3

I remember the first time I really looked at this beatitude.[11] *Blessed* seemed like such an odd word; *poor in spirit* wasn't very positive; and I had no clue what the *kingdom of heaven* was. So I wasn't even understanding half of what this particular verse meant. Since then, however, it has become very significant to me. This one little statement has impacted my prayer life and relationship with God. It has especially affected how I live in community. I believe Christ wants this beatitude (or *beautiful attitude*) to be a hallmark of his *kingdom community*. But before we can get there, we first need to understand it. Then we will be set free to live it.

Blessings and the Poor in Spirit

The Greek word translated *blessed* is *makarios*. It literally means to be happy, a certain freedom from anxieties, a deep joy flowing in a person who is blessed. As funny as it sounds, there is also a congratulatory aspect to this word, as if Jesus were saying "yes" or "good job" to those who possess these qualities. If you live out these beatitudes, you are entering the good life, the kingdom life of God. As one commentator put it, "… you won't be a loser…" if you live this kind of life.[12] The qualities that Jesus talked about in the Sermon on the Mount are to be emulated and lived out, because they lead to the good life, the kingdom life, the community of God.

He [Jesus] was not talking about *material* poverty, but about the value of *spiritual* poverty—the neediness of our inner person, our spirit, or soul.

And what's the first quality of the kingdom community that Jesus wanted to congratulate us for? *Blessed are the* ***poor*** *in Spirit. Poor*— that just doesn't sound right, does it? Why would Jesus value poverty? Wouldn't Jesus rather have us be strong in spirit, or rich in spirit? Wouldn't that lead to a life that God blesses, a rich community life?

But Jesus didn't use any of those words. He simply said *poor*. Do you know what the Greek word for *poor* means? It means just that—*poor*. It means destitute, reduced to begging, needy, lacking in necessities. The more you think about it, the worse it gets. Yet, we should note that in this context, Jesus was referring to a certain kind of poverty. In Matthew 5:3 he was not talking about *material* poverty, but about the value of *spiritual* poverty—the neediness of our inner person, our spirit, or soul.

What does this spiritual poverty look like? Simply, it is people who see or acknowledge their desperate need for God. The *New Living Translation* (NLT) translates verse 3 like this: *God blesses those who realize their need for him.*

Roman Catholic Bishop Robert F. Morneau commented on this concept of spiritual neediness: "In our more honest moments, we recognize our profound neediness, our intellectual limitations, our spiritual inadequacy, our moral failures. In our helplessness, we turn to God." [13]

---

11. "Beatitudes" is the term commonly used to describe Jesus' statements in Matthew 5:3-12 that begin with the Greek word translated "blessed," "happy," or "to be congratulated."

12. Richard T. France in *New Bible Commentary: 21st Century Edition*, section on *Matthew*, Leicester, England: Intervarsity Press, p. 911.

13. Morneau, Bishop Robert F. "God in Our Midst: The Beatitudes' Promises", *Every Day Catholic* newsletter. URL: http://www.americancatholic.org/Newsletters/EDC/ag0102.asp January 2002.

When we get real with God and take an inventory of our soul, we begin to see our desperate need for him. Jesus challenges us to be a community that is candid about our weaknesses and shortcomings. He also wants us to be honest about our sins, our jealousy and hatred, our bitter and unforgiving hearts. He calls us to be a people who authentically share our insecurities, our lack of faith and our pride. If you ever hear a person pray a *poor in spirit* prayer out loud, you will know it and remember it.

This attitude, or quality, is something that God has always valued. Throughout the Old Testament, God pled with his people through his prophets, *turn your hearts to me.* In the Old Testament book of Joel, we see people acting as if everything were okay between them and God and among themselves. But God didn't think so. He begged his people to do a soul check, to take an honest look at their hearts. Reading Joel, we constantly find these words: *MOURN, WAIL, DESPAIR, GRIEVE … declare a holy fast…call a sacred assembly…return to me* (God)…. The problem was (and still is) that people responded outwardly, going through the religious motions; but deep within their hearts, they remained the same.

Jesus challenges us to be a community that is candid about our weaknesses and shortcomings.

Rend Your Hearts

An old custom among the Jewish people was to rip a portion of their garments (like a shirt or jacket today) as a symbolic act of the loss or pain they were experiencing. This is still practiced today. At a funeral, a Jewish man might rip his garment as an expression of sorrow, an outward symbol of the pain within. The problem in Joel's day was that they were "ripping their garments," but it wasn't a true representation of their heart attitude. So God said,

> **Rend your heart and not your garments….**
>
> *Joel 2:13*

This is similar to David's famous prayer.

> **The sacrifices of God are a broken spirit; a broken and contrite heart….**
>
> *Psalm 51:17*

God is saying to us that he wants our hearts. He wants us to be real, broken, acknowledging and confessing our shortcomings and struggles. This is the way of the kingdom.

In spite of all, there is the possibility of a blessing. Joel said that if you do this,… *Who knows? He may turn and have pity and leave behind a blessing* (2:14). Joel's words may sound ambiguous, but Jesus removes the doubt. He promises that we will be blessed if we live like this.

For Ours Is the Kingdom of Heaven

This kind of brokenness and authenticity may seem strange in the church today. Many of us grew up believing that for church you put on your "Sunday best." That didn't mean just your clothes, but your appearances as well. Heaven forbid that you would let a struggle or difficulty be known! If you did, you might get kicked out. Without a doubt, grace and forgiveness must be an integral part of any community that is serious about sharing their brokenness. For too long the church has been graceless in its approach to the hurting and wounded. Tragically, many churches have concentrated on appearances, not authenticity.

For some of us, this kind of authenticity just hasn't been a part of how we operate. My own denomination (Reformed Church in America) is still made up of a lot of Dutch folks. I was talking with some people about this kind of brokenness when one of my more frank (yet extremely humorous) leaders simply said, "Eric, we're Dutch, we don't do that. We're the frozen chosen." I agreed, but I commented in return that if being vulnerable and honest is biblical, then regardless of our comfort level, we had better start living this way—that is, if we want to receive the promised blessing.

We will not only miss out on the blessing, but we will miss out on what Jesus promised at the end of the beatitude. He said if we lived like this, then ... *[ours] is the kingdom of heaven.* Wow! That is pretty significant. Think about this amazing kingdom that we have been studying. Now, why would Jesus promise the kingdom to people who are simply *poor in spirit*?

We can't pray... the Kingdom of Heaven into areas of need for one another, unless we confess our sins to each other.

Look at the following passages of Scripture that relate to what we are talking about. They are community passages. They talk about how we care for each other.

> **Carry each other's burdens, and in this way you will fulfill the law of Christ.**
>
> *Galatians 6:2*

> **Therefore confess your sins to each other and pray for each other so that you may be healed.**
>
> *James 5:16a*

Consider these Scriptures from the reverse angle. **First**, there is no way that we can *fulfill the law of Christ* (or his beatitude) if others are not sharing their burdens with us and if we don't allow others in on our struggles.

Second, we can't be healed if we don't *pray for each other*. We can't pray the presence and power of God or pray the Kingdom of Heaven into areas of need for one another, unless we confess our sins to each other. We haven't wanted to "wear our hearts on our sleeve," but by not doing so we have caused ourselves and others to miss out on the blessings of the kingdom.

In one of the churches where I served, a beloved elder was diagnosed with cancer. It came as quite a shock to our community of faith. The elders surrounded him and prayed for him. I prayed for him after services one Sunday. On another Sunday, a close friend felt that we needed to go to the elder's house and pray healing prayers for him and his family. This was the third time I was going to lay hands on him and pray for him; and, to be honest, I was feeling a little sensitive regarding their level of privacy. I am a firm believer in persistent and continual prayer, but I wondered if

Phil and his wife needed some space and privacy. I did go with my friend, but I brought up my hesitation. Phil assured me that he welcomed as much prayer as he could get. I thought he was just being polite, so I brought it up again. And at one point, Phil made a statement that struck me. He began talking about how in the past he had been a very private person, but now he was different. He said, "Eric, I can't afford to be private."

Phil couldn't afford to miss out on the support and encouragement of a loving community. He couldn't afford to miss the power of healing that is part of a praying community. He couldn't afford *not* to be poor in spirit. I don't think any of us can afford to miss out on that. You see, Phil and his wife were allowing themselves to be fully embraced by God and his people, and …*theirs is the kingdom of heaven.*

Ⓡ Reflection

This is a good beatitude to memorize.

> **"Blessed are the poor in spirit, for theirs is the kingdom of heaven."**
> *Matthew 5:3*

Take a moment to meditate on the words, asking yourself some important questions:

Have you opened your life up to a small community of people?

Are you living as a *poor in spirit* person?

Have you allowed others in so that they might walk with you and pray for you?

Is there something in particular you need to share within your community, allowing others to invite the kingdom into your life?

Phil and his wife were allowing themselves to be fully embraced by God and his people.

Day 23 A Gifted Community

Follow the way of love and eagerly desire spiritual gifts

Ian, a young adult friend, was preparing to move down to the San Diego area with us to begin a new church. Although a relatively young believer, Ian had a unique passion for the Lord. He had been given the gift of tongues but handled this gift with surprising maturity. He used this gift to encourage his personal prayer life, but was careful not to allow it to cause confusion within the general body of believers. Sometimes Ian would pray in tongues under his breath during prayer meetings, but always in a way that was not distracting.

> Despite our limited understanding and focus, God chose to bless us through the gifts he had given.

One night we were praying together as a potential launch team. We had done a short meditation, worshiped some, and were praying. The prayers grew with intensity, and the Holy Spirit seemed to be stirring. Ian happened to be sitting next to me and he whispered, "Eric, I think the Lord wants me to pray in tongues—out loud. Would that be okay?" The gift of tongues was not common in our church. Yet knowing Ian, and being sensitive to the context, it seemed appropriate along with some explanation. I said a few words about the gift and Ian's leading and then allowed him to pray. Ian prayed in tongues for maybe two or three minutes. When he had finished, I shared a little bit about the gift of interpretation of tongues and invited the group to listen to see if anyone would give the interpretation. This was also not a common gift in our community. But I did know that another person present, Brian, had used this gift of interpretation some in the past.

After a few moments, Brian felt led to share the interpretation. As I listened to the interpretation, I was so blessed by the beauty of the message. It was full of encouragement for us as a team, admonishing us to stay focused on the Lord as we ventured into the new endeavor. After Brian stopped, we began as a group to pray in response to the words that were spoken.

This experience was so memorable to me because we were a community who didn't talk much about the gifts of the Spirit, let alone use them very often. And yet, despite our limited understanding and focus, God chose to bless us through the gifts he had given. Not only were we tremendously blessed by manifestations of the Spirit through one another, the experience placed in me a vision and hunger for more. My hunger was to be part of a community striving to walk in all the gifts of the Spirit. I longed to be part of a community growing in their understanding, discovery and practice of these gifts. I believe that this is how God intended his community and church to be. He planned for us to operate in his spiritual gifts as we seek to bring kingdom transformation to the world and within one another. But if we are going to be a community that is walking in the gifts of the Holy Spirit, we need to understand them first.

Gifts of the Spirit[14]

There are three major lists of gifts in the New Testament.

In Romans 12:3–8, we have the first list that some call "gifts of the Father." God has given each of us a *measure of faith* (verse 3) and of *grace* (verse 6), so Paul exhorts us to use the different gifts we have been given for the good of all. We are to live out our gifts by serving, giving, encouraging, etc. These gifts named in the Romans passage appear to relate especially to daily life in and around the church.

> Paul emphasizes that each of us has been given a portion of grace, and calls us to use it.

In Ephesians 4:11–13 we have the second list of gifts. Again Paul emphasizes that each of us has been given a portion of grace, and calls us to use it. The famous British teacher and writer, John Stott, calls this "serving" grace as opposed to "saving" grace.[15] The gifts listed in this passage appear to be given by Christ Jesus (verse 7), and some call them "office-based." The list includes apostles, prophets, evangelists, pastors and teachers. The purpose of these office-based gifts is to *prepare God's people for works of service, so that the body of Christ may be built up* (verse 12).

The third major list is found throughout 1 Corinthians 12. Paul talks of some office-based gifts in verses 27 and 28, as well as some service-based gifts, such as helping and administration. In verses 7–10, however, Paul speaks of gifts that are *manifestations* of the Spirit. The unique feature of these gifts appears to be that they are given specifically by the Holy Spirit for a community gathered in the presence of God. I do not mean to say that this is the only context for using these gifts, but the primary one.

Many of us feel less comfortable with these manifestations of the Spirit. They are more foreign to us than, say, the gifts of *mercy* or *encouragement*. These manifestations of the Spirit are often included on spiritual gift assessments, but somehow they never quite fit right on a questionnaire. I mean, do you really need a questionnaire to ask if you have the gift of tongues? From my perspective, the best way to identify and grow in these manifestations of the Spirit is to experience them in community, while the community is in the presence of God.

Let's take a moment now to look at the nine gifts listed in 1 Corinthians 12:7–10. In terms of titles or terminology for the gifts, I will use the New King James (NKJV) translation, simply because I like the word choices better:

14. I am indebted to Dr. Paul Walker and his article, "Holy Spirit Gifts and Power," for my approach to this section and have adapted many of his definitions of the gifts. Dr. Walker's article appears in *Spirit-Filled Life Study Bible*. Nashville: Nelson, 1991, p. 2018-2026.

15. *The Message to the Ephesians: God's New Society*. London: InterVarsity Press, 1986, p. 155.

> **But the manifestation of the Spirit is given to each one for the profit *of all*: for to one is given the word of wisdom through the Spirit, to another the word of knowledge through the same Spirit, to another faith by the same Spirit, to another gifts of healings by the same Spirit, to another the working of miracles, to another prophecy, to another discerning of spirits, to another *different* kinds of tongues, to another the interpretation of tongues.**
>
> *1 Corinthians 12:7–10*

Today in our opening story about Ian, we have already seen two gifts in action.

Tongues

This is the gift of speaking supernaturally in a language not known to the individual. The Greek word translated *tongues* is *glossolalia* and is also used to mean *languages* or *dialects*. In the New Testament we see disciples speaking in other human languages previously unknown to them like at Pentecost (Acts 2:4–6), or in heavenly languages that Paul calls *tongues of angels* (1 Corinthians 13:1). There are both private and public uses for this gift. In its private use, people exercise this gift primarily in personal times of prayer and worship. Many who have this gift and use it in this way testify that it allows them to grow in intimacy with God. They may know the content of their prayer, but not have a literal word-for-word understanding. People may also use the gift of tongues in public settings, such as worship services or small groups. This is what Ian did. And Paul talks of the importance of having someone gifted with *interpretation* so the body can be blessed. (See 1 Corinthians 14:5 and other related verses in this chapter.)

This is not healing accomplished by medicine or the natural powers of the body to heal itself, but rather healing done supernaturally by the Spirit of God.

Interpretation of Tongues

This gift is obviously the ability to understand and interpret the language that is given through the gift of tongues. Brian used this gift. He explained that he didn't translate every individual word that Ian spoke, but rather shared his internal sense or knowledge of what God had said through the spoken tongue.

Faith

This is a special form of faith that goes beyond natural faith and saving faith. Some believers may have a trust that seems beyond normal. They lead us in specific situations, as they express no doubt but have an unwavering faith about what God will accomplish. I have seen this gift expressed in different people in different situations, and usually they are a huge comfort to those of us struggling to trust God.

Healing(s)

This gift seems fairly obvious, but there are some unique things about how it is listed. The NKJV keeps the double plural *gifts of healings* from the original Greek. The plural suggests that there are many sicknesses and diseases, so we interpret that the gift is related to the healing of many disorders. This is not healing accomplished by medicine or the natural powers of the body to heal itself, but rather healing done supernaturally by the Spirit of God. I am not suggesting that God does not work through modern medicine. I only want to point out that there is a difference.

This gift is specifically related to miraculous works of the Spirit that are beyond the capability of ordinary medicine. The next gift is similar but different.

Working of Miracles

Literally, the Greek words for *working of miracles* could be translated *deeds of power*. These are manifestations of power beyond the ordinary working of natural law. It is a divine enablement to do something (other than healing) that could not be done naturally. Supernatural healings are miracles, too, of course. But it seems that this term, *deeds of power*, refers to actions like calming of storms or walking on water, such as we see in the lives of both Jesus and Peter.

Prophecy

This gift is mentioned in numerous places in the Old and New Testaments and has numerous expressions in the Body of Christ. The simplest definition is this: a divine message given to a believer by the Holy Spirit, often relating to a given situation or context. Sometimes the prophecy may come as a prediction of the future, such as with the Old Testament prophets or in the life of Agabus (Acts 11:28).
But many times prophecy is an indication of the will of God in a given congregation. I have personally experienced this in preaching and writing.

We are meant to discern and distinguish rightly spoken words from those that are off the mark.

Discerning the Spirits

This is the ability to detect what the spirits are doing and how they affect the circumstances or motives of people. In the New Testament we are encouraged, as the body of Christ, to *...test the spirits to see whether they are from God...* (1 John 4:1). It is a mistake to take all concepts offered to us—whether through gifts, messages or counsel—and assume they are accurate. We are meant to discern and distinguish rightly spoken words from those that are off the mark. We will learn more of this another day.

Word of Wisdom

This gift is a Spirit-directed utterance or word of counsel that is given in a specific situation and appears to impart the mind, purpose and way of God. I have experienced this most during meetings as leaders reflected on a particular situation, and then one person would give an insight that brought clarity and understanding in a profound way. I have seen people chosen as elders because they expressed this gift—whether they realized it or not!

Word of Knowledge

This is a supernatural revelation of information pertaining to a person or event, given for a specific purpose, usually relating to an immediate need. This gift may be experienced as a word or a picture, or even a physical or spiritual impression given for guidance to meet the particular need.

Learning to Operate in the Gifts

I have taken the time to explain the gifts of the Holy Spirit because many Christians have very little understanding of what they are. Paul tells us twice to *eagerly desire* the gifts (1 Corinthians 12:30; 14:1). We neglect to eagerly desire the gifts, and I think we often don't recognize them in operation. We may actually have experienced a gift like a *word of knowledge*, but we didn't know it. I decided that I wanted to start eagerly desiring the gifts of the Holy Spirit. I began praying for them, studying them and trying to be sensitive to how they operated.

Around the time when I began praying for the gifts, after a particular Alpha program night, some leaders were gathered in prayer. We were trying to follow the Spirit in terms of praying for various needs of the leaders in the circle. While we were praying, I felt an impression on my leg as if someone had put their hand on my knee.

I looked up expecting to see Helen, a secretary at the church who was sitting next to me, trying to get my attention. But Helen's hands were folded in prayer. I closed my eyes again thinking it must have been some kind of fluke. A few moments later I got the impression in the same place, but again when I looked up, Helen still had her hands folded. I reasoned what possibilities there were to explain this. Maybe Helen was playing a trick on me during prayer, or she was getting fresh with me! But since Helen was past 70 years of age, I figured those possibilities were unlikely. "It must just be some static clinging on my pant-leg," I reasoned. So I adjusted my pants and resumed praying. Sometimes I think God looks down and shakes his head at us, wondering when we are going to get it!

We neglect to eagerly desire the gifts, and I think we often don't recognize them in operation.

A third time I got the impression on my leg. As I looked up, it dawned on me that perhaps this was the Spirit nudging me to pray for someone's knee. The only problem was that I didn't know of any knee injuries in this small group of leaders. I also thought the probability of me looking silly was extremely high if I were to ask. Nonetheless, since I was feeling slightly guilty for being so slow to catch on, I decided to step out in faith.

Continuing in an attitude of prayer, I told the group that I had an impression that we should pray for someone's knee and was wondering if anyone had recently had a knee injury. Mary, one of the leaders, said, "Well, yes, during volleyball over the weekend I injured my knee." Breathing a sigh of relief, I said, "Well then, let's pray for Mary's knee."

Eagerly Desire

Some of my most memorable small group experiences have been during those times when the gifts of the Holy Spirit were operating among us. There seems to be a divine synergy that Paul refers to in 1 Corinthians 12:12-26 when he illustrates the gifts as operating like different body parts, and how they are all meant to work together. It's similar to athletes who have trained the different parts of their bodies to work together so they can compete at the highest levels. They experience a certain excitement, a sense of awe and wonder. That's exactly what I have felt.

We have been studying the task of being part of an advancing kingdom. That kingdom is moving within us and through us by the presence and power of the Holy Spirit. We have received not only the Gift, but also gifts from the Gift. He gives in order to advance the Kingdom of God. If we expect to be a part of this kind of kingdom work, we must be operating as empowered disciples who are learning to use these divine gifts.

Kingdom Questions

Have you ever eagerly desired the gifts of the Holy Spirit?

Have you ever been in a mature and growing community of faith? A group that is learning to recognize the gifts of the Holy Spirit in each other? A group that offers a safe place for people to grow in using these gifts?

That kingdom is moving within us and through us by the presence and power of the Holy Spirit.

What would a kingdom community look like that eagerly desires the gifts in order to advance the kingdom?

Ministry Time

Pray this verse into your life

> **Follow the way of love and eagerly desire spiritual gifts....**
>
> *1 Corinthians 14:1*

Share with the heavenly Father what you want this to look like for you personally, and for your small group.

Day 24 | A Listening Community

Speak, Lord, for your servant is listening

Are you listening? I know you are reading, but that's different. You can read without listening. Listening seems to be a key component in a lot of things we do—like worshiping, having a conversation, praying, sitting in a lecture, sitting on the shores of an ocean. But we can do all these things without really listening. In fact, we can hear but not really be listening.

> The question is not whether God is actively speaking to us. The question really is whether or not we are listening.

I wonder if you've ever stopped to think of this basic Bible teaching: God is speaking. Yes, he has spoken, especially through creation, his Word and his Son. But Scripture also teaches that he *is* speaking, right now. The question is not whether God is actively speaking to us. The question really is whether or not we are listening. So, I ask you again, "Are you listening?" If we are not truly listening, we definitely need to learn how. True listening lies at the heart of a dynamic Christian life and a dynamic community of faith.

A Little Boy Learns to Listen

There is a classic story of listening tucked away in the Old Testament. We probably heard it as children, but we need to read it anew and really listen. It is the story of little Samuel, who was the miracle child of his parents. If you recall, his mother Hannah was barren and couldn't conceive. But God graciously opened her womb to conceive Samuel. His name means "heard of God," because Hannah asked and God heard her prayer. After Hannah weaned Samuel at the age of three or four, she dedicated him to the Lord, to serve in the tabernacle at Shiloh. We pick up the story when Samuel was still a boy.

> **The boy Samuel ministered before the LORD under Eli. In those days the word of the LORD was rare; there were not many visions. One night Eli, whose eyes were becoming so weak that he could barely see, was lying down in his usual place. The lamp of God had not yet gone out, and Samuel was lying down in the temple**

of the LORD, where the ark of God was. Then the LORD called Samuel. Samuel answered, "Here I am." And he ran to Eli and said, "Here I am; you called me." But Eli said, "I did not call; go back and lie down." So he went and lay down. Again the LORD called, "Samuel!" And Samuel got up and went to Eli and said, "Here I am; you called me." "My son," Eli said, "I did not call; go back and lie down." Now Samuel did not yet know the LORD: The word of the LORD had not yet been revealed to him. The LORD called Samuel a third time, and Samuel got up and went to Eli and said, "Here I am; you called me."

Then Eli realized that the LORD was calling the boy. So Eli told Samuel, "Go and lie down, and if he calls you, say, 'Speak, LORD, for your servant is listening.'" So Samuel went and lay down in his place. The LORD came and stood there, calling as at the other times, "Samuel! Samuel!" Then Samuel said, "Speak, for your servant is listening."

1 Samuel 3:1–10

The turning point for Samuel is intriguing. He learned to listen.

This may strike you as a very quaint story of a clueless boy, but it is more than that. In some ways it is a picture of us, a picture of our lives of faith. Some of us are serving the Lord in our little corner of the kingdom, but haven't learned yet to listen—really listen.

Look now at the first sentence of this passage. Notice how Samuel was actively ministering before the Lord. He was probably serving in many ways, attending to and assisting in the rituals and functions of the tabernacle. Samuel was even sleeping near where the actual ark of God was kept. And yet, we are told in verse 7 that Samuel *did not yet know the Lord*. He was serving and living a very religious life, but despite that he did not know the Lord.

The Hebrew word used here for *know* is *yada'*. When Scripture uses this term, it often refers to a personal knowing or experience between two people. It is often an intimate knowing. For example, Genesis 4:1 uses this word when it tells us, *And Adam knew Eve, his wife; and she conceived, and bore Cain....* (NKJV) This is a very personal knowledge and experience between two people. We can know God personally (without the physical intimacy, of course). In fact, he wants us to know him personally and therefore reveals himself to us.

Probably many of us in the United States can relate to Samuel carrying out his religious duties, but not really knowing God personally. In a nation or community such as ours, we can grow up in the faith, so to speak—doing the practices, doing the rituals of the faith. We can attend church, serve in a variety of ways, even go through confirmation or catechism—and yet still not *know* God in a personal way.

The turning point for Samuel is intriguing. He learned to listen. Through learning to recognize God's voice, he stepped into the know. To have a personal relationship with God we don't have to hear an audible voice like Samuel did. Many disciples experience more of an internal knowing, such as a mental impression. For some, the words of Scripture jump off the page and go straight to their hearts. For others, it is the voice of a preacher or teacher. When a word is spoken, it's as if it were earmarked just for them. Sometimes God brings people into the know through visions and dreams. I don't think it really matters how we hear God's voice. What matters is that in some way, somehow, we step into the know.

Yes, we need to recognize God's voice calling us to receive him as Lord and Savior. But we also need to recognize God's voice of guidance and direction. This is one of the primary roles of the Holy Spirit in our lives (John 14:26). He is our counselor. He desires to speak to us, so that we might *know* him more and know his will.

Notice from the last part of chapter 3, verses 19–21, how this was true of Samuel. He didn't just hear God's voice once and then he was done. He learned to hear and obey his voice on a regular basis. Samuel's ministry as a prophet flowed out of a deep personal knowledge of God. An integral part of Samuel's faith and personal relationship with God was listening.

We also need to recognize God's voice of guidance and direction.

God Breaks His Silence

Earlier in chapter 3, verses 11–14, God had spoken a word of judgment against Eli and his greedy sons who were serving as priests. At the strong prompting of Eli, Samuel had overcome his fear and faithfully related God's devastating and fateful word to the old priest (verses 15–18).

Now look at the contrast between verse 1 and verses 19 and 21 regarding the Lord's voice:

> **...In those days the word of the Lord was rare, there were not many visions.**
>
> *1 Samuel 3:1*

> **The Lord was with Samuel as he grew up, and he let none of his words fall to the ground....The Lord continued to appear at Shiloh and there he revealed himself to Samuel through his word.**
>
> *1 Samuel 3:19, 21*

So, as we read in verse one, God had not been saying much. This in itself seems ironic, because the town of Shiloh was the worship center for the Hebrews in those days. The tabernacle was there, and God was supposed to be present. Yet apparently not many folks were listening. I don't think there were many people in the know. Not many were actively listening for the word of the Lord. And we know for sure that Eli's sons certainly weren't! (verse 13)

By the end of the chapter, though, we see a change. God broke the silence. Through this young teenage boy who had learned to listen, he began to speak again to Israel. God appeared and revealed himself in Shiloh. As 1 Samuel 4:1a tells us … *Samuel's word came to all Israel.*

What a difference listening made! Samuel grew from a clueless boy, to a man of God. Israel, a nation starved for the voice of God, became a people filled with the words of God—all because a boy learned to listen and obey.

God Wants to Speak to You

Here's the thing! We can read Samuel's story and think,

***Well yeah, sure,
God spoke to Samuel, but he was a prophet
in the Bible. I'm just an everyday person who shops at
Walmart. I don't think the God of the universe
really wants to get personal and speak to me.
Maybe to pastors or leaders today,
but certainly not me!***

This *knowing* of the Lord would be for everyone.

Will you believe me if I tell you that God wants to get "up close and personal" with you?

Will you balk if I tell you that the God of the universe wants you to **KNOW** him personally—to break the silence with "li'l old ordinary you", to build an intimate and personal relationship?

Will you trust me if I prove it to you in Scripture? Remember, you made a commitment to conform your thinking to the Word of God.

Think back to Day 17 when we talked about the Holy Spirit, the promise of the Father poured out on his followers. Now read what Jeremiah prophesied about the coming of a new day, a New Covenant.

> **"...I will put my law in their minds and write it on their hearts. I will be their God, and they will be my people. No longer will a man teach his neighbor, or a man his brother, saying, 'Know the LORD,' because they will all know me, from the least of them to the greatest," declares the LORD.**
>
> *Jeremiah 31:33–34a*

Did you notice our little word in that passage? Yes, that same Hebrew word *know* appears there. Jeremiah prophesied that in this new day, the knowing of God wouldn't just be for prophets or pastors, not just for priests or kings. This *knowing* of the Lord would be for everyone ...*from the least of them to the greatest*.... And remember, the new day that Jeremiah foretold is the time of the New Covenant that we are living in right now!

Jesus brought this new day. He established this New Covenant in his blood. His death and resurrection paved the way for the Father to pour out the promised Holy Spirit at Pentecost (Acts 2). As a result, every single disciple could know the presence and guidance of the Spirit. That is why Jesus could say so confidently that his followers would know his voice, even after he was taken from them.

> **"I am the good shepherd; I *know* my sheep and my sheep *know* me—just as the Father *knows* me and I *know* the Father—and I lay down my life for the sheep. I have other sheep that are not of this sheep pen. I must bring them also. They too will listen to *my voice*, and there shall be one flock and one shepherd."** (emphasis added)
>
> *John 10:14–16*

We are meant to be disciples that know the voice of our Good Shepherd. But God's desire is not just to speak to us as individuals. He also wants to speak to us as a community.

A Word-Filled Community

This kind of dynamic listening characterized the New Testament church.

The Scriptures talk about a new covenant community where the word of God is frequently heard and acted upon. This is the kind of community that we are meant to be today—a people who are gathered around his revealed word, Scripture; and at the same time listening for his voice and following his guidance. We embrace this truth not only as the wisdom of Scripture, but also as the revelation of the Spirit.

In Day 23, we talked about the manifestation of the Spirit's gifts. The operation of those supernatural gifts depends on us listening for God's voice. If you want to receive a *word of knowledge* or of *wisdom*, you need to listen. If God is going to speak a prophetic word through you or interpret a tongue through you, you have to be listening. Imagine a small group or house church in the Greek city of Corinth. The Holy Spirit manifested these gifts as believers worshiped together and prayed for each other. How incredible it must have been to hear someone share a *word of knowledge* meant for you in your life's circumstances!

This kind of dynamic listening characterized the New Testament church. Whether in Corinth or in Jerusalem, there were communities of believers filled with the words and guidance of the Holy Spirit. Take another example from the church in Antioch. Look at how they listened and hear what they heard:

> **In the church at Antioch there were prophets and teachers.... While they were worshiping the Lord and fasting, the Holy Spirit said, "Set apart for me Barnabas and Saul for the work to which I have called them." So after they had fasted and prayed, they placed their hands on them and sent them off.**
>
> *Acts 13:1–3*

From reading the New Testament, you can't say that the *word of the Lord was rare* in that day, like it had been before Samuel (1 Samuel 3:1). The words of the Lord filled his church. God was speaking to them through the power of the Spirit and the gifts he had given.

We are meant to be a community like that. We are meant to be a community filled with the words of God for each other and for the world.

Beginning to Listen

The next time we get together as a small group, we will practice listening to God together. But for now we need to start learning to listen personally, in our own one-on-one time with the Lord. I would like to suggest Samuel's key phrase as our framework for listening:

We are meant to be a community filled with the words of God for each other and for the world.

Key Phrase of a Christian Disciple—
Speak, Lord, for your servant is listening.

Speak, Lord

When we turn to the Lord and say, "Speak, Lord," we are really trying to do two things:

- **Believe** that the Lord is actively speaking and wants to speak to us.
- **Ask** him to begin revealing himself to us.

We can miss the voice of God because we don't believe or expect this kind of divine leading from him. But now we know differently. We know that God does indeed desire to speak to us, to lead us, to guide us in this life—even in specific and personal ways. Believing and asking is the way to start.

Your Servant

When we call ourselves his servants, we are committing ourselves to **obey and submit** to what he says, to the direction he gives. This is a crucial piece of listening for the voice of our Shepherd. He wants to speak to those who are not only listening, but to those with the willingness to obey. Jonah was a man who had the listening part down, but not the obeying part. Look where that landed him! We definitely want to model Samuel, not Jonah. God longs for us to become servants of his Word, cooperating with his kingdom work.

Is Listening

Listening is really an ongoing activity. It takes time and focus to actually get quiet enough to hear the Lord. We lead busy lives, don't we? One of the hardest things to do in our culture is to shut everything off and listen. But if we really want to listen, we have to quiet the noise around us and within us, and turn the ears of our hearts to heaven.

Ⓡ Reflection

Please take a few minutes right now and follow the wisdom of our key phrase. Think of an issue that you need clarity on, something that you would like the Lord to speak to you about. Name the issue out loud, and then pray, "Speak, Lord, for your servant is listening."

DAY 25 | A DISCERNING COMMUNITY

Do not believe every spirit, but test the spirits

I have known Dale for most of his life. He is a good friend who discovered the Lord—or "stepped into the know"—a little while after college. Single, working in business and living in a suburb of Chicago, Dale had no idea of the significant adventure God had planned for him—taking a new job in Georgia, just outside of Atlanta. He knew no one, but trusted God as he launched himself out into new frontiers in January of 1991.

> The counsel wasn't stated as opinion or something to pray about, but as a "word from the Lord."

Dale connected with a church and began singing in the large choir. At this time, he really desired a life-long companion and asked the Lord to bring him to a new relationship in his new home. Jeanne was a beautiful woman of God who also sang in the choir. On a church retreat, they began a relationship and started falling in love. As I talked with Dale, it seemed like this had God's fingerprints all over it. Their love was growing, and Dale was feeling more and more like he was ready to pop the question.

But they hit a very significant snag. Some of the people closest to her shared some shocking news. Both her sister and her close friends felt as though the Lord had given them counsel and direction that she should break things off with Dale. The counsel wasn't stated as opinion or something to pray about, but as a "word from the Lord."

First, Jeanne's sister Ruth stated that she had received a picture of Jeanne crying and weeping because of Dale. Ruth interpreted this picture as what Jeanne's life would look like if she continued in the relationship and eventually married Dale. According to Ruth, the Lord had revealed to her that Dale had some unconfessed homosexual experiences in his past. This, she assumed, would lead to a marriage of strife and pain for Jeanne. If that weren't bad enough, listen to the rest: Jeanne's close friends and spiritual mentors, Bill and Grace, declared that when they had been praying for her and Dale, the Lord had revealed Dale to be a violent person. They believed that Dale struggled with anger. Bill and Grace told Jeanne that if she were to marry Dale, it would be a marriage spoiled by violent behavior and brokenness.

As you can imagine, this was very disturbing news for Jeanne. Not only were these folks close to her, but they were part of her believing community. They expressed these views as *impressions* and *words* from the Lord and expected Jeanne to act on them—and fast. She decided to talk them over with Dale first, before she acted on them.

Dale gave me a call in desperation. The relationship and their future were on the brink of destruction. I still remember his words:

***"What am I supposed to do, Eric?
I have denied the accusation of homosexual experiences, but how do I prove something like that to people who are convinced they have heard from God?
Also, how can you deny a picture of the future when no one knows for sure what the future looks like?"***

These communities were filled with the Spirit and sought to live with the Spirit at their center.

Now what do you say to all this? What counsel would you have given to Dale and Jeanne?

The Necessity of Testing

One way I could have reacted was simply to deny any validity to the claims of Ruth, Bill and Grace. I could have labeled them as crazy and ungodly, and dismissed altogether their ability to hear from God. This was certainly a temptation to me, because their counsel seemed so disconnected from who Dale was and the strength of the relationship. All those who knew Dale well knew he had zero indication of a confused sexuality or a problem with violence.

However, I chose to tackle the issue in a different way. I encouraged Dale and Jeanne to practice a very important spiritual principle found in the New Testament. Rather than blindly accepting the counsel given, because it was attached to the-Lord-told-me language, I advised them to test these *words*.

In the New Testament, we see new and growing Christian communities struggling with a variety of issues, everything from theological questions to practices and rituals of the faith. These communities were filled with the Spirit and sought to live with the Spirit at their center. The apostles who wrote to these communities encouraged godly thinking and practices. They exhorted them to mature in their use of their spiritual gifts and the ministry of prophecy. But along with such encouragement, they emphasized the need for testing and discernment.

Here is what the Apostle John said about this:

> **Dear friends, do not believe every spirit, but test the spirits to see whether they are from God, because many false prophets have gone out into the world.**
>
> *1 John 4:1*

John encouraged the Christian community not to take things at face value. That is, don't accept every *discernment* or *word* or *impression* hook, line and sinker. The apostles did not deny that people were led and guided by the Holy Spirit in these ways. On the contrary, they wanted disciples to grow in listening to God. They cautioned, however, about false prophets who can lead people astray.

Not only are there false prophets, but there are also Christians who will get it wrong sometimes. We are a fallen people. Though we have been redeemed and saved, the old nature still clings. Sanctification is a process, and we are all still on the road. Even well-meaning disciples may get things wrong. At times, pastors may pastor poorly, elders may shepherd with wrong motives, wise Christian counselors and mentors may give wrong advice, and prophetically gifted people may hear or interpret words and impressions wrongly. This is the reality of life for God's covenant people. Until the kingdom comes in fullness, we will all suffer from the stain of sin. We need to learn to operate in the tension produced by a kingdom that is here already, but not yet in its fullness. That means, through the Spirit, we must always test and discern our leadings and understandings.

Even well-meaning disciples may get things wrong.

Not only are we a fallen people, but there are multiple voices out there. I have heard a Christian speaker, Ted Kallman, talk about the "four voices in our heads".[16] This has helped me process and grow in my own listening to God. Consider Kallman's four voices:

- **Voice of the Holy Spirit**. God speaks in many different ways—an audible voice, like Samuel heard; mental and sensory impressions; the *still, small voice*. We know his voice is always good and right.
- **Voice of the enemy**. He is the father of lies, and he works by twisting the truth and burrowing lies deep into our thinking. We know his voice is always false, and intended for confusion and harm.
- **Voice of others**. These voices not only represent the things that people are currently saying to us, but also and especially the things spoken to us in the past that have stuck in our souls. These are the "tapes" that keep playing in our minds, whether we recognize them or not. They can be good or bad, hopeful or harmful.
- **Voice of our conscience**. These are the things that we tell ourselves, over and over. Again, they can be good or bad. They can sow life and our true identity within us, or break us down and rob us of our sense of worth or significance.

Part of the process of spiritual growth and maturity is learning to differentiate among these voices—recognizing and holding on to the good while rejecting the lies.

Handling Fire with Care

My friend Tom was a pastor of a nearby congregation and spoke often about the person and work of the Holy Spirit. Tom was in his sixties, and his journey toward life in the Spirit included many wounds and hurts. At one time, he pursued more charismatic expressions of the faith but, as he put it, he got burned by a lot of the extremism. He shared with me that, for several years afterwards, he had turned away from seeking more of the Spirit.

16. Ted Kallman, from his presentation and self published book, *Stark Raving Obedience*, 2007.

As Tom has grown in his faith, he has learned to strike a balance between seeking more of the Holy Spirit and operating with wisdom and discernment. This is an important tension that I believe we need to live with as Spirit-filled Christians. It is part of living in the *in-between times* of the kingdom. Listen to the balance that the Apostle Paul promotes in the Thessalonian community:

> **Do not put out the Spirit's fire; do not treat prophecies with contempt. Test everything. Hold on to the good. Avoid every kind of evil.**
>
> *1 Thessalonians 5:19–22*

In verse 19 Paul likens the Spirit to *fire*. Fire is a tremendous power, and necessary for certain aspects of living. Prior to electricity, people would not have survived without it. Yet if we do not handle fire with care, we can very easily be burned.

This is analogous with the work and ministry in the Spirit. As we have seen, life and ministry in the Spirit are powerful and significant. Yet if we lose respect for either the power of the Spirit, or for our propensity to use our good gifts in ungodly ways, we get burned, and burned badly.

Our human tendency is to want to control, rather than be led by what happens.

Once burned, there is the temptation to just avoid fire altogether. It would have been understandable for Dale to avoid these kinds of *leadings* and *impressions* after his experience. But the Apostle Paul says emphatically not to go to that extreme. Don't fall into the temptation to *treat prophecies with contempt* (verse 20). Because of our own bad experiences or inexperience, we may treat these kinds of *leadings* with disdain, disrespect, or scorn. We need to respect the New Testament truth that we are all—great and small—filled and empowered by the Spirit. We are called not to reject this kind of ministry, but to test it.

And in our testing, we are also cautioned: *Do not put out the Spirit's fire* (verse 19). Our human tendency is to want to control, rather than be led by what happens. But the Spirit has his own will and sometimes chooses to operate beyond our established guidelines and traditions. Again, Paul's exhortation is to **test**, **not squelch**, and to **discern**, **not disdain**. To the Corinthian church Paul said:

> **Two or three prophets should speak, and the others should weigh carefully what is said.**
>
> *1 Corinthians 14:29*

There is a humble weighing of what is shared. And after we have weighed, tested and discerned what the Spirit is saying, we need to hold on to the good and avoid what is fleshly. We need to do this as individuals, and especially as a community of faith.

Essay or Multiple Choice

So if we are called to test, weigh and discern, what does this look like? To me the questions in the testing process (discernment) are more like essay questions rather than multiple-choice. It's not so much a check-the-box experience as it is a dialogue.

Scripture. Usually the first test is Scripture. We must hold all of our *leadings* up to the light of Scripture. If there is anything inconsistent with it, you know it is not from the Lord. As people of the Book, we need to submit humbly to the authority of Scripture, which reveals God's good and perfect will.

Community. I repeat, community is vital to our growth as Christians. We need the freedom and permission to express hesitations and struggles to one another. We also need the humility to realize that we might be in error and allow others to correct us. This is part of being a mature Christian—always to be willing to admit a wrong or a miss.

Prayer. Additional prayer and reflection are often crucial. We need to process what we think we have heard, especially related to bigger decisions. As I do this, I often have the impression that I am holding a *word* in my hands before God, turning it over, and looking at it from different angles.

Circumstance and Confirmation. I do believe in the open and closed doors perspective. God does use circumstances to confirm or deny what we believe to be his will.

Is it loving? The question that is always good to ask is, "Is it loving?" Yes, sometimes we need to proceed in tough love, but I have found the question to be a check to some of my thoughts, actions and attitudes. If we do not think or speak in love, chances are we have not heard the voice of God.

If we do not think or speak in love, chances are we have not heard the voice of God.

The End of the Story

You are probably wondering what happened with Dale and Jeanne. Well, they did test and discern the perspective of her friends and family. They did exactly what we are talking about; they sought to *test the spirits*. As they prayed and discussed the validity of the *words* and *impressions* given, they realized that the likelihood was very high that people's own motives and impressions (and even jealousies) could enter into any *leading*.

In the end, Dale and Jeanne decided to get married. They have been married over fifteen years and have three wonderful kids. Dale has not developed a propensity for anger or reflected any confusion over his sexual identity. Praise God for the spiritual principle of discernment.

Ⓡ Reflection

Please take a few moments to meditate on the following verse of Scripture:

> **Love must be sincere. Hate what is evil; cling to what is good.**
> *Romans 12:9*

DAY 26 | A WORSHIPING COMMUNITY

…since we are receiving a kingdom that cannot be shaken, let us be thankful, and…worship…

So what is it, this thing we call worship? One Thursday evening I was filling in for our worship director. To begin our worship team practice, I decided to start with a little devotional. With the adults and teenagers of the band gathered around, we turned to the story of Jesus interacting with the Samaritan woman at the well.

> **"…Believe me, woman, a time is coming when you will worship the Father *neither on this mountain nor in Jerusalem.* You Samaritans worship what you do not know; we worship what we do know, for salvation is from the Jews. Yet a time is coming and has now come when the true worshipers will worship the Father in *spirit and truth,* for they are the kind of worshipers *the Father seeks.* God is spirit and his worshipers must worship in spirit and in truth."** (emphasis added)
>
> *John 4:21–24*

Many Christians may go through the motions of worship, the rituals of worship, without really worshiping.

I have always been intrigued by this passage because, as far as I know, it is the only place that tells us that God the Father is *seeking* something. He is looking for what Jesus calls *true worshipers*—those worshiping *in spirit and in truth.* I thought my question to the worship team was simple: "What does it mean to worship in spirit and in truth?"

After some limp guesses and a short discussion, it was clear that no one on the worship team really had any idea what that meant. I was very surprised. These folks were leading our congregation in worship, and yet they didn't have a clue what it was they were supposed to be doing. The focus was pretty much on notes and chords and that was it.

The members of this team were not unique in their lack of understanding. Many Christians may go through the motions of worship, the rituals of worship, without really worshiping. God is seeking those who get it—those who understand what it means to worship *in spirit and in truth,* right here, right now. Jesus wants us to get it. And that is one of the reasons why this discussion with the Samaritan woman is recorded in Scripture. Jesus pointed the woman, as well as us, to a new reality of worship, a new community of *true worshipers.*

What Mountain? I Don't See a Mountain...

Did you notice that in the midst of the discussion with the Samaritan woman regarding worship, Jesus talked about two locations—a mountain (Mount Gerizim) and Jerusalem (built on the Temple Mount)? There is another passage of Scripture essential to our understanding of worship that also refers to mountains. The writer of Hebrews clarified where we go when we do this thing called worship.

> **You have not come to a *mountain* that can be touched and that is burning with fire; to darkness, gloom and storm; to a trumpet blast or to such a voice speaking words that those who heard it begged that no further word be spoken to them.... But you have come to *Mount Zion*, to the heavenly Jerusalem, the city of the living God. You have come to thousands upon thousands of angels in joyful assembly, to the church of the firstborn, whose names are written in heaven. You have come to God, the judge of all men, to the spirits of righteous men made perfect, to Jesus the mediator of a new covenant, and to the sprinkled blood ....** (emphasis added)
>
> *Hebrews 12:18–19; 22–24*

Jesus pointed the woman, as well as us, to a new reality of worship.

All this talk of various mountains might be confusing. Let's try to understand the various mountains involved in these two passages of Scripture.

While talking with the Samaritan woman, Jesus referred to **Mount Gerizim** (*this mountain*, John 4:21). This was the Samaritan place of worship. They believed this mountain was a sacred place and even went so far as to build a temple of worship on it in 400 B.C. This was a huge point of contention between the Samaritans and the Jews, so much so that the Jews would later destroy this temple. They believed that Jerusalem (specifically the temple) was the only appropriate place of worship.

The Temple Mount (John 4:21). When Jesus referred to Jerusalem, he was probably contrasting Mount Gerizim with the Temple Mount in Jerusalem. This was the location of the temple of God that Herod had rebuilt. Built on a hill in Jerusalem, it was commonly known as the Temple Mount. Isaiah 2:3 says, *Come, let us go up to the mountain of the Lord.*

Mount Sinai (Hebrews 12:18). The author of Hebrews also talked about two mountains. The first was Mount Sinai. All the chilling language he used in 12:18-20 recalled the experience of the Israelites when they received the Law from God on Mount Sinai (see Exodus 19:10-25). God's awesome presence terrified the Jews. So they asked Moses to be their mediator in order to avoid stepping into the presence of God on the mountain.

Of the three mountains just mentioned above, which one are we supposed to go to for worship? In John 4:23, Jesus told the woman that things were changing. True worshipers would no longer go to Mount Gerizim, or to the Temple Mount. According to the passage in Hebrews, people wouldn't go to Mount Sinai either. Rather, there is a fourth mountain, a spiritual mountain—a mountain in heaven.

Mount Zion in Heaven (Hebrews 12:22). This is where God truly is. Rather than a chilling experience of gloom, the work of Christ has transformed our worship into a beautiful experience of holy awe. We cannot see this mountain with our physical eyes, but it is just as real as the other three. The book of Hebrews gives us a glimpse of what this mountain of worship actually looks like.

Imagination Station

As we unpack this glimpse of the heavenly mountain in Hebrews 12, create a picture in your mind. Allow the words of Hebrews to impress upon your mind's eye the actual worship taking place at this very moment:

The work of Christ has transformed our worship into a beautiful experience of holy awe.

...thousands upon thousands of angels in joyful assembly... (Hebrews 12:22). In Revelation 5:11 (another glimpse of heavenly worship), John described *ten thousand times ten thousand* angels encircling the throne. Imagine a host of angels as far as the eye can see—an ocean of worshipers, bowing in reverence, lifting their voices in adoration and praise.

...to the church of the firstborn whose names are written in heaven... (Hebrews 12:23). Incredible as it may seem, this is a reference to you and me, to Christians from around the world entering this spiritual place of worship. *Firstborn* suggests our privileged position as heirs of the heavenly Father together with Christ. Whether we realize it or not, when we worship we are really part of this heavenly assembly.

...to God, the judge of all men... (verse 23). The eternal and one true living God, who is judge over every man and woman, is sitting upon the throne. He is at the center of this worshiping assembly. He is the focus. He is King of the Mountain.

...to the spirits of righteous men made perfect... (verse 23). These are the people of faith who have gone before us. They are living their reward of righteousness and faith in the presence of God.

...to Jesus, the mediator of a new covenant, and to the sprinkled blood... (verse 24). Jesus is the one who brought the change. We no longer approach a physical place on Earth with fear and trembling. But in new covenant worship, we now enter the heavenly realms with joy and thankfulness, in reverence and awe. His sprinkled blood gives us confidence.

> **Therefore, brothers, since we have confidence to enter the Most Holy Place by the blood of Jesus ... let us draw near to God with a sincere heart in full assurance of faith....**
>
> *Hebrews 10:19, 22*

Do you see it? Remember that the author of Hebrews is not giving a glimpse of what is to come. He is revealing a glimpse of the new reality of worship. This is not the assembly that we will enter into after we die. I encourage you, "Climb the mountain" right here, right now.

Not Practice, but the Real Deal

Today we often talk about worship as practice for our arrival in heaven. But that's not correct. According to the New Testament, Jesus has paved the way for us to get off the practice field and into the actual game. We are not preparing to worship the king on his holy mountain. We are actually ascending the spiritual mountain and entering into the very real presence of our king—but only if we are worshiping *in spirit and in truth.*

In Wayne Grudem's *Systematic Theology*, he comments on this Hebrews passage:

> "This is the reality of new covenant worship: it actually is worship in the presence of God, though we do not now see him with our physical eyes, nor do we see the angels gathered around his throne or the spirits of believers who have gone before and are now worshiping in God's presence. But it is all there, and it is all real, more real and more permanent than the physical creation that we see around us, which will someday be destroyed." (p. 1007)

We are actually ascending the spiritual mountain and entering into the very real presence of our king.

We have talked about getting heaven down here; but in this instance the emphasis is getting Earth-bound people to heaven. The rituals of worship are not the goal; they are the avenues. Our rituals and practices—in music, prayer, the Word—are intended as pathways up the mountain.

Early in my marriage, I discovered the things my wife didn't like. One was reading the newspaper at dinner. She did not buy my argument that I could simultaneously carry on a conversation with her while reading the paper. (She was right, of course!) Now think about me for a moment. I am going through all the rituals of a dinner conversation: There I am, sitting at the table, eating and drinking, even talking and listening. But if I am reading the paper at the same time, I am not having a conversation with my wife, am I?

The same is true of worship. I can be standing in a church, even singing songs. But if I am reading the bulletin or thinking about the crockpot stew cooking at home, I am not truly entering into worship. I am not ascending the mountain. I am simply hanging out at the foot of the mountain while others around me are climbing. How many of us are stuck at the bottom of the mountain because we have never known there was a mountain to be climbed?

Climbing in Spirit and in Truth

Returning to John 4:24, we notice that Jesus pointed out two essential elements of true worship. If we want to be true worshipers, we must have both. God is seeking those of us who have both. These two elements are spirit and truth.

You may ask me, "What does spirit-and-truth worship look like?" A passage from 1 Corinthians has really helped me understand. The Corinthian church struggled in the area of worship and spiritual gifts. So in order to clarify, Paul shared some of his personal experience.

> **So it is with you. Since you are eager to have spiritual gifts, try to excel in gifts that build up the church. For this reason anyone who speaks in a tongue should pray that he may interpret what he says. For if I pray in a tongue, my spirit prays, but my mind is unfruitful. So what shall I do? I will pray with my spirit, but I will also pray with my mind; I will sing with my spirit, but I will also sing with my mind.**
>
> *1 Corinthians 14:12–15*

Paul taught some important things about worship in this passage. First, part of who we are engages God on a different level. He calls it *spirit*. There is more to worship than our reasoning and understanding. Paul said that worship is not just about praying with the mind (truth). We should *pray with [our] spirit and sing with [our] spirit*. Paul says that when he prays or sings with his spirit, his mind is *unfruitful*. But that is not a bad thing. This is a spiritual element of worship that is good and right. Jesus even said it was necessary if we are to be *true worshipers*.

This is a spiritual element of worship that is good and right.

Of course, this does not discount worshiping with our minds, or *in truth*. Paul says the answer is to do both. We can engage God with both our minds and our spirits. We know the God whom we worship, because Jesus has revealed him (John 10:37–38). Jesus has revealed the Father to us so that we might worship him *in truth*. But Jesus has also enabled us to be *born again*, to experience a spiritual birth in which our spirits come alive (John 3:3, 6). Energized by his Spirit, we can worship him with our spirits.

For me it was significant simply to realize that there was some part of me that worshiped—a part that I could never completely understand. But even if I didn't understand completely, I did begin to sense when I was worshiping in my spirit and when the Spirit of God was brooding over me.

Men and women of the Bible got this idea of worshiping in the spirit. We might call it soul worship. The psalmist wrote,

> **As the deer pants for streams of water, so my soul pants for you, O God. My soul thirsts for God, for the living God.**
>
> *Psalm 42:1 2a*

Mother Mary sang,

> **"… My soul glorifies the Lord and my spirit rejoices in God my Savior, …."**
>
> *Luke 1:46–47*

Worship with All You Are

Please look again at the simple diagram that helps us see who we are.

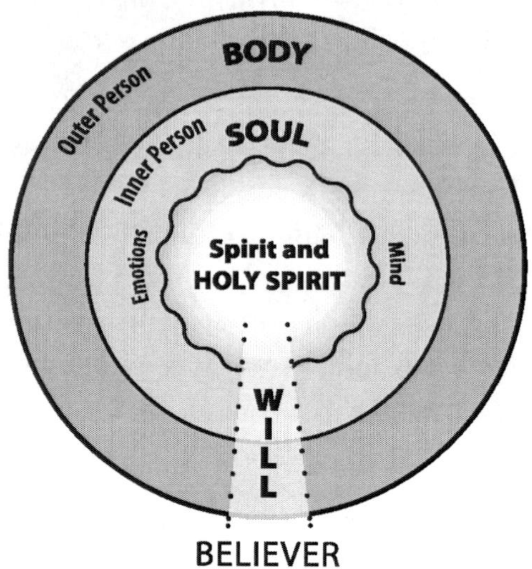

Don't practice, but *do* it.

In light of this diagram, read this Scripture.

> **"Love the Lord your God with all your heart and with all your soul and with all your mind and with all your strength."**
> *Mark 12:30*

Obviously, Jesus is describing our whole being. God desires worshipers who love and worship him with their whole selves.

Kingdom Questions

Don't practice, but **do** it. Reflect on the Hebrews 12:22-24 passage about worship and enter in.

What posture will you assume so that you can worship him with your strength?

What aspect of who he is will you focus on, so you can worship him with your mind?

What emotion will you allow to flow toward him that will enable you to worship with your heart?

What prayer will you pray to invite the Spirit of Christ to connect with your spirit?

Right now, right here, worship him *in spirit and in truth.*

Days 27 & 28 | A Kingdom Community

...for theirs is the Kingdom of Heaven...

Midway through seminary I decided to start a different kind of small group. In the church where I interned, there was a small cadre of people yearning to grow more in experiencing the presence and power of the Spirit. We called our little gathering "Creating Space for the Spirit", and decided we wouldn't have much of an agenda. Our longing was just to have the Spirit lead us.

> ...a Holy Spirit-presence-based community ... ready to minister and pray the kingdom into any area of life....

For each gathering, I asked a different person to lead with a brief meditation from Scripture. Then we worshiped together. I led with my guitar and a few songs. From that point on, the Spirit led us. Sometimes a person would share an issue they were struggling with, and we would pray over them. At other times, someone would sense that we were supposed to pray for another person in the group. After asking a few questions, we prayed into whatever area was appropriate.

The extraordinary part of this kind of humanly unscripted small group was that the Holy Spirit always came with his particular agenda. If we truly gave him the space to lead, he would direct us to the area of need to pray for. We never knew what to expect!

You have been reading about different aspects of what I call a kingdom community. This is a Holy Spirit-presence-based community that is ready to minister and pray the kingdom into any area of life that he directs us to. Today I want you to practice the same thing in your small group gathering. Please follow the very general guidelines of this kingdom community that you have read so far, and seek to let the Spirit lead where he wants you to go.

Reviewing Some Aspects of Our Kingdom Community

Now let's take a few moments to review some of the aspects of a kingdom community that we have talked about this past week.

A Worshiping Community. Remember the spiritual truth that worship is not just practice for heaven; it's the real deal today. When we truly worship, we enter the very presence of God right here, right now. Seek to worship him not only with your mind, but with your spirit as well—with your whole being.

A Listening Community. Listen! Allow the Holy Spirit to lead into the places he wants to go. Learn to discern his voice and his way. Lay your own agendas aside and give the Spirit space to operate, to direct.

A Broken Community. Try to be open and honest with your community. Share some of the areas you are struggling in. By opening ourselves up for others to pray, we advance the reality of the kingdom in our lives.

A Gifted Community. Recognize and affirm the gifts the Spirit has given you. Use them to edify the community of Christ. By humbly learning and growing in our gifts together, we can bless and advance the kingdom.

A Discerning Community. Seek never to undermine or doubt the Holy Spirit, but ask for wisdom, discernment and love as you minister to one another. Ask for the faith to take risks and obey what you believe the Spirit is saying. But do all this humbly—always ready to be corrected or redirected.

By opening ourselves up for others to pray, we advance the reality of the kingdom in our lives.

Ministry Time

Your small group leader will serve as the facilitator, gently leading you in this time of ministry. Simply follow the general outline of the characteristics of the kingdom community, and commit to following where the Spirit leads.

Worship through Music. The small group facilitator will have asked someone beforehand to lead with a guitar, piano or simply with their voice. Or, you may just listen to a few worship songs on a CD. Try to establish a mood of quiet reflection.

Listening Prayer. The small group facilitator will pray to bind or stifle the voice of the enemy and the untrustworthy voices of our conscience. Then, take a few minutes as a group to quietly listen. Who or what does the Spirit want us to pray for?

Authentic Sharing. This is the time to risk, honestly sharing needs for prayer. These may be a physical need, an emotional or relational need, or a spiritual need. During this time, don't ask to pray for someone else who is not a part of your small group. The focus is to be on the group members who are present. It is always appropriate to ask to be filled again with the Spirit. (See Days 20–21.) You may also want to ask for more clarity about a certain spiritual gift, or to receive one. This would definitely be a part of *eagerly desiring the gifts*. It is usually best to have two or three people share a need and then pray for them as a whole group, one by one. It is common to ask the person being prayed for to sit in the center, and also to request permission to lay hands on him or her.

Operating in the Gifts. In beginning to pray for a person, the group should ask God to help them exercise their gifts in the best way. While praying, seek to be led by the Spirit. Is he giving someone a word or impression? Is he showing someone a picture or vision? Should you lay hands on the person for prayer (if you haven't yet)?

Discerning during the Ministry Time. Normally, after a few have prayed or shared words or impressions, I ask the person being prayed for if any of those prayers or words particularly connected with them. I may also ask the person if she or he has received any insight or understanding. I also continue listening in order to discern the next step. Do we need to pray further into a particular area? Do we need to listen a bit more? Is it time to go to the next person who shared a need? The small group facilitator will guide this process.

Continue listening in order to discern the next step.

Week Five | With the Kingdom Comes Healing

And a woman was there who had been subject to bleeding for twelve years, but no one could heal her. She came up behind him and touched the edge of his cloak, and immediately her bleeding stopped.

Luke 8:43–44

Day 29 | Wounds that Heal

By his wounds we are healed

Once there was a pastor who moved into my geographical area to take a denominational position for church planting. He was a unique Reformed pastor, known not only for his vision and work in the area of church growth but also for healing. I felt led to ask him to begin a coaching relationship with me, primarily concerning the concept of the kingdom. Although I realized that the Lord had shown me much about the kingdom through Scripture, I was unsure what to do with this knowledge. I think the Holy Spirit nudged me to seek out Tim. Perhaps he could provide some wise counsel.

> So many weird and unbiblical practices seemed to be associated with healing and with those in the Christian world who promoted it.

As Tim and I began to connect, he became very excited about the discoveries in the kingdom that I was sharing. At one point he said, "You know, Eric, the kingdom is the language that is used in healing ministry." I don't remember my exact response but it was along the lines of, "I think I'll just stick with kingdom ministry and not so much with healing ministry."

You see, at that point in my study of the kingdom, I understood very little in terms of its relationship to healing. Not only did I lack understanding, but also willingness. To be honest, I didn't really want to get into healing ministry. So many weird and unbiblical practices seemed to be associated with healing and with those in the Christian world who promoted it. I had also seen people hurt through many teachings about healing—people left to feel inferior, or responsible for their sickness or lack of healing. I just assumed that healing ministry would be better left alone.

However, I had a growing problem. As my understanding of the kingdom grew, I began to realize how central healing and restoration were to the Kingdom of God. I also continued to struggle with how healing had played such a significant role in the life and ministry of Jesus. This put me in a dilemma. Was I going to honor my commitment to Jesus and his kingdom and follow wherever he led? Or would I let my significant hesitations and concerns hold me back? I decided to pursue the truth of Scripture despite my discomfort. I would like to ask you to do the same.

I don't know if you share those reservations regarding healing, but if so, I would challenge you to push through them for the sake of truth. Recommit to following Christ and living biblically even in areas that seem confusing and disconcerting. In the next couple of days, we will look at some different aspects of healing and the kingdom. I have found some of these aspects to be both foundational and inspirational. These truths have allowed me to seek to grow in the ministry of healing, even while pushing through hesitations and questions. My hope is that they will do this for you as well.

If Jesus is our model in all things, then the right place to begin is with his life and ministry. Specifically, we need to see how healing relates to his prophetic calling.

The Suffering Servant

Although the book of Isaiah was written over 600 years before Jesus was born, more than any other book in the Old Testament, it speaks prophetically about his life and ministry. We have already looked at Jesus' prophetic job description (Isaiah 61:1–4 and Luke 4:17–21; see Day 9). In Isaiah 53 there is another key passage known as the "Suffering Servant." Some call this section the "Gospel in the Old Testament" because it reveals so much of what God's suffering servant would accomplish. Please read this very sad and yet inspirational description of Christ.

> He was pierced and wounded so that we might be healed and receive peace.

> **He was despised and rejected by men, a man of sorrows, and familiar with suffering. Like one from whom men hide their faces he was despised, and we esteemed him not. Surely he took up our infirmities and carried our sorrows, yet we considered him stricken by God, smitten by him, and afflicted. But he was pierced for our transgressions, he was crushed for our iniquities; the punishment that brought us peace was upon him, and by his wounds we are healed.**
>
> *Isaiah 53:3–5*

It is amazing to reflect on these passages of Scripture in the light of Christ Jesus' sacrifice. He became a man of sorrows so that we might become a people of joy. He became a man from whom others hid their faces so that God might shine his face upon us. He was crushed and broken so that we might be made whole. He was pierced and wounded so that we might be healed and receive peace. What a savior!

This prophetic description of the suffering servant's calling was very significant for the early church. As the writers of the New Testament later reflected on the significance of Christ's life and ministry, it was to this passage that they turned for understanding. In fact, two different writers referred to these verses for understanding and clarity, but they emphasized two different aspects of the passage.

Peter and Forgiveness

In his first letter, the Apostle Peter reflected on how we are called to live as chosen people, following the example that Christ set. Specifically, he reflected on the example of Jesus' suffering and also looked at what his suffering accomplished.

> **He himself bore our sins in his body on the tree, so that we might die to sins and live for righteousness; by his wounds you have been healed.**
>
> *1 Peter 2:24*

Notice what Peter emphasized here. He referred to Christ's death as the substitution for our own. On the cross (figuratively speaking, *tree*), he took our stuff, our junk, all the things that separate us from our Holy God. It was really our price to pay. *We* should have been the ones on the *tree*, but the suffering servant absorbed our sins into his own body. Like the sacrificial lamb in the times of the Old Testament, our punishment was transferred to him. Here Peter emphasized the part of Isaiah 53 that talked of the forgiveness Christ had accomplished.

> **...he was pierced for our transgressions, he was crushed for our iniquities...**
>
> *Isaiah 53:5*

Like the sacrificial lamb in the times of the Old Testament, our punishment was transferred to him.

When Peter quoted the word *healed* from Isaiah, he was speaking of a spiritual healing, or healing of the soul. The Greek word that is used in this verse is *iaomai*. It can mean a physical or spiritual healing. In 2:24, Peter's language obviously pointed to the spiritual, i.e.... *bore our sins... so that we might die to sins and live for righteousness....* We have been set free from the penalty of sin and have received his salvation.

This emphasis that Peter took from Isaiah is what I have understood for a long time as a Christian. It can be summed up in the simple statement often used, even in our larger culture, "Christ died for our sins." This is part of the atonement ("at-one-ment," i.e., bringing together those who have been separated or estranged). We were separated from God but through Christ we are reconciled. And, according to Peter, we can now live as God intended, dead to our sins but alive to his righteousness.

It was Peter's emphasis that I have long understood and talked about when referring to what Christ accomplished on the *tree*. But I completely missed what Matthew emphasized in his Gospel. You see, Matthew quoted from this same passage of Isaiah, but with a slightly different emphasis, one that we shouldn't miss.

Matthew and Healing

By quickly looking through the eighth chapter of Matthew's Gospel, we can see that it is a series of stories about healing. These stories relate to Jesus' healing ministry. The chapter starts with a man with leprosy. He knelt before Jesus and said,

…"Lord, if you are willing, you can make me clean."

Matthew 8:2

Here we learn a little of Jesus' heart and compassion through his simple, but beautiful words of assurance, *I am willing*. Then, he healed the leper (8:3).

Next comes the story of an officer in the Roman army, a centurion. He came to Jesus because his servant was paralyzed and in great pain. Jesus agreed that he would go to heal him. The centurion, however, gave a surprising answer. In effect, he said, "Don't bother coming, since I believe you can just speak the word, and my servant will be healed." Astounded at the soldier's faith, Jesus subtly suggested that this Gentile soldier would have a place at the feast in the Kingdom of Heaven (verse 11). By the way, Jesus healed the servant in a long-distance miracle, just as the centurion believed he would in Matthew 8:13.

Next is the account of Peter's mother-in-law (8:14–15). While she lay in bed with a fever, Jesus touched her hand and healed her. After this, in the evening, many others came for healing. It is at this point that Matthew quoted the familiar Isaiah passage, helping us to understand part of the significance of Jesus' death on the cross.

Not only did Christ die for the forgiveness of our sins, but also for the healing of our *infirmities* and *diseases*.

When evening came, many who were demon-possessed were brought to him, and he drove out the spirits with a word and healed all the sick. This was to fulfill what was spoken through the prophet Isaiah: "He took up our infirmities and carried our diseases."

Matthew 8:16–17

Notice the emphasis that Matthew brought here to the Isaiah passage, which is different than Peter's emphasis. Not only did Christ die for the forgiveness of our sins, but also for the healing of our *infirmities* and *diseases*. Matthew applied the Greek word *iaomai* in the context of physical and emotional healing—to be cured or made whole.

Isaiah said of the suffering servant, *Surely he took up our infirmities* (physical ailments) *and carried our sorrows* (emotional struggles) (Isaiah 53:4). Matthew pointed out that Christ came to reverse all the effects of sin, to redeem the whole person. This includes physical and emotional sickness and distress. On the cross, Christ Jesus provided not only for our spiritual needs, but also for our physical and emotional needs. He heals our broken relationship with God, and also our broken bodies and emotions; he heals all that we are. Jesus came fulfilling his Suffering Servant call. He did that on the cross, and also in his daily ministry of healing and restoration. The Isaiah passage points us to the significance of the cross, as well as to the daily life and ministry of Jesus. In both his life and death, Jesus fulfilled his calling.

Jesus the Healer

I once listened to a pastor talk about the healing ministry of Jesus. He spoke of a very personal interaction between Jesus and himself in prayer. While talking with the Lord, he felt as though Jesus had challenged him with this statement: "You have received me as your savior, but not as your healer." As you can imagine, this was a significant moment in his faith journey. Jesus had revealed to him part of his desire for his life. Jesus wanted to play the role of healer, but the pastor had not sought him for this, or even believed in him for such a thing. The pastor had limited Jesus to a role that did not include present-day physical and emotional healing. When this godly man began to seek the healing ministry of Jesus in his own life, he found that Jesus began to play that role.

As the church, we have usually been taught and trained to see the Suffering Servant from Peter's emphasis. Of course, this is an important emphasis that we must not neglect. Christ's death on the *tree* in our place is foundational to our profession of the Christian faith. The atonement is indeed central to the faith.

However, I think that the church in general has missed or neglected Matthew's emphasis. Jesus not only came to take away sin, but also to remove all the effects of the Fall. True, Jesus came to seek and save the lost; but he also came to heal the lost. And just as Jesus saves people today through his church, so he desires to heal people today, also through his church.

Jesus not only came to take away sin, but also to remove all the effects of the Fall.

The early church understood this. They proclaimed Jesus as Messiah and savior of the world. But they also offered healing. The miraculous ministry of Jesus continued through the early church (see the accounts in the book of Acts). The Lord often used healing to draw people to him as savior.

Just as healing was part of Jesus' ministry and calling, so it is a part of his church today. His desire is that we receive him not only as savior, but also as healer. I admit that it's a little scary to talk this way, but I believe this is what Jesus intended for the church. The early church saw him as their healer. Today, I don't think we have fully turned to Jesus as our healer, even though this is God's desire.

Kingdom Questions

How does Jesus' calling, spoken thousands of years ago, relate to you today?

Do you think he desires to heal you today? Is he willing?

What would it take for you to turn to Jesus as your healer, to seek his healing emotionally and physically?

What obstacles remain that prevent you from actively pursuing his personal healing?

Go to him in prayer!

Day 30 | Following the Stream

Streams of living water will flow from within

Recently I heard a pastor praying for healing. He invoked that phrase we so often hear, *if it is your will….* Why do we pray that way? I think it's because we don't want to give false assurance to people, so we use this as our explanation (through prayer) of why God doesn't heal everyone.

> The question of his will is not really about *if*, it is actually more about *when*.

This is a very real and practical question regarding healing, but I don't think that invoking God's divine will is the right answer to it. **The question of his will is not really about *if*, it is actually more about *when*.** In order to understand more about God's divine will in regard to healing, we must follow the stream.

Have you ever followed a stream? When my family lived in Michigan, we took an annual trip to our favorite place in Michigan, Sleeping Bear Dune. There is a stream flowing into Lake Michigan at the part of the beach where we liked to go. We put on water shoes, grabbed some buckets and nets and followed the stream up from the lake. The kids hunted for various things like little fish, cool-looking rocks, and even some crawdads. Each year it was a fun journey of discovery.

Today I would like us to follow a stream. This, too, is a journey of discovery; and we might just find some interesting and unexpected things along the way. But instead of starting at the end of the stream and working our way up, I want to start at the beginning. The beginning of our stream is in a very special place. It's a place that was lost to us many years ago, but we can still get a glimpse of it, if we really want to. The beginning place of this stream is in a garden. In fact, the stream watered the garden and was God's provision for all that lived there.

In the beginning, …the earth was formless and empty, darkness was over the face of the deep…. (Genesis 1:2) There was no land, and there were no streams. But we are told that the Spirit of God hovered above the waters. He hovered with a life-giving purpose.

At first, when God created the land, there was no source of water to nourish life. So, we are told he created streams.

> **...but streams came up from the earth and watered the whole surface of the ground.**
>
> *Genesis 2:6*

It was after this that God created a man and placed him in a garden in Eden. A river ran through it—*a river watering the garden flowed from Eden* (Genesis 2:10). This is the stream we are looking for; it's our stream—the stream that was given to us originally. This stream was full of life and it nourished all the vegetation, animals and humans that were created and lived in the garden. Apparently, this stream even watered the tree of life at the center of the garden. God's perfect will for us is to live near this stream of life.

Yet, as we know, things changed. Adam and Eve disobeyed God, and because of their sin, they were driven from this well-nourished garden—driven from a reality of perfect union with God. In the garden, near the stream, was life in complete wholeness, the complete blessing of God. But then they entered a new life, a new reality, shut out from the tree of life and the stream that nourished it.

God's perfect will for us is to live near this stream of life.

Adam and Eve entered a dry and difficult life; they entered a desert. This was a land that was not well watered, but cursed. It only produced edible plants through toil and hardship in the midst of thorns and thistles. It was a new life outside of the garden, away from the stream in Eden. In that reality they lived and died, and into that reality we all are born.

In the Desert and the City

That is how life was for Adam and Eve and their descendents. It was not God's perfect will. It was a life in the arid regions, away from God's presence, away from the living streams. In those desert regions, there was a constant longing for the lost river in the garden, just as in our hearts today there is a thirst for the stream of life. How we long to drink from it! Adam and Eve have passed this thirst on to all their descendents. It lies deep within our souls. But if we listen closely enough, we can follow the stream through the words of others.

If we really listen, we can hear this longing in the voice of the psalmist as he tenderly reveals the yearnings of his heart.

> **There is a river whose streams make glad the city of God, the holy place where the Most High dwells.**
>
> *Psalm 46:4*

The psalmist understood his longing, and understood the source—much like the Samaritan woman at the well. When a strange Rabbi talked of the *living water* that would quench her thirst, she knew enough to ask,

> **..."Sir, give me this water so that I won't get thirsty and have to keep coming here to draw water."**
>
> *John 4:15*

That same thirst exists in men and women today, just as it did in ancient times. You can hear it from the heart of the modern psalmist crying out in a loud voice, "But I still haven't found what I am looking for." The thirst is alive and strong today, just as it always has been.

The stream not only flows through the desert, but we can also follow it through the city of Jerusalem, the city of God. The psalmist tells us,

> **As the deer pants for streams of water, so my soul pants for you, O God. My soul thirsts for God, for the living God....**
>
> *Psalm 42:1–2*

So there is a city and a river runs through it. Yet, there is a curious thing about Jerusalem. Unlike many great cities in the world, there is no actual stream that flows through it. But the psalmist insists that there is a stream, one that flows with the presence of the Most High. It is not a physical stream that brings in commerce to fill the city with worldly wealth. It is a Spirit stream that makes the poor man rich and the broken man whole.

It is a Spirit stream that makes the poor man rich and the broken man whole.

It is not just the longing for this stream that we can experience. In sacred moments, we can also drink from its waters. Because God is so gracious, his river of life is not completely lost to us. He allows us to actually sip from Eden's stream. Even in the desert regions, he allows his people to sample the river of life. By his grace we can kneel down to drink, stretching out to reach the flowing waters. He beckons us to

> **Taste and see that [he] is good...**
>
> *Psalm 34:8*

He invites us to

> **"Come, all who are thirsty, come to the waters..."**
>
> *Isaiah 55:1*

And when we drink, this water is not without effect. The stream flows within us and brings newness of life. It produces purpose and strength in us. As the psalmist said when he talked of its effects on the righteous and God-fearing person:

> **He is like a tree planted by streams of water, which yields its fruit in season and whose leaf does not wither. Whatever he does prospers.**
>
> *Psalm 1:3*

Blessings and health and goodness flow to us from this stream. He restores our souls as he leads us beside the quiet waters as it says in Psalm 23. And as we seek to live near the stream, he brings the fullness of a well-nourished life, producing fruit in the seasons he has designed.

The Stream Flows Inward

We have discovered that God has graciously allowed his living waters to flow beyond the garden. Even in Genesis we are told,

> **A river watering the garden flowed from Eden; from there it was separated into four headwaters.**
>
> *Genesis 2:10*

No matter where lost souls may find themselves, this river can flow to the four corners of the world. We have seen it in the desert and in the city. But there is one more place where we must find it, a place that can't be lost to us. It is the most important place—the place of the soul.

In ancient times, the people of God prayed and longed for God's living waters. They used symbols and ceremonies to express that longing. One of those ceremonies was done annually at the Feast of Tabernacles. Leading a procession, a priest would dip a golden pitcher into the pool of Siloam and then bring the water back to the altar at the temple of God. As the people gathered with anticipation, he would pour the water from the pitcher into silver bowls with holes in them. The water would flow over the altar out toward the people. It was a powerful symbol and a prayer for God's flowing favor to come to his people. Some Bible scholars think that it was at this moment when Jesus gave the invitation:

We ourselves become part of the living stream for others.

> **..."If anyone is thirsty, let him come to me and drink. Whoever believes in me as the Scripture has said, streams of living water will flow from within him."**
>
> *John 7:37–38*

Incredibly, Jesus referred to himself as the source of the stream. Just as God the Father had been inviting people to come to him to drink, so now Jesus invited all to do the same. Jesus not only taught about the source, but also about the flow. The flow is not just through a garden or a city, but the river runs through us—at least, through those of us who are thirsty!

Not only does the stream of Eden flow from within us, but in some amazing way, it will flow from us for others to drink. We ourselves become part of the living stream for others. We are not just in the garden drinking from its stream, but we become part of it.

It looks like Jesus was referring to Isaiah 58:11.

> **The Lord will guide you always; he will satisfy your needs in a sun-scorched land and will strengthen your frame. You will be like a well-watered garden, like a spring whose waters never fail.**
>
> *Isaiah 58:11*

In a *sun-scorched land* we become the *well-watered garden*, because the living streams are flowing in and through us. The promise is for us. The only question is whether we are thirsty or not. Are you thirsty enough to come?

Wading into the Deep End

As wonderful as the promises in John and Isaiah are, they don't represent the end of the stream. They don't symbolize the larger body of water into which the stream flows. This, we have not known yet. Even if we are living in such a way that the waters are flowing through us, we are still moving down the stream. There is a deeper place. Our feet won't be able to touch the bottom at one point, and we'll have to tread water. We are first given a glimpse of this place, a promise of these deeper waters of life, in a prophetic vision of the prophet Ezekiel.

In chapter 47 of Ezekiel, we find the prophet being led by an angelic guide into a brief experience of the river of God. The water was flowing from the temple of God, the dwelling place of the king. The guide led Ezekiel down the course of the stream, measuring its depth. At first the water was ankle deep, but as Ezekiel continued, it grew deeper—knee-deep, waist-deep—and finally Ezekiel waded in over his head. This was a river that no one could cross. The angel led Ezekiel to the river bank; he wanted to make sure that Ezekiel saw the impact of the waters.

> **He asked me, "Son of man, do you see this?" Then he led me back to the bank of the river. When I arrived there, I saw a great number of trees on each side of the river. He said to me… "When it empties into the Sea, the water there becomes fresh. Swarms of living creatures will live wherever the river flows. There will be large numbers of fish, because this water flows there and makes the salt water fresh; so where the river flows everything will live…. Fruit trees of all kinds will grow on both banks of the river. Their leaves will not wither, nor will their fruit fail. Every month they will bear, because the water from the sanctuary flows to them. Their fruit will serve for food and their leaves for healing."**
>
> *Ezekiel 47:6–12*

This prophecy describes the time when the lost stream of Eden will be found again, bringing full restoration for the people of God.

This prophecy describes the time when the lost stream of Eden will be found again, bringing full restoration for the people of God. The salty curse and all the devastation will be removed; the salt water will become fresh. The leaves of the trees will produce healing. From the fruit trees to the fish, this picture reveals the heart of God—restoration of what was lost, fullness of life, healing for his people. This is God's bottom line, and we long for its fulfillment. Toward these deep, healing waters we keep flowing.

Another glimpse of this full restoration appears in the very last chapter of Scripture. On this occasion, an angelic guide is leading the Apostle John.

> **Then the angel showed me the river of the water of life, as clear as crystal, flowing from the throne of God and of the Lamb down the middle of the great street of the city. On each side of the river stood the tree of life, bearing twelve crops of fruit, yielding its fruit every month. And the leaves of the tree are for the healing of the nations. No longer will there be any curse….**
>
> *Revelation 22:1–3*

See the consummation of this stream? God and the Lamb are its source, and it flows through the new city where we will one day live. The tree of life is still planted near the stream, but this time it stands on both sides, more easily accessible to all of God's people. The trees bear abundant fruit—not just in season, but every month. Finally and completely, the salty curse is removed and the leaves of the trees are intended for the healing of the nations.

This is a picture of God's kingdom fully restored, and a river runs through it. When the waters flow in utter fullness, then the Kingdom of God will have been fully restored. As Zechariah prophesied,

> **On that day living water will flow out from Jerusalem, half to the eastern sea and half to the western sea, in summer and in winter. The Lord will be king over the whole earth….**
>
> *Zechariah 14:8–9*

It is on these shores that we are called to live—when our thirst is finally quenched, when the lost river of Eden is found again. In the living streams of his favor, God will delight to see his children splash and play. As it was in the beginning, he will once again delight in watching his children drink afresh from the streams of living water.

His desire now is that we are all in the flow toward this end—healing and restoration.

In a sense, we will end where we began—God's perfect will completely revealed in our lives, his will of healing and wholeness. His desire now is that we are all in the flow toward this end—healing and restoration in his presence.

We know his will in terms of healing; he has revealed it. His desire is that we are all healed. Ultimately, every single one of his children will be healed of every ailment, disease and deformity that have plagued us since the Fall.

The question then is not *if* healing is God's will. He has already told us it is. What we don't know is the *when* of God's will. We can give assurances of healing to any child of God, because either in this life or the next, God has promised it to us. The healthy tension that we have to face in praying for healing is a kingdom tension—the *already but not yet* tension of the kingdom having come, but not yet fully consummated (see Day 10). As we pray healing for our brothers and sisters, we usually don't know if God will bring kingdom fullness into a person's life here on Earth, or if complete restoration will wait until the New Heaven and the New Earth.

No matter the tension, we are called to join him in his work. And that work is leading people to drink from his healing stream, here on Earth and in the promised New Heaven.

Ⓡ Reflection—Think Over This Invitation

Do you know that there is one final invitation in Scripture? It is one that completes God's revealed Word to us and echoes through every generation and every heart. This is an invitation to be heard and received. Listen and respond as you sense his presence in your heart.

> **The Spirit and the bride say, "Come!" And let him who hears say, "Come!" Whoever is thirsty, let him come; and whoever wishes, let him take the free gift of the water of life.**
>
> *Revelation 22:17*

Are you thirsty? . . . Then come.

Are you thirsty?
. . . Then come.

Day 31 | All Things Made Whole

I am making everything new!

When I went to college I considered myself a Christian; but I didn't attend church very often and my main group of friends didn't think of themselves as Christians. My parents, however, were Christians; and occasionally, they would talk with me about the faith. My perspective on Jesus was formed from what my parents shared, what I heard every now and then in church, and some sporadic opinions picked up at school. I had never actually read the story of Jesus in Scripture for myself; I'd only heard snippets at church.

> ...my perspective of Jesus and his influence on my life was very limited.

My impression of Jesus was that he was a very nice guy—oh yeah, and the Son of God as well! He taught about loving everyone, even your enemies. I thought of him as a kind of social-worker-Jesus, teaching people to forgive, love, and sacrifice for each other. I also assumed that his death on the cross was his ultimate act of love.

Most of these things are true, but it is clear that my perspective of Jesus and his influence on my life was very limited. My idea of the basics of the faith was: 1) believe in Jesus and, 2) try my best to do the right thing. Then, I was good to go! I didn't think he cared much about the specifics of my life, like how much I partied on the weekends, or any goals for my future. As long as I was generally a good person and stayed out of trouble (I wasn't very good at that!) I figured I was on the right track.

When I got to college, though, the Holy Spirit began nudging me to look for some of the deeper things in life. I figured there had to be more to it than simply having a good time. So, of course, on my quest for truth and meaning, I joined a social fraternity. A logical step, right?! But also during that first year, I heard about a group of guys doing a Bible study in my dorm. One of them invited me and I gave it a shot. In hindsight, it wasn't that great of a Bible study. The leader had a little trouble linking all of the random thoughts and opinions together. Nonetheless, it was in that Bible study that, for the first time, I read the story of Jesus for myself. It was in that reading that my view of Jesus began to quickly expand.

I soon realized that my impression of Jesus had been quite distorted. He amazed me—what he taught and what he did. It struck me that he never backed down to the religious leaders, but gave brilliant answers to the questions that had been meant to trap him. He was zealous for God, his Father, his house, his glory, his calling. And I was astounded that he seemed to be very interested in my life. It was as if he was calling me along with his disciples, *Come, follow me.* (Matthew 4:18)

One night, during my freshman year, I went to a field on campus to confess. I confessed that though I claimed to be a Christian, I wasn't really living like one, at least how I thought Jesus would define it. And I told Jesus if I could really follow him like he invited me to, then I would. I promised that I would give him everything, every area of my life, whether it was partying, girls, grades, profession—whatever. You see, Jesus moved from being just a part of my life and thinking, to become the center of it all. Actually, that is the only acceptable place for him. Sure, he did want me to stay out of trouble, but I soon realized he wanted so much more for me. He himself was and is so much more.

Nothing is Beyond Jesus

Jesus moved from being just a part of my life and thinking, to become the center of it all.

One of the exhilarating things about the story of Jesus is how the people around him realized, in greater and greater measure, that he was over all things in life, not just one little section. Jesus was a prophet but he was far more than an ordinary prophet. He was a king but much more than any old king. He was the Messiah, as well as the very creator and sustainer of life. Nothing was outside the sphere of Jesus' influence. For him, nothing was outside the realm of possibility.

Chapter 8 in the Gospel of Luke illustrates an exciting and extraordinarily active time during the ministry of Jesus. Look at how the chapter begins.

> **After this, Jesus traveled about from one town and village to another, proclaiming the good news of the kingdom of God. The Twelve were with him.**
>
> *Luke 8:1*

Jesus was teaching and training the Twelve for ministry by modeling how to do it. Through these activities, he also revealed who he was and what he was capable of doing. Following along in the chapter (after the parable of the sower, verse 16) we see Jesus performing successive miracles. The first miracle involved nature. A ferocious storm had started battering the disciples while they were in the middle of a lake. They woke Jesus, because they feared for their lives, and he exerted his authority over nature by calming the storm with a single rebuke. The disciples went through their own shock and awe experience.

> **...In fear and amazement they asked one another, "Who is this? He commands even the winds and the water, and they obey him."**
>
> *Luke 8:25*

Why were the disciples so astonished? Jesus had expanded their limited belief of who he was and what he was capable of. It appeared to be a dramatic gesture, but for Jesus it was just the simple extension of his Spirit-given power.

When Jesus and his disciples had crossed the lake, they arrived at the region of the Gerasenes. There, a demon-possessed man was waiting to greet them. But this wasn't just any old demon-possessed guy. He was called Legion because he didn't have merely one demon, but many. A typical Roman legion was made up of 6,000 men, so this guy had some serious problems. Apparently, the town had tried to keep him under control by chaining him and placing guards around him. But the legion of demons would drive him to break the chains and live naked in the graveyards. Don't you wonder how long he had been collecting demons in the graveyard?! He wasn't simply a demonic challenge; he was the granddaddy of demonic challenges. Yet, Jesus had full authority and control even to command this legion of demonic beings and force them out of the man.

This show of power so frightened the people of the region that they didn't even ask Jesus who he was or why he possessed such power. Seized by fear, they asked the King of Glory to leave them. Jesus granted them their request because he never forces himself on anyone. Through this incident Jesus demonstrated his power and authority over the demonic.

...his power extended even to the dead.

Next, in verses 43–48, Luke told the beautiful story of a woman's healing. Apparently, in that day and age, there was no medicinal support for her condition.

> **And a woman was there who had been subject to bleeding for twelve years, but no one could heal her. She came up behind him and touched the edge of his cloak, and immediately her bleeding stopped.**
> *Luke 8:43–44*

Then, Jesus stopped his procession through the throngs of people pressing against him and asked, *Who touched me*? The disciples were confused, because basically everyone was touching him; but they learned that Jesus had power that a person could access through faith and action. And so, as Jesus did throughout his ministry, he demonstrated his power and authority over every kind of sickness and disease.

The chapter ends climactically with the story of a father named Jairus and his dying daughter. Jairus had come to fetch Jesus because his daughter was deathly ill. But while they were on the way back to his house, the girl died. Someone came from the household and said,

> **..."Your daughter is dead...don't bother the teacher any more."**
> *Luke 8:49*

There was the assumption that Jesus' authority was limited to the living, but he knew differently. At this critical juncture, Jesus looked Jairus in the eye and said,

> **..."Don't be afraid; just believe, and she will be healed."**
> *Luke 8:50*

What did Jesus ask this shocked and grieving father to believe? That his power extended even to the dead? Jesus healed the daughter and there were her parents—overwhelmed and astonished witnesses to Jesus' authority over life and death.

In just this one chapter, Jesus demonstrated to his disciples that his power and authority extended to all areas of life. With him, there would be no limits, no compartmentalizing of life's challenges. Jesus related to all that was before him. He was at the center.

I have noticed in my own faith that I often don't live this way. I fail to look to Jesus for everything. In our culture, we are trained to turn to other places first before Christ. If we are struggling with sickness or an ailment, we turn first to our physicians. We only turn to the Great Physician if our earthly ones can't do anything about it. For emotional pain or distress, we turn to our counselors and psychologists, neglecting the role of the Holy Spirit as our counselor and guide. When faced with societal ills and injustices, we turn to politicians rather than our King. When facing global issues, we turn to education and information, neglecting the Creator of the World.

Please don't misinterpret what I am saying. I am not devaluing any of these areas, such as education or counseling. They certainly have tremendous value for us. But what is at issue is that we have prized these so highly that we are in danger of compartmentalizing Christ Jesus and his power. We find partial answers or partial cures in these areas, so we never even go to ask Jesus to come and face our struggles with us. As a community of faith, should he not be the first one we turn to with every ailment, conflict and injustice? Jesus came to bring a kingdom of restoration and healing, but even we, his followers, haven't turned to him with all our needs. Shouldn't we be the first to reach out and touch him with faith? Shouldn't we be the first to *not be afraid, but just believe*? (Luke 8:50)

In our culture we are trained to turn to other places first before Christ.

Sozo: A Greek Word Enlarges Our Understanding

Before we leave Luke 8, I want to point out a significant word used in this chapter that has great value for our understanding. The word in Greek is *sozo* and has a variety of meanings in that language. It is often translated *to save*, but also means *deliver*, *heal*, *restore health*, and *make whole*. This word is used four times in Luke 8, and in the different stories, the different nuances of meaning become clear. Look at the following examples:

In the story of salvation—

> **"Those along the path are the ones who hear, and then the devil comes and takes away the word from their hearts, so that they may not believe and be *saved*."** (emphasis added)
>
> *Luke 8:12*

In the story of deliverance—

> **Those who had seen it told the people how the demon-possessed man had been *cured*.** (emphasis added)
>
> *Luke 8:36*

In the story of healing—

> **"Daughter, your faith has *healed* you. Go in peace."** (emphasis added)
>
> *Luke 8:48b*

In the story of new life—

> **Hearing this, Jesus said to Jairus, "Don't be afraid; just believe, and she will be *healed*."** (emphasis added)
>
> *Luke 8:50*

Is it fair to say that our understanding and ministry have often been limited to the first example of *sozo* above? We see Christ today as administering salvation in the classical sense, being "*sozo*-ed" from our sins and granted eternal life. This certainly is a huge and important aspect of the ministry and purpose of Christ and the church. But, it is not the only purpose. If we simply stick to only one aspect of *sozo*, we limit his mission and purpose—we limit the mission and purpose of his church today.

Think of the shades of meaning for the word *sozo*, as used above, and read Luke 19:10 with fresh understanding. Jesus said,

> **"For the Son of Man came to seek and *save* what was lost."** (emphasis added)

Praying for physical healing can be very confusing and challenging.

Jesus never meant to be limited to one area of life; he brings his power and authority to all areas of life. He came to redeem and to restore everything, all of creation. That is the kingdom message, isn't it? This was and is Jesus' mission—the restoration of all of creation, all areas of life.

> **He who was seated on the throne said, "I am making everything new!"**
>
> *Revelation 21:5*

He has commissioned his church to this *sozo* mission, to seek and to *sozo* the world. He told them to preach the kingdom and heal the sick. This is our mission of *sozo* in the complete sense of the word. This is a holistic ministry that relates to every area of life. Jesus has come for the whole person, the whole of creation.

Called to a Holistic Ministry

I have good friends, Bill and his wife, Katie. Bill is a pastor and Katie is a physician. Recently when I called Bill, he shared a story about a couple that had been coming to his Alpha course who were not yet Christians. They asked Bill if he would pray for physical healing, and Bill said, "Maybe later." On the phone, Bill said to me, "You know, Eric, I don't like praying for healing for folks, especially a couple like that who have so many other big issues to deal with."

I can understand where Bill was coming from. Praying for physical healing can be very confusing and challenging. Sometimes it feels like more than we signed up for as Christians. Yes, we have believed that Jesus died to save us. We have even realized that we are called to share the good news of the cross. But praying for each other for physical healing? Well, for some of us, it just feels a little "out there." It seems so much simpler and more straightforward to stay focused on getting people saved, spiritually speaking.

Bill was my friend, but I thought I would tease this out a little. I responded to him by saying, "You know, Bill, you have a problem." He asked, "What's that?" I stuck my neck out and said, "I know you want to be like Jesus as a pastor and as a disciple, and Jesus prayed for healing all the time. Sometimes he did it regardless of a person's living situation or spiritual state."

Not only have we too narrowly defined what it means to be saved, but we have also allowed that narrow definition to limit our calling and mission in the world. Yes, God's call is to be saving souls with him, but it is also to bring the restoration of the kingdom—a restoration of the whole person.

An interesting sidelight is that Bill's wife Katie takes some risks in her calling. She doesn't just treat people medically, but when appropriate she prays over people, asking for the healing power of God to invade their lives. It's her desire to have Christ at the center of her medical ministry.

God's call is to be saving souls with him, but it is also to bring the restoration of the kingdom—a restoration of the whole person.

Kingdom Questions

In what ways has your understanding of Christ been limited?

How is he calling you to expand your perspective of who he is?

In what ways have you limited the ministry of Christ in your own life?

Are you ready to step into a more holistic ministry through the power and authority of Christ?

What are your fears in all of this?

> **"But for you who revere my name, the sun of righteousness will rise with healing in its wings. And you will go out and leap like calves released from the stall."**
>
> *Malachi 4:2*

Talk to Jesus about your questions and fears.

Day 32 | Faith Matters

According to your faith will it be done to you

A dear woman recently told me the sad story of her husband's death a number of years ago. Although a committed and serving member of their congregation, she had to overcome significant hurt inflicted by well-meaning church members throughout the process of her husband dying. A member of the congregation had come to their home and talked about having believing faith. He assured them that if they just kept on believing, healing would result. The husband, of course, sought to do all the things this man had suggested, but to no avail. He died. And worse yet, the wife told me that her husband had died believing he lacked the faith to be healed.

Reading through the Gospels, we must conclude that we do have a part to play in the kingdom ministry of healing.

Stories like these have caused many, including me, to erect significant roadblocks against anything remotely connected to miraculous healing. At one point, I concluded that I would never talk about faith as it related to healing! I wanted to avoid any chance of hurting others in the ministry of the kingdom. It seemed better just to stay focused on God's healing stream and on...*by his stripes we are healed* (Isaiah 53:5). I didn't want to meddle with people's faith. I just wanted to affirm God's desire and power to heal today. It seemed so much safer than talking about how our faith relates to healing.

Yet, as with most works of God in this world, he calls us to cooperate with him. This is certainly true in the ministry of healing. When we read through Scripture it's clear that Jesus included people in partnering with God the Father in this ministry—challenging them in the deepest places of their faith. Reading through the Gospels, we must conclude that we do have a part to play in the kingdom ministry of healing. Whether we are comfortable with it or not, our faith really does matter in the equation of God's healing work.

Faith Matters

Faith does matter! Jesus continued to make this point as he interacted with people who needed healing. If we look at his healing ministry, he never just touched people and poof! they were healed, and then went on their merry way. No, Jesus seized those moments for our benefit, using one powerful event after another to further expand our understanding.

Often, Jesus focused his teaching about healing around the idea of faith. In evangelical circles, we don't like to talk about "proportions of faith," but Jesus did. He was disappointed with the smallness of people's faith. To a sinking Peter, who had lost his focus, Jesus said,

> **..."You of little faith ... why did you doubt?"**
>
> *Matthew 14:31*

Peter had it, he was walking on the water; but then he allowed fear and doubt to shrink his faith, and Jesus was disappointed. Today, Jesus might say, "Don't you trust me?"

From Jesus' perspective, another attitude that betrayed a lack of faith was worrying. To those who worry about clothes and meals for the day, he said,

> **..."Oh you of little faith!"**
>
> *Luke 12:28*

Often, Jesus focused his teaching about healing around the idea of faith.

Again, it's like he said, "Don't you trust me?"

Jesus said our focus shouldn't be on these insignificant things. Instead, focus on the big stuff, his big idea,

> **. . . "seek his kingdom...."**
>
> *Luke 12:31*

Faith doesn't just matter with regard to miraculous feats, or the material things in life. Faith especially matters, it seems, in healing people. Jesus made faith part of the process in God's healing work. Remember the woman who had suffered with bleeding for twelve years? She pushed through the crowd and touched his cloak and was healed. Jesus affirmed her part in the process,

> **..."Take heart, daughter ... your faith has healed you."**
>
> *Matthew 9:22*

When the blind beggar, Bartimaeus, kept shouting out to Jesus despite the rebukes of the crowd, Jesus healed him. Not only that, he affirmed the part Bartimaeus had played.

> **"Go... your faith has healed you."...**
>
> *Mark 10:52*

When the leprous Samaritan returned and bowed at Jesus' feet to give thanks for his healing, Jesus affirmed this foreigner's role in his own healing,

> **..."Rise and go; your faith has made you well."**
>
> *Luke 17:19*

Jesus summed up this whole matter of faith and healing in his response to the blind men in Matthew 9. These two had been persistently following Jesus and calling out, *Have mercy on us, Son of David!* (verse 27) Jesus went indoors and still the blind men followed. Then Jesus taught them (and us) through his questioning.

> **..."Do you believe that I am able to do this?"**
> **"Yes, Lord,"... Then he touched their eyes and said, "According to your faith will it be done to you"; and their sight was restored....**
> *Matthew 9:28–30*

Jesus' question was about their faith. Their answer was a statement of faith. Then, Jesus affirmed that faith is an important part of the healing ministry. It is our part; it is how we cooperate with him. It is important in the advancement of the Kingdom of God. Faith is not the only part of the healing process, but it is a very significant part. Faith is how we cooperate with the power and actions of God to heal us.

Amazing Faith

Throughout Jesus' ministry, people were amazed by his power—the miracles and healings experienced because of him. Even the twelve disciples, who saw everything day after day, continued to marvel. People were also astonished at his teaching. He spoke with such authority and wisdom that people realized there was something different about him. (Mark 1:22)

Faith is how we cooperate with the power and actions of God to heal us.

But did you know that on occasion Jesus himself was amazed? Yes, it seems surprising that the Son of God would ever be amazed, but we are told twice that he was. In both instances it was in regard to proportions of faith. And this amazing faith came from the least expected people.

A Roman soldier, a centurion who was sympathetic to the Jewish people, had a dying servant; so, on his behalf, a contingent of Jewish elders asked Jesus to help. But as they started for the soldier's house, he sent friends to say,

> **"...I do not deserve to have you come under my roof...."**
> *Luke 7:6*

The Roman officer so believed in the authority and power of Jesus that he just asked him to say the word and his servant would be healed. (verse 7)

Here was a non-Jew, a Roman soldier, who trusted Jesus to heal his servant via a long-distance miracle. The centurion not only showed surprising humility, but also surprising confidence in the authority and power of Jesus to heal. When Jesus heard this,

> **...he was amazed at him and turning to the crowd following him, he said, "I tell you, I have not found such *great faith* even in Israel."** (emphasis added)
> *Luke 7:9*

How cool would it be for Jesus to look at our faith and be thrilled by its depth, its confidence and humility?

Yet, we can amaze Jesus with our faith in another way. Jesus astonished the community in which he grew up by his teaching and miraculous works. They marveled at his teaching and power, yet they took offense at him. They couldn't get past his earthly roots to see God's calling in his life. This affected Jesus and his ministry. We are told,

> **He could not do any miracles there, except lay his hands on a few sick people and heal them. And he was amazed at their *lack of faith*....** (emphasis added)
>
> *Mark 6:5–6a*

I sometimes fear that we amaze Jesus more with our lack of faith than the opposite!

Many Christians in the evangelical world shy away from discussions about faith and proportions of faith because they have seen or been hurt by so-called faith healers, or some poor theology about the importance of faith.

However, it is a huge mistake to neglect the role of faith in the bringing of the kingdom. It is clear that Jesus has called us to greater faith. He looks for it in his followers and even from seekers.

> ...it is a huge mistake to neglect the role of faith in the bringing of the kingdom.

> **And without faith it is impossible to please God...**
>
> *Hebrews 11:6a*

Without faith, we cannot join him in the kingdom ministry, but **with** faith, we can move mountains. (Matthew 17:20) **Through** faith we can conquer kingdoms. (Hebrews 11:33)

How then do we understand this faith that Jesus looks for? How do we live the faith in such a way that Jesus would be amazed by it?

Growing in Faith

Scripture teaches us that faith is given by God. It is a gift of grace (Ephesians 2:8), but we are called to cooperate with this grace. Just as with any gift, we have to receive and open it. This cooperation with God's gracious gift of faith isn't just a one-time thing; it is pictured in Scripture as a continuous cooperation. God warned through Isaiah of the importance of standing firm in our faith.

> **..."If you do not stand firm in your faith, you will not stand at all."**
>
> *Isaiah 7:9*

Perseverance and persistence were blessed and encouraged by Jesus throughout the Gospels. On the contrary, doubt and lack of (or little) faith, were discouraged. Jesus exhorted us to have faith that would overcome doubt.

> **I tell you the truth, if anyone says to this mountain, "Go, throw yourself into the sea," and does not doubt in his heart but believes that what he says will happen, it will be done for him.**
>
> *Mark 11:23*

Evidently, part of Jesus' disciple-making process was to stimulate faith. His desire was for the disciples' faith to grow as they saw and experienced more of the ministry of the kingdom. Jesus sometimes got frustrated with their lack of faith. After they had been with him for a while, experiencing his power and teaching, the disciples still didn't realize his authority and power over all things, including a raging storm. They woke him, afraid for their lives in the midst of the storm. After calming the waves, Jesus said to them,

> **"Why are you so afraid? Do you still have no faith?"**
>
> *Mark 4:40*

We might paraphrase Jesus' words today as, "When are you going to get it?!" or "When are you going to trust me for everything, not for just a few things?"

I am sure the disciples realized this tension within Jesus. They were dull at many points, but they must have gotten Jesus' emphasis on the role of faith in the ministry of the kingdom. At least, they got it enough to ask Jesus to increase their faith. (Luke 17:5)

I think this is a legitimate request for a disciple. If we want to push into kingdom work, we will need not only to persist in faith, but persistently ask for an increase. May he grant us the strength to live into the measure of faith he has given.

> We are not supposed to have faith in ourselves or our own worthiness or giftedness.

A Starting Point

A confusing thing about faith is that we forget who the object of our faith is. We are not supposed to have faith in ourselves or our own worthiness or giftedness (or lack thereof). Doubt creeps into our lives when we focus on whether we personally deserve God's healing touch, or whether we deserve to be used by him to minister healing to others. I can settle that doubt right now: You're not worthy! But God's ministry is not based on your worthiness or righteousness; it is based on his power and authority. Remember the Roman soldier? He was fully aware of his unworthiness, but still had complete confidence or faith in the authority and power of Jesus. That is great faith. Jesus used the Twelve to do all sorts of kingdom ministry, and it certainly was not based on their maturity or righteousness. It was based on their growing faith in him, his power and authority.

Jesus clearly directed us to the object of our faith.

> **"Have faith in God."…**
>
> *Mark 11:22*

He also told us,

> **…"anyone who has faith in me"…**
>
> *John 14:12*

I think this is a great starting point for us in terms of faith. We need to focus our faith primarily on Jesus. Not doubting does not mean denying physical realities or symptoms. Not doubting is having an unwavering confidence and faith in the person of Christ. Our faith is meant to be rooted in a relationship of trust in God. We don't trust a formula. We don't place our hopes in a certain method, but in a person. Our faith is rooted in a relationship with an all-powerful God, who can do anything he wants; and his desire is to bring healing and restoration. We must retain a persistent trust in Jesus, regardless of circumstance or results. This is the kind of faith that amazes Jesus.

One of my favorite stories from the Old Testament is found in the third chapter of Daniel. The three friends of Daniel, Shadrach, Meshach and Abednego, refused to worship pagan gods or the 90-foot idol that King Nebuchadnezzar had set up. The king had commanded them to worship it or be thrown into a blazing furnace. Listen to their response and tell me if you would consider it great faith.

> **Shadrach, Meshach and Abednego replied to the king, "O Nebuchadnezzar, we do not need to defend ourselves before you in this matter. If we are thrown into the blazing furnace, the God we serve is able to save us from it, and he will rescue us from your hand, O king. But even if he does not, we want you to know, O king, that we will not serve your gods or worship the image of gold you have set up."**
>
> *Daniel 3:16–18*

Jesus was amazed by their great faith.

Was this a statement of great faith? Absolutely! Notice it wasn't about results; they weren't exactly sure what was going to happen. But at the same time, they were expectant. They entrusted their lives and well-being into God's hands, their God who had complete power and loved them. I wouldn't be surprised if Jesus was amazed by their great faith. Maybe that is what he talked with them about when he joined them in the furnace. (verse 25)

This is the kind of faith that Jesus blesses and affirms in the Gospels. It is this persistent, expectant and humble faith that Jesus was looking for—a faith rooted in a relationship with God.

Ⓡ Reflection—Faith Like a Soldier

Now look again at the faith story of the Roman centurion in Luke 7:1–10. Observe carefully who this man was.

What was admirable about his faith?

What was it about his actions and words that led Jesus to comment on the greatness of his faith?

Respond in prayer by asking Jesus to help you have a faith that he would affirm and bless, and maybe even be amazed by.

Day 33 | Listening for the Stream

Pray over him and anoint him with oil

> Community is meant to provide encouragement and support....

We have been talking about some pretty incredible stuff regarding healing. God has given us a glimpse of his healing stream that continues to flow through his world. We've seen the searing stripes crisscrossing the back of his suffering servant—a costly provision for our healing. Jesus brought *sozo* to apply to all areas of our lives, and now we have begun to learn the importance of faith in God's process of healing. How then do we live in response to these amazing truths? Head to the hospitals in twos? Purchase a tent and begin a healing ministry? Meet with the pastor and inform him or her that we now know what is missing in our community of faith? May I humbly suggest that we hold off on these ideas right now? Instead, let's begin by doing one simple thing—*listening*.

Remember, Jesus is the king of the kingdom; he is the one with the master plan of advancement. He is the one who gives the direction and guidance. We need to listen to his direction, his plans and his guidance in our lives. Remember his promise that we would recognize his voice? He has spoken truth to us and given us tools. But he's done that so that we might follow him into ministry—not use these gifts independently, apart from his counsel and direction.

Let's not begin by just listening ourselves. Let's enter in from the very first by listening *in community*. When we begin to live into new truths and gifts that God has given us, community becomes vitally important. True community is meant to provide encouragement and support, especially when we struggle, or grow and get discouraged. True community also provides accountability and correction, in case we stray into some unbiblical places.

Today we will walk through a very simple process of listening and praying in community as it operates in the area of healing. This is not meant to be a formula, but a suggested flow for how our time in community might look when we pray for healing. This time through we will do it personally and, in the next small group time, we will practice it together—in community.

Listening In Community

In his letter, the Apostle James wrote some very practical instructions for Christian living. Much of it involved getting along in community. For instance, when believers struggle with sickness, James tells them to call others, to get into community.

> **Is any one of you in trouble? He should pray. Is anyone happy? Let him sing songs of praise. Is any one of you sick? He should call the elders of the church to pray over him and anoint him with oil in the name of the Lord. And the prayer offered in faith will make the sick person well; the Lord will raise him up....**
>
> *James 5:13–15*

Notice a couple of points from this passage. When James talked about responding to trouble or happiness, he mentioned an individual's response. But when he talked about dealing with sickness, he directed us to get into community, specifically a mature community of believers. Elders were presumably the most spiritually mature in the context of the early church, likely more comfortable and experienced in praying for healing.

Have you ever noticed how, when people came to Jesus for healing, he often began by asking them a question?

James also directed the community about what to do for sick people.

> **...pray over [them] and anoint [them] with oil...**
>
> *James 5:14*

This is not just any kind of prayer, but a prayer offered in faith—faith in God's will and purpose—faith in his active kingdom work—faith in his overcoming the results of the Fall, including sickness and disease.

Verse 15 records a powerful promise. We don't know the details or the timing of God in fulfilling that promise. That is really his deal. We do know, however, that healing is God's provision, it is his will. This is the foundation for our prayers.

When you come together next time as a group, practice the following simple approach to prayer for healing. One part flows after the other. It is based on the idea of *listening in community*:

1. Listen to the person in need
2. Listen to the Holy Spirit
3. Listen to the community
4. Listen to the Spirit again

1. Listening to the Person in Need

Have you ever noticed how, when people came to Jesus for healing, he often began by asking them a question? I have wondered what Jesus was listening for. In my view, Jesus wasn't merely listening for the disease that needed healing. I think he must have been listening for more.

For example, think of the blind man who was making a nuisance of himself by yelling out for Jesus to have mercy on him in Luke 18. The crowd rebuked him and told him to quiet down, but he shouted all the louder. Jesus stopped walking, had the man brought to him, and asked,

> **"What do you want me to do for you?..."**
>
> *Luke 18:41*

Wouldn't you say that the answer to Jesus' question was fairly obvious? At this point, was Jesus really wondering why this blind guy was shouting over the noise of the crowd? If my very verbal (and "mistress of the obvious") young daughter had been there, she would surely have piped up right then and said, "Jesus, he wants you to make him see!"

When the blind man stated the obvious, Jesus responded,

> **..."Receive your sight; your faith has healed you."**
>
> *Luke 18:42*

Jesus wasn't listening for the obvious; he was listening to so much more. In this particular instance, he was listening for the man's faith and for his sincere desire to be restored.

Jesus...was listening for the man's faith and for his sincere desire to be restored.

See the contrast between the crowd's reaction to the shouting of the blind man and Jesus' response. The crowd saw a nuisance; Jesus saw an opportunity—the opportunity to bring the Kingdom of God into the man's life. Jesus saw the blindness for what it was, an affliction issuing from the Fall, part of the kingdom of darkness.

One of the results of this kingdom study will be revealed in how you listen to the people around you. For example, I'd been sitting at the Panera Bread restaurant one day, working on this manuscript, when I heard and saw something from the kingdom of darkness. A woman had come in with her two kids to have coffee with another woman, probably her mother. Right away she started talking about the rash on the body of one of her two boys. It had persisted for many months. They pulled up his shirt so the grandma could see. (Yes, I was eavesdropping. Was this bad? I couldn't help it. I was listening for the kingdom!)

The kingdom train of thought began in my head—

Are there skin rashes in heaven? No!

Was this skin rash part of the Kingdom of God or of darkness? Darkness, of course!

Does God desire to heal and restore? Absolutely!

Will this woman think I am crazy if I launch into a homily on the healing power of God? Yes!

God, what do you want me to do?

Listen now... wait...be open to opportunity... listen...

As we mature as Christians, we need to listen from a kingdom perspective. What is of God and what is of darkness? When people share struggles or a hurt, we need not only to listen to them, we need to listen to the Lord. This leads to step two—focusing on the leading and direction of the Holy Spirit.

2. Listening to the Holy Spirit

I recently noticed the motto of a ministry organization: "Staying one step behind the Holy Spirit." I love that! We can get in trouble when we try to stay one step ahead of the Spirit. We need to ask many questions:

Are we supposed to pray right away for healing, restoration of this ailment?

Lord, how are you leading this time?

Do we need to pray for strength and perseverance?

Is there something else going on that is related to the physical ailment?

Do we need to pray for peace or clarity?

Do we need to pray through an area of bondage?

As we mature as Christians, we need to listen from a kingdom perspective.

In Jesus' healing ministry, he made it clear that he wasn't merely self-directed, but was following and emulating the works and words of the Father. He told us that he was constantly doing what he saw the Father do. Jesus said,

> **..."The words I say to you are not just my own. Rather, it is the Father, living in me, who is doing his work."**
>
> *John 14:10*

> **..."These words you hear are not my own; they belong to the Father who sent me."**
>
> *John 14:24*

As Jesus interacted with people, there seemed to be this constant listening for the work and words of the Father. He did the Father's work and spoke his Father's words.

We need not only to listen to the person in need, but at the same time, to listen to the Holy Spirit and his direction.

Father, how would you have us pray?
Is there a truth or a promise to pray from Scripture?
Is there something else you want us to focus on in prayer?
Is there a lie that we need to pray truth into?
Is there a blessing we need to give thanks for?
What are you saying? What are you doing?
How do we join and cooperate with your work?

These are good questions to listen for while people share their stories. They are also good for specific, silent listening prayer. We tend to jump right into prayer, but as a group it is good to take some time to listen before praying. This might mean beginning with a few minutes of silence, with all knowing that this is a time to listen.

You, as a group, have been growing in your understanding of the gifts of the Spirit. Now is the right occasion to listen for a *word of knowledge* or *wisdom*. Now is the time when God will use the different gifts of the community to bless, heal and restore another member of the Body of Christ.

3. Listening to the Community

Let me repeat—there is power in community. This is partly because of the opportunity for all the gifts of the Spirit to play a role in the ministry of the kingdom. When I lead and facilitate a time of healing prayer, it is usually at this point that I may say something like this:

> "I want you all to continue to listen on behalf of [the person we are praying for]. Listen for a word from the Lord, an impression, a Scripture he may lay on your heart, or a way he wants you to pray. If you feel led, go ahead and speak it out."

Many times, as you give the Holy Spirit space to work in and through the community, there comes a rich time of direction and prayer. I have found that often the person being prayed for receives tremendous blessing. It's not just having a community of friends listening on his/her behalf, but having the Lord speak and direct through those gathered.

There are two elements crucial to this time of listening as a community—humility and patience. This is especially important for a body of believers who are just beginning to operate in the gifts of the Spirit. There must be the humility to realize that sometimes a word or picture is indeed from the Lord, but sometimes it's not. It's a miss. We have to share our thoughts humbly, respecting the fact that we are still a fallen people. We have not been fully restored. This admonition should not keep us from moving ahead or being bold; but we must always be on guard against arrogance.

There are two elements crucial to this time of listening as a community—humility and patience.

Patience is the other essential characteristic for a listening community. A word or impression shared might not make complete sense at the moment, but perhaps it is something to hold onto and ponder. It may be a small part of what God is doing, and the other parts have not yet been revealed.

After some direction and prayer by the community, I will often ask the person who is being prayed for what they are thinking or feeling. Did they connect with a particular impression or prayer that was offered? If so, why? Do they have a sense of how we should continue to pray for them?

This leads to the final element.

4. Listening to the Spirit Again

Sometimes the Spirit has already provided further direction at this point through the person or a member of the community. Sometimes the group may need to listen more. The timing of healing prayer ministry seems to depend on a variety of things. Is there a sense of completion and freedom for the facilitator to close? OR, is the prayer time flowing into many aspects of the person's life—emotions, spiritual struggles, physical ailments? If so, the community should continue following the prayer stream.

Of course, if the person being prayed for is not familiar with this kind of prayer, he or she may soon get tired. Just take a break.

One of the most important things I've discovered in healing prayer is that people are given permission to return and ask for further prayer on the same issue. This may be how the Spirit leads, and the community should commit to pray again for this person. Think of what a powerful element this can be, if the community perseveres and sees an answer unfold right before them. Remember, perseverance is a key characteristic for prayer.

Perseverance is a key characteristic for prayer.

Ⓡ Reflection—Listening Today

We are not in our groups yet, but please try to continue growing in this today. Take a few moments to think of one of your personal ailments or struggles. No need is too large or too small. Rather than pray a short, thirty-second prayer for healing, begin by listening. Try to follow the steps that we have outlined above. When you get to step 3, Listening to the Community, focus on the gifts of the Spirit. Let the Father, Son and Holy Spirit be your community.

Days 34 & 35 | A Community of Restoration

Is any one of you sick?... call the elders...to pray

At one of the churches where I served on staff, there was an elder, Wendell, who had studied healing for more than forty years. As people found out about this, they began to approach him for prayer. Wendell sought to take James 5:13–16 literally and invited these folks to attend our elders' meetings. It was a wonderful growing experience for our whole staff and elder team. I wouldn't say that we had this healing ministry thing all figured out, but we simply sought to obey God's word in James. Whenever we prayed for someone, I always got the sense that this was one of the most important things the leaders in God's church could do—pray for his kingdom to come and his will to be done in the life of his people.

> Invite the power of God to heal, restore and renew.

This week you have been reading about healing. Even though we have looked at some foundational aspects of healing, I don't imagine we have it all figured out either. But the question is, despite incomplete understanding and remaining unanswered questions, will we still seek to obey Scripture and pray for one another?

To be honest, for several years now, I have been studying and seeking to practice healing ministry; and I don't think I will ever have it all figured out. Still, I have decided that I will continue pursuing and praying for healing. Why? Because that is what Jesus wants us to do.

You, as a small group, may have already been praying for healing for one another without calling it a healing ministry. This is exactly what a kingdom community is supposed to do. We aren't just meant to empathize with one another; but to invite the power of God to heal, restore and renew. So now, today, this is what we will seek to do.

 Ministry Time—Listening Prayer

In Day 33, I suggested a very simple format for listening prayer. This framework is not meant to control the direction of the ministry time, but to be a simple guide or flexible structure. Your small group facilitator will lead you through this time of praying for one another. Following is the suggested flow—

Begin with Scripture Meditation

Have someone read James 5:13–15a aloud. Read it through once. After a few moments of silence, read it again.

> **Is any one of you in trouble? He should pray. Is anyone happy? Let him sing songs of praise. Is any one of you sick? He should call the elders of the church to pray over him and anoint him with oil in the name of the Lord. And the prayer offered in faith will make the sick person well; the Lord will raise him up….**
>
> *James 5:13–15*

Don't be afraid to receive what the Holy Spirit may communicate.

As we approach the prayer time, let's remember, that the more we get to know each other in our small groups, the easier it will be to share our personal needs and struggles.

1. Listening to the Person in Need

The facilitator can begin by asking if anyone has come with a desire to be prayed for about a particular ailment or illness. Keep in mind that this is not the time to ask for prayer for someone outside of the group. Instead, try to stay focused on ministering to one another. It's only necessary to ask enough questions of the person in need to get the group praying in the right direction.

It may also be helpful to ask not only the *what* questions of healing, but also the *why* questions. Does the person feel that their struggle or ailment is connected to any other event or relationship in their life? For example, an accident, a divorce, an argument, service in the military.

2. Listening to the Holy Spirit

In the past days, we have sought to grow in this spiritual discipline. As a group, listen for his still small voice. Do you hear a word or have you received an impression? Was there anything in the person's sharing that caught your attention? Don't be afraid to receive what the Holy Spirit may communicate.

3. Listening to the Community

As you begin to pray, continue to listen to the Holy Spirit, and also to the community. Does something that is prayed ring true to you? In what direction do you sense the Spirit leading? Do you feel a need to follow up in prayer in a particular area?

The facilitator may simply ask the group if anyone has heard a word and urge them to share it. Sometimes these are simply short phrases or even just one word. For example, *jealousy, grief, fears of dying, carrying a heavy pack.*

4. **Listening to the Spirit Again**
   This is a continuous process, and we need to keep listening to the Spirit through each step. But sometimes it is important to give the group permission to listen in silence again, and simply wait. It is also helpful to look for outward signs of the Spirit's presence and work. These signs don't always come, but often they do. They may include things like emotions or tears by the person being prayed for, or by those who are praying. Sometimes the Holy Spirit may express his presence through heat on the hands of those who are praying. Sometimes it may be as subtle as the slight shaking of a person's hand or another part of the body.

Try this too— Listening to the Person in Need Again

I have found it is usually healthy and helpful to ask the person who is being prayed for what they are experiencing. Are we praying in the right direction? Does he or she sense a direction for continuing our prayers?

You don't need to be nervous or afraid. Remember, this is simply obeying Scripture and trusting God that his promises are true.

...ask the person who is being prayed for what they are experiencing.

Week Six | The Missional Kingdom

Day 36 A Refreshing Message

Day 37 Evangelism Unplugged

Day 38 Did Jesus Read Her Mail?

Day 39 Philip the Listener

Day 40 An Inspired Cup of Cold Water

Days 41 & 42 Listen and Act

"Everyone who drinks this water will be thirsty again, but whoever drinks the water I give them will never thirst. Indeed, the water I give them will become in them a spring of water welling up to eternal life."

John 4:13, 14

Day 36 | A Refreshing Message

...that times of refreshing may come from the Lord

For most of my active Christian life, I have loved sharing my faith. In his classic, *How to Give Away Your Faith*, Paul Little likened evangelism in the Christian faith to the fizz in Pepsi. It can be tremendous! Sharing Christ with folks in whom God is stirring can be one of the most exciting experiences in this world. Of course, there have been times of frustration and sadness for me in sharing my faith. And there were those times when I wish I had done and said things differently. Yet, I have had the honor of leading many people to Christ during my Christian life.

Sharing Christ with folks in whom God is stirring can be one of the most exciting experiences in this world.

I remember first learning how to explain the gospel message, the good news. Over time, Christians have developed many ways of explaining the good news, but I really took to One Verse Evangelism, also known as the Bridge Diagram. I liked it because of its simplicity and because I am a visual learner. Developed by a Navigator staff person, Randy Raysbrook, it spells out the gospel by walking a person through one verse.

> **For the wages of sin is death, but the gift of God is eternal life through Christ Jesus our Lord.**
>
> *Romans 6:23*

Often, when I've explained the Christian faith using this verse and the Bridge Diagram, people would say, "Wow, no one has ever explained things like that before." I place a high value on being able to explain the gospel in clear and understandable ways that invite people to respond.

I believe that God has definitely worked through me using this little One Verse Evangelism. However, as I have studied the kingdom, God has challenged my presentation of the gospel. When I compare my witness and outreach to the scriptural model, I am forced to conclude that my message has been very limited in scope.

So, What Is the Good News Anyway?

For most Christians today, when we think of the gospel or good news, we think of Jesus and the good news that he died on the cross and rose from the dead. That is certainly central to the good news and how it is presented in the New Testament. The apostles held up Jesus as the center of the good news they proclaimed.

> **Day after day, in the temple courts and from house to house, they never stopped teaching and proclaiming the *good news* that Jesus is the Christ.** (emphasis added)
>
> *Acts 5:42*

A little later, we see Philip sharing with the Ethiopian eunuch.

> **Then Philip began with that very passage of Scripture and told him the *good news* about Jesus.** (emphasis added)
>
> *Acts 8:35*

Jesus didn't just ask people to intellectually affirm the message of the kingdom…

Jesus was and is the good news that we share. Note, however, that when Jesus shared the good news, he didn't begin with himself. He actually began with the kingdom. We read this in a number of places in the Gospels.

> **"The time has come," he said. "The kingdom of God is near. Repent and believe the *good news*!"** (emphasis added)
>
> *Mark 1:15*

> **But he said, "I must preach the *good news* of the kingdom of God to the other towns also, because that is why I was sent."** (emphasis added)
>
> *Luke 4:43 (see also Luke 8:1; 16:16)*

> **Jesus went through all the towns and villages, teaching in their synagogues, preaching the *good news* of the kingdom and healing every disease and sickness.** (emphasis added)
>
> *Matthew 9:35 (see also Matthew 4:23)*

So what was the good news regarding the kingdom? First of all, remember that even though Jesus was stretching and challenging the people's view of the kingdom, at least they knew it meant restoration. When God brought the kingdom for his people, it meant peace (*shalom*) and prosperity; it meant justice and freedom; it meant the world made right at every level of society; it meant the restoration of all things. That was certainly good news!

And Jesus didn't just ask people to intellectually affirm the message of the kingdom; he called them to change their lives. He challenged them to repent (do a 180° turn) and begin to follow him as disciples. He invited them to enter the Kingdom of God right then and there by a new birth, to be born again by the Spirit, just as he had told Nicodemus (John 3:1–21).

When I compared what Jesus proclaimed to my own presentation of the gospel, I realized how limited was the good news that I had shared. You might even say I was simply selling "afterlife insurance." I tried to get people into heaven, but had missed the aspect of the Kingdom of Heaven invading lives in the here and now. I invited people to embrace eternal life, but had missed the new life in the Spirit.

Joe and the Spirit

Joe was pretty new to the church. Someone told me that he had been part of our Families Victorious group and was now trying out our Sunday morning service. I met Joe after one of our services and he asked if we could get together and talk through some stuff. I could see in Joe's demeanor that he was seeking something.

Joe came to my office that next week and shared his story. He had spent much of his adult life struggling with drugs and alcohol—a pretty hard life, including incarceration. During his last time in jail Joe had begun talking and praying with a chaplain. Soon he started on the journey to find God and walk with him, but by now he had a very basic, yet awesome, question. After sharing his story he asked, "So how do I do it? What else am I supposed to do as a Christian?"

I invited people to embrace eternal life, but had missed the new life in the Spirit.

You see, Joe had stepped away from the drugs and alcohol. He had removed a lot of the junk in his life, but somehow knew there was something more to it—something he hadn't figured out yet.

Well, as you might guess, I began my response with sharing the Bridge Diagram. I worked through Romans 6:23. When I got to the response part, I shared the three words that I usually use: "admit, believe, and receive." Then Joe gave a very interesting response. He said, "I think I have done the 'admit' and 'believe' part, but not the 'receive' part." I don't think I will ever forget his response. It implied two very important things. One was that Joe had not yet personally received Christ into his heart. No one had led him in a personal prayer of commitment to Jesus.

Secondly, he was not just longing for the forgiveness and removal of his past stuff. Joe wanted to receive whatever it was that would enable him to live as a Christian.

Of course, I talked with Joe about praying to receive Christ personally and he was ready. But I felt that was an incomplete answer to his question, "How do I do this?" Joe needed to hear more than just,

> **For the wages of sin is death, but the gift of God is eternal life in Christ Jesus our Lord.**
>
> *Romans 6:23*

Joe was looking for more than the washing away of his sin and gaining eternal life in the distant future. He longed for a new life now—the life that God wanted him to live in his present reality.

Joe and I began to talk about the Holy Spirit of God, an essential person in the fulfillment of God's promises. I explained that the sacred words don't just include forgiveness and wiping away of sin, but also the gift of his Spirit—the Spirit of Christ dwelling in us, guiding in all our daily activities. The Holy Spirit would empower Joe (and us) to fight the temptations of the flesh and live out his kingdom purposes.

The desire of Jesus is to baptize us with his Spirit, so that we might live a new life, a different life, as his new creations.

> **Therefore, if anyone is in Christ, he is a new creation; the old has gone, the new has come!**
>
> *2 Corinthians 5:17*

Joe and I talked about what it means to be a *new creation*. We also discussed Romans 8:1–17 that describes life in the Spirit. What a contrast there is between living according to our sinful nature and living according to the Spirit!

This is what Joe had been looking for—not just the good news of forgiveness in the gospel, but also the good news of freedom in the Spirit—not just salvation in the afterlife, but also the abundant life of Christ day by day.

What a contrast there is between living according to our sinful nature and living according to the Spirit!

And so I led Joe in a prayer to personally receive Christ into his heart. Then I laid my hands on him and prayed for the infilling presence of the Holy Spirit in all his life. Joe entered the kingdom and began living in it!

Early Invitations

If we look carefully at the early gospel invitations recorded in the book of Acts, we see that the first disciples invited people to far more than the removal of sins for the purpose of eternal life. Peter and John had healed a crippled beggar on their way to the temple. The man got so excited that he jumped all around attracting a crowd in the outer temple courts. Peter seized this opportunity to share the good news right there in the temple. Read his invitation to repent.

> ***Repent*, then, and turn to God, so that your sins may be wiped out, that times of *refreshing* may come from the Lord, and that he may send the Christ, who has been appointed for you – even Jesus. He must remain in heaven until the time comes for God to *restore* everything, as he promised long ago through his holy prophets.** (emphasis added)
>
> *Acts 3:19–21*

In this invitation, Peter emphasized three aspects of salvation—three blessings or realities of the Kingdom of God that people would experience if they repent and turn to God.

1. **Repent...that your sins may be wiped out...** (verse 19)
   I love the phrase *wiped out.* The Greek word is *exaleipho.* It doesn't just mean to "wipe away," but to "erase" and "obliterate." God doesn't mess around with our sin; he doesn't merely overlook it. He gives us a good scrubbing!
   Our sin is the greatest barrier in our relationship with God, so he obliterates that barrier. As a result, we can walk in a personal, intimate relationship with him. What good news! The obliteration of sin is an essential part of the gospel, but there's more.

2. **...that times of refreshing may come from the Lord...** (verse 19)
   What a neat phrase to include as part of the invitation to turn to God. On my computer, I can right click on the initial screen and go to "refresh." This action straightens everything up and cleans up the icons. Through daily use, things get out of kilter, don't they? Peter knew that and invited the crowd to be spiritually refreshed, to experience rest and relief in their lives, allowing God's Spirit to straighten out the aspects of their lives that have gotten out of kilter. This was not an invitation for future "refreshment" (he will get to that) but a renewing today, right now. I wonder if Peter learned this invitation from Jesus when he said,

   > **"Come to me, all you who are weary and burdened, and I will give you rest. Take my yoke upon you and learn from me, for I am gentle and humble in heart, and you will find rest for your souls. For my yoke is easy and my burden is light."**
   >
   > *Matthew 11:28–30*

   This is available to all people who turn to God and that is very good news!

Peter invited his listeners into God's grand scheme of restoring all creation.

3. **...that he may send the Christ... [when] the time comes for God to restore everything...** (verses 20–21)
   Now, that is kingdom language and Peter's listeners would have understood it as such. Remember, this was what the Messiah, the anointed king, was meant to do. Peter invited his listeners into God's grand scheme of restoring all creation. This was what the prophets had talked about and the people expected. It's such a different picture of heaven or eternal life than we normally hear about. But heaven is not a stagnant reality that we hope to enter someday when our lives are all said and done. It is a present reality that is coming here; and we want to be a part of it. Peter invited them to become a part of God's great restoration project. He invited them to receive, in the present day, God's obliteration of their sin and refreshment of their soul and spirit—to taste kingdom life. He also invited them to participate in God's act of restoration by living in such a way now that they might be a part of the future kingdom—to experience everything made new. This too is very good news!

The last verses in the book of Acts sum up the message that another great apostle taught—an invitation to the kingdom.

For two whole years, Paul stayed there in his own rented house and welcomed all who came to see him. Boldly and without hindrance, he preached the kingdom of God and taught about the Lord Jesus Christ.

Acts 28:30–31

Refreshing Our Own Invitations

Compared to Peter's, any invitations I have extended to people have been half-baked. Yes, I have invited people to experience forgiveness, but not the kingdom life of refreshment and restoration. How sad that I have communicated such a limited version of the good news! Many of us may be guilty of not sharing the full message of Jesus Christ, the good news of the kingdom. From now on, let us share not only the forgiveness of sins in Jesus Christ, but also the way into kingdom life.

Reflection

What a contrast there is between living according to our sinful nature and living according to the Spirit!

Take a few moments to re-read Peter's invitation in Acts 3:19–21. Before we can invite others to receive this good news, we must be sure of experiencing it ourselves. Perhaps you need to receive a time of refreshment for your soul, to receive the hope of the restoration of all things.

Day 37 Evangelism Unplugged

...not with wise and persuasive words, but with a demonstration of the Spirit's power...

As I mentioned in Day 36, when I compared my own outreach and witness with Scripture, I came to the conclusion that my presentation of the gospel message was very limited, so I determined to expand its scope. I also came to a second conclusion, one that is perhaps more difficult to resolve. By comparison, my outreach had been done with very little power. If we look at the witness of the early church, it comes across as energized and vibrant, clearly directed and empowered by the Spirit of God. Jesus had done what he promised he would do according to Luke 24:49—clothe them with power from on high.

> If we want to see the multiplication of the kingdom that Jesus talked about, we need to reconnect to the power source—the Spirit of Christ.

Yet, today's evangelism in the Western world often looks to me like something unplugged and powerless. Rather than being clothed with power, it feels like a wet blanket has been thrown over us. At times, the witness of the church comes across as judgmental and negative, failing to reflect the Spirit of Christ in communicating the truth. At other times, it appears formulaic and without authenticity. When it should ring true in the ears of listeners, it sounds hollow. I believe that our evangelism today desperately needs to be plugged back in. If we want to see the multiplication of the kingdom that Jesus talked about, we need to reconnect to the power source—the Spirit of Christ. There are three primary ways to plug back in.

Reclaiming the Spirit in Evangelism

I have not only sought to grow personally in evangelism, but I have taught numerous classes on evangelism. I have trained and demonstrated how to grow in the skills of relational evangelism by sharing our testimony and sharing the gospel. All these things were valuable and good; but until I started studying the kingdom, I never really understood the role that the Spirit of Christ is intended to play in evangelism. On occasion, I would give lip service to the Spirit, but then quickly get back to the strategic skills. For Christ, however, the Spirit is the prime initiator in our witness. Yes, the Spirit is given to bring intimacy and sanctify our lives, but another primary reason Jesus sent his Spirit was to empower our witness. As he said goodbye to his disciples, he told them,

> **"But you will receive power when the Holy Spirit comes on you; and you will be my witnesses..."**
>
> *Acts 1:8*

The Spirit is at work in many ways in our lives as believers. He acts in and through us. But the Spirit also works in the lives of non-believers. He is drawing and nudging, convicting and pricking hearts. Jesus said,

> **"When he [the Spirit] comes, he will convict the world of guilt in regard to sin and righteousness and judgment...."**
>
> *John 16:8*

This means that the Spirit is the one who does the primary convicting. He is the one who readies the hearts of those we love. This means that, apart from the work of the Spirit, people cannot see themselves as they truly are, lost in sin, guilty as charged. Only the Spirit can cause people to see their need for the righteousness of Christ. Only the Spirit can bring awareness of our separation from the Father. Most of us know this as Christians, but we don't live it out when it comes to evangelism.

I think that many of our attempts at evangelism and outreach today are ineffective because we don't practice this primary command of Christ—first wait and pray.

A former senior pastor of mine often told the story of his evangelistic zeal when he first became a Christian in college. So passionate was he to share his faith that one day, in the middle of the cafeteria at his dorm, he stood up on his chair, and, with Bible in hand, said in a loud voice, "If anyone would like to know how to become a Christian, I will be sitting right here every day, at the same time, at this same table." And that is exactly what he did; he sat at that same table, at the same time—all by himself. You see, he was trying to barge into people's lives on his own time, in his own way. He wasn't following the Spirit.

This is not to say that we don't have a role to play, and we will talk much more about it later this week. But first of all, we need to know that we are called to cooperate with the Spirit, allowing him to move and guide us into the areas where he is working.

When the disciples watched Jesus ascend into heaven, they could have gone right out and started announcing Jesus' resurrection and ascension from the rooftops. But they didn't because Jesus didn't tell them to. He gave them strict orders to wait and pray.

> **"...Do not leave Jerusalem, but wait for the gift my Father promised ... you will receive power when the Holy Spirit comes on you; and you will be my witnesses...."**
>
> *Acts 1:4, 8*

Jesus instructed the disciples to wait for the power, not to jump ahead without the Spirit. He is the one at work in the unbelievers that we will someday talk with. But the Spirit's job is also to come in power upon us. Then we will be ready for the work he has called us to. Just like the TV, we must be plugged in before we can work.

I think that many of our attempts at evangelism and outreach today are ineffective because we don't practice this primary command of Christ—first wait and pray.

This is not just for empowerment but also for direction, for his clear guidance. He doesn't want us to be cruising off the road in our ATVs where he is not at work. Our job is to follow his path.

Hurry Up and Wait!

Once, when I met with a group of pastors regarding evangelism, the lead pastor asked us to take our evangelistic temperature. In other words, were we living evangelistically, with passion? Although evangelism had been one of my red-hot passions, I had to confess that day how cold I felt. The business of ministry had certainly taken its toll. And I wasn't the only pastor with a similar confession.

The lead pastor simply gave us this direction, "For those of you who are feeling pretty ice cold right now, would you simply commit to pray for those in your life who do not yet know Christ? Before you do anything else, before you take any action, would you simply commit to waiting in prayer on a daily basis?" I felt sad to realize that in my own life I had fallen out of the spiritual discipline of waiting in prayer for my non-Christian friends and neighbors. No wonder I was cold!

We in the Western church have not trusted the power of God to meet the needs of people.

Within a week of making that commitment, God provided a divine moment for me to serve one of my neighbors—just what I had been praying for. It was a kingdom opportunity that I would have surely missed had I not been waiting in prayer, a simple random act of kindness that blessed my neighbor.

Would you commit to wait in prayer for two or three friends or family who do not yet have a relationship with Jesus? The first step in doing that is to plug back into the power source. Find the outlet in the upper room and simply plug in. Then, wait.

Demonstrating the Spirit in Evangelism

The Spirit's desire is to be our power source, the prime initiator in our witness. So let's acknowledge our need and, then, trust him. Trust his great love for those who do not know him. Trust him to guide us as we seek to advance the kingdom. That is probably the easier part. The bigger challenge is trusting that he will empower us and demonstrate his own power whenever we share his good news. This is where the rubber meets the road. Will we trust his leadership as we pass on the message of restoration, healing and renewal to those we love? That is a little scary!

Speaking personally, I have not done this well. In the past I did not train people to even consider this aspect of evangelism. To me it seems that we, in the Western church, have not trusted the power of God to meet the needs of people. We have not truly responded to Christ's call to preach the kingdom and heal the sick. We have not proclaimed the Kingdom of God well, let alone demonstrated the presence of the kingdom. But Jesus did! In Luke 9 we saw how he trained and sent the Twelve to spread the kingdom through proclamation and demonstration. And then in Luke 10, we watched him do the same with the Seventy-two. After Christ's resurrection and ascension that is exactly what the early church did as well.

Empowered Community

The disciples were not just given boldness to proclaim the gospel, but also power to demonstrate it. At the end of Acts 2 we catch a glimpse of what the early church looked like.

> **Everyone was filled with awe, and many wonders and miraculous signs were done by the apostles.**
>
> *Acts 2:43*

Small groups have been another passion of mine. Much of my training of leaders came from Acts 2:42–47. I trained my leaders to focus on the different aspects of this community, such as fellowship, discipleship, worship, service and evangelism. But for all my training and talk, I simply skipped the *many wonders and miraculous signs*. The community of faith that I taught lacked the power component. I left it out, and that was not right.

Not only was the early community of faith and fellowship power-packed, so was their witness!

The early church was *not* an unplugged community. Not only were they energized by love and fellowship, those believers experienced significant supernatural activity. In the past, I would skip over that. Did you? But now, from a kingdom perspective, we realize that the miraculous signs and wonders were essential to the early church. They demonstrated the new reality of what they proclaimed.

Empowered Paul

Not only was the early community of faith and fellowship power-packed, so was their witness! Paul figured this out early in his life. He wanted to make sure the Corinthians knew the source of his evangelistic zeal.

> **My message and my preaching were not with wise and persuasive words, but with a demonstration of the Spirit's power, so that your faith might not rest on men's wisdom, but on God's power.**
>
> *1 Corinthians 2:4–5*

Can you say that about your own evangelism? Wouldn't you like to? For Paul, it wasn't just about reasoning in the synagogues and engaging in philosophical argument in the market place. For him, spreading the gospel meant a demonstration of God's power in both word and deed.

Empowered Philip

When Stephen was martyred (Acts 7) and the church was scattered, the disciples carried the gospel out from Jerusalem. But see, they didn't just preach the kingdom; they demonstrated the kingdom—they lived it out. Their message was not a powerless discourse of Bible references and theological statements. The Spirit's power was actually demonstrated through their message. Acts 8 describes Philip's power-filled ministry in Samaria.

When the crowds heard Philip and saw the miraculous signs he did, they all paid close attention to what he said. With shrieks, evil spirits came out of many, and many paralytics and cripples were healed. So there was great joy in that city.

Acts 8:6–8

Notice how they were not just *hearing* the message, they were *seeing* the message; they were experiencing the kingdom in word and deed.

The early church got this connection. They clearly saw the connection between the empowering presence of the Spirit and evangelism. When they faced persecution from the religious leaders of their day, they prayed to God for greater boldness. But that wasn't their only prayer. Listen to what else they asked for.

Now, Lord, consider their threats and enable your servants to speak your word with great boldness. Stretch out your hand to heal and perform miraculous signs and wonders through the name of your holy servant Jesus.

Acts 4:29–30

Is it time to plug in and trust God to meet the needs of his people with his power, through us?

Have you ever prayed that prayer before? I myself have prayed for boldness, insight and wisdom; but prior to my study of the kingdom, I don't remember ever asking for miraculous signs and wonders. What do you think? Is it time we started praying more like the early church? Is it time to plug in and trust God to meet the needs of his people with his power, through us?

Proclaiming the Spirit in Evangelism

We learned in Day 19 that the Holy Spirit isn't just the primary evangelist in the world, he is also a central part of the message. A huge part of what makes the New Covenant new is that life in the Spirit is available to every believer, male or female, young or old. The Spirit should also be a central aspect of the message that we proclaim, a huge part of the kingdom life that we offer to the world.

When Peter first proclaimed the gospel he gave an invitation to respond:

…"Repent and be baptized, every one of you, in the name of Jesus Christ for the forgiveness of your sins."

Acts 2:38a

But we must not stop there. We need to continue as Peter did,

"And you will receive the gift of the Holy Spirit. The promise is for you and your children and for all who are far off—for all whom the Lord our God will call."

Acts 2:38b–39

Peter didn't want them to miss out on the receiving part; he didn't want them to miss out on the power source.

 Ministry Time—Prayers for Power

I think the most appropriate response to this day is to wait in prayer. Begin by choosing three or four friends and family members who don't know Christ. Wait in prayer for them. After that, open your Bible and meditate on the early church's prayers and proclamations.

> **"... enable your servants to speak your word with great boldness. Stretch out your hand to heal and perform miraculous signs and wonders through the name of your holy servant Jesus."**
>
> *Acts 4:29–30*

> **..."Repent and be baptized, every one of you, in the name of Jesus Christ for the forgiveness of your sins. And you will receive the gift of the Holy Spirit. The promise is for you and your children and for all who are far off—for all whom the Lord our God will call."**
>
> *Acts 2:38–39*

...meditate on the early church's prayers and proclamations.

Day 38 Did Jesus Read Her Mail?

I can see that you are a prophet

During my years at seminary, I developed an enjoyable friendship with my classmate and intellectual sparring partner, Chris. Chris was a high-octane personality filled with faith and an undeniable zeal for God's Word. His background was different from mine and we enjoyed talking through matters of the faith from our particular perspectives.

He [Chris] felt everything was fair game for us as followers of Christ.

One day we were talking about evangelism, a subject that I was pretty passionate about. I had even formed some surefire beliefs. This conversation sticks in my mind because we had a key disagreement. We both wholeheartedly agreed that Jesus had much to teach us about evangelism, but I argued that there were some limitations for us that Jesus didn't have. Chris disagreed. He felt everything was fair game for us as followers of Christ. Let me explain.

Jesus and the Woman at the Well

Our disagreement centered on the story of Jesus and the Samaritan woman at the well. Let's take a moment to read the interaction between Jesus and this Samaritan woman:

> **When a Samaritan woman came to draw water, Jesus said to her, "Will you give me a drink?"....**
>
> **The Samaritan woman said to him, "You are a Jew and I am a Samaritan woman. How can you ask me for a drink?" (For Jews do not associate with Samaritans.)**
>
> **Jesus answered her, "If you knew the gift of God and who it is that asks you for a drink, you would have asked him and he would have given you living water."**
>
> **"Sir," the woman said, "you have nothing to draw with and the well is deep. Where can you get this living water? Are you greater than our father Jacob, who gave us the well and drank from it himself, as did also his sons and his flocks and herds?"**
>
> **Jesus answered, "Everyone who drinks this water will be thirsty**

> **again, but whoever drinks the water I give him will never thirst. Indeed, the water I give him will become in him a spring of water welling up to eternal life."**
>
> **The woman said to him, "Sir, give me this water so that I won't get thirsty and have to keep coming here to draw water."**
>
> *John 4:7, 9–15*

Now there are some absolutely wonderful aspects about this story. From this interaction, we can learn a lot from Jesus regarding evangelism. We see him crossing cultural barriers for the sake of reaching out in love, and astutely linking the woman's physical need for water with a spiritual one. Jesus creatively pointed the woman to a greater reality—a place that would quench the thirst of her soul.

All of this was great, and Chris and I agreed completely. But it was the next few verses in the story that threw us for a loop. You see, Jesus continued by challenging the woman in a brand new way.

According to the New Testament, Jesus did all the things he did because he was anointed with the Spirit.

> **He told her, "Go, call your husband and come back." "I have no husband," she replied. Jesus said to her, "You are right when you say you have no husband. The fact is, you have had five husbands, and the man you now have is not your husband. What you have just said is quite true." "Sir," the woman said, "I can see that you are a prophet."**
>
> *John 4:16–19*

Wow! How is that for an evangelistic technique? The question is, how in the world did Jesus know all of those personal details about her life? There are really only three options. The first is that, prior to this meeting, Jesus was somehow able to locate where she lived and spy on her. Perhaps he read her mail, went through her garbage and interviewed some neighbors. Well, okay, based on what we know of Jesus' moral integrity, this is not a likely explanation.

The second option is the most obvious. Jesus knew these details about this woman's life because he was God. It makes sense. God knows all things. Jesus is God. Jesus can know the details of anyone's life. This was my perspective, my belief. And here is where Chris and I disagreed. His comment to me was, "Why don't we learn from this way of evangelism just like we do from the other things in the story?" I responded with a snort! "Don't be ridiculous. He is God. We are not. We can't do stuff like that."

Chris argued for a third option, one that relates to our discussion in Day 16, *You Have an Anointing*. There we discussed Jesus' power source. For many of us, it was natural to assume that Christ's power source was directly linked to who he was and his divinity; that he did all his miraculous acts through his divine nature. But according to the New Testament, Jesus did all the things he did because he was anointed with the Spirit (see Luke 4:18; Acts 10:37–38).

As we looked at the New Testament with this question in mind, we concluded: Jesus came as the God-man (Philippians 2:6–7) but lived as a man who was anointed by the Spirit of God to do the work of the kingdom. He was anointed and empowered with the same Spirit that now anoints and empowers us.

This conclusion is not limited to physical healings and spiritual deliverances. What we need to do is apply this truth to every aspect of our understanding of Jesus' life, including evangelism. Just as Jesus healed the blind because of the anointing of the Spirit, so he was given spiritual insight into the Samaritan woman's life due to that same anointing. He read her mail (spiritually speaking) because he was operating under the direction and guidance of the Spirit. The Spirit who anointed and empowered Jesus in evangelism is the same Spirit who now desires to anoint and empower us for evangelism. Chris was right. It only took *me* five years of studying the Kingdom of God to give *him* credit.

Turning the Gifts Outward

If we choose the third option, we acknowledge that Jesus operated as a Holy Spirit-filled man, ministering to the Samaritan woman by the presence of the Spirit and the gifts of the Spirit. Considering the list of manifestation gifts that we studied, from 1 Corinthians 12 in Day 23, we can see that Jesus probably received a *word of knowledge* regarding the woman's life. He was given divine insight into her personal life, and it drew her to the Father. Later she would invite the townspeople to come and see Jesus.

> **"Come, see a man who told me everything I ever did. Could this be the Christ?"**
>
> *John 4:29*

> The Spirit who anointed and empowered Jesus in evangelism is the same Spirit who now desires to anoint and empower us for evangelism.

Talk about evangelism! Not only was this word of knowledge a powerful impetus to the Samaritan woman's own faith, but it enabled her to be a witness to the whole town, including her friends and family.

Not only have many of our churches neglected the spiritual gifts, but we have not thought much about them in terms of evangelism. How powerful would it be if we started seeking to use the spiritual gifts in the area of outreach? This is what Jesus and the early church did. When he performed a miracle, all the people flocked around him. Jesus never struggled to draw a crowd.

People were drawn to Jesus' authoritative teaching, but many simply came to him to be healed. The spiritual *gifts of healings* were certainly at work in Jesus and the early disciples. After Pentecost, on their way to the temple, Peter and John used the healing of the lame man as an opportunity to share the gospel with the amazed crowd (Acts 3).

But it wasn't just healings that the early church used for gospel outreach. It was also other spiritual gifts. The first presentation of the gospel by the early church resulted from the extraordinary event of Pentecost. What an attention getter! Though at first the onlookers may have thought people were drunk, they quickly changed their minds as they heard Peter's powerful message.

When the Apostle Paul talked about spiritual gifts in the community, he encouraged the pursuit of the gift of prophesy over tongues for many reasons. One of them was because of the value of prophesy (or a prophetic word) in outreach.

> **So if the whole church comes together and everyone speaks in tongues, and some who do not understand or some unbelievers come in, will they not say that you are out of your mind? But if an unbeliever or someone who does not understand comes in while everybody is prophesying, he will be convinced by all that he is a sinner and will be judged by all, and the secrets of his heart will be laid bare. So he will fall down and worship God, exclaiming, "God is really among you!"**
> *1 Corinthians 14:23–25*

Keep in mind that the churches Paul wrote to were primarily house churches. Now, picture your small group (you probably meet in a house). You are ministering to one another in the gifts of the Holy Spirit, just as you have learned. Then, imagine inviting a couple of non-Christian friends to one of your gatherings, and they have the chance to experience that kind of gift-based ministry. How powerful would that be? Non-believers experiencing the presence of the Spirit firsthand! They might even exclaim, "God is really among you!" (But if you get all whacky, they might respond, "You are out of your mind!")

Non-believers experiencing the presence of the Spirit firsthand! They might even exclaim, "God is really among you!"

"Well, You're Gonna Be!"

I knew an elder at a former church who got involved in the healing ministry as a young adult. When Bob was in college, he attended a Derek Prince healing service.[17] Bob told how Prince had invited a number of people forward to be healed (he chose specific people as he was led by the Holy Spirit). Bob was one of those invited forward.

Bob continued the story. "Yeah, my back was healed, but that was almost insignificant compared to what happened to the guy next to me. The guy had one leg that was shorter than the other. When Prince got to the man, he asked if he had faith to be healed. The man said, 'Well, I guess that would be a *no* because I am not a Christian, I am not a believer.' Prince smiled at him and said, 'Well, you're gonna be!'"

Derek Prince was right. The man was healed and became a believer. This is what Paul is talking about. When the power of God is manifested through the spiritual gifts, people recognize his existence. Kingdom evangelism demonstrates the power of God as a witness to his reality and work in this world.

Listening Like Jesus

Remember Jesus' discipleship plan? He modeled the life and ministry that he called his disciples to. His desire was that we would live like him, whether it was in our community of faith or in outreach. We are called to be continually conformed to the likeness of Christ (Romans 8:29), and to reflect how he reached out to people in the power of God.

17. An Englishman, Derek Prince, was known for his international healing and deliverance ministry from the 1970s until his death in 2003.

If we want to become more like Jesus in our outreach, we need to begin listening like he did. In Jesus' life, we see a powerful dynamic at work. Jesus explained to us that he was continually listening and learning from the Father. In the Gospel of John, we find this active listening to the Father.

Listening to the revealed Word

We know that before and during Jesus' ministry he studied deeply the revealed Word of God. Jesus studied the Scriptures, learning from the Father and preparing to speak what the Father revealed, and doing the Father's will. Jesus wanted us to know that his words were not his own. He would only speak the words the Father had taught him.

> **..."When you have lifted up the Son of Man, then you will know that I am the one I claim to be and that I do nothing on my own but speak just what the Father has taught me."**
>
> *John 8:28*

There is a power that many Christians deny themselves by not meditating daily on the Scriptures.

This was a powerful dynamic in Jesus' life. He had studied and meditated on God's words, God's plans, God's deeds. Now, as he lived and ministered, he spoke from what he knew, what he had been taught. This revealed his union and intimacy with the Father.

> **"For I did not speak of my own accord, but the Father who sent me commanded me what to say and how to say it. I know that his command leads to eternal life. So whatever I say is just what the Father has told me to say."**
>
> *John 12:49–50*

This is a very practical example for us. We need to listen to the Scriptures. If we want to be like Jesus, then we need to study and meditate on the revealed Word of God. Listening to the Word of God is meant to be the same powerful dynamic in our lives as it was in his. The Spirit's job is to illuminate the Scriptures. As we meditate on them, we will be able to speak into the lives of both believers and non-believers what we have been taught.

This is the primary way the Spirit has spoken to me personally—through the Scriptures. There is a power that many Christians deny themselves by not meditating daily on the Scriptures. But there is another aspect of listening that Jesus modeled for us. It is listening for the freshly spoken Word of God. Some would call it the "still small voice" of the Holy Spirit. It is the revelation of God in the moment.

Listening for a fresh word

Jesus didn't just speak the words that he had been taught. He also seemed to speak from a fresh revelation of the Spirit. Again, Jesus shares more words about himself.

> **"I tell you the truth, the Son can do nothing by himself; he can do only what he sees his Father doing, because whatever the Father does the Son also does. For the Father loves the Son and shows him all he does...."**
>
> *John 5:19–20*

Jesus' words here give us the impression that as Jesus lived and ministered to people, he actively looked to the Father for direction and guidance. As he spoke with people, he kept one ear open toward them and one ear toward heaven. As he moved and interacted with people, he kept looking to the Father for his immediate will, his direction in the moment, his desire in a particular instance.

This ongoing communication was so close and intimate that Jesus said,

> **"Don't you believe that I am in the Father, and that the Father is in me? The words I say to you are not just my own. Rather, it is the Father, living in me, who is doing his work."**
>
> *John 14:10*

Even Jesus did not march to his own drumbeat. He listened to the rhythms of heaven. His words and works were the Father's words and works—not because he was the divine Son of God, but because he was filled with the Spirit of God. Incredibly, this dynamic is true of the Spirit of God as well.

> **"But when he, the Spirit of truth, comes, he will guide you into all truth. He will not speak on his own; he will speak only what he hears, and he will tell you what is yet to come."**
>
> *John 16:13*

As he spoke with people, he kept one ear open toward them and one ear toward heaven.

The main way to follow Jesus in this dynamic is to actively listen to the Father as we interact and minister to those around us. It means keeping one ear to the ground of heaven and remembering that the Father is speaking. He desires to speak into the lives of people a fresh word, a revelation.

Ⓡ Reflection

Tomorrow, Day 39, we will focus on this kind of ongoing listening, but as we close this day, I want you to meditate on some Scripture. These Scriptures describe this intimate relationship between us and our Trinitarian God—Father, Son and Holy Spirit. These words can only be understood as the Spirit seals them deep in our hearts.

> **"And I will ask the Father, and he will give you another Counselor to be with you forever—the Spirit of truth....he lives with you and will be in you. I will not leave you as orphans; I will come to you....On that day you will realize that I am in my Father, and you are in me, and I am in you....If anyone loves me, he will obey my teaching. My Father will love him, and we will come to him and make our home with him."**
>
> *John 14:16–18, 20, 23*

Day 39 | Philip the Listener

The Spirit told Philip, "Go to that chariot and stay near it."

One of the unsung heroes of Scripture was a guy by the name of Philip. This Philip wasn't one of the original twelve apostles, but he actually got more attention in the Scripture than many of them. Playing a significant role in the early church and the spread of the gospel, the story of Philip's ministry dominates the whole eighth chapter in Acts.

Philip is the only one in all of Scripture to be specifically named an *evangelist.*

Philip also had a unique honor bestowed upon him. Though many people in the early church were probably considered evangelists by calling or office, Philip is the only one in all of Scripture to be specifically named an *evangelist*. In the book of Acts we read,

> **Leaving the next day, we reached Caesarea and stayed at the house of Philip the evangelist, one of the Seven. He had four unmarried daughters who prophesied.**
>
> *Acts 21:8–9*

This should cause us to sit up and pay attention. What was it about Philip that the Lord would bless him with being the only person in Scripture named as an evangelist? What can and should we learn from him regarding evangelism? How did Philip fulfill our shared call to extend the message of the kingdom paired with Christ's redemptive work on the cross? To me it looks like Philip did evangelism like Jesus; his life reflected what we can call *listening evangelism*.

Evangelism Like Jesus

When Stephen was martyred, the church was scattered (Acts 7:59–8:1). Before Paul's conversion, he harassed any disciple of Jesus he could get his hands on. It was a dangerous time, but God used this persecution to spread the church geographically. The disciples fled to the highways and byways but while so doing, shared the faith. Philip fled to Samaria, where he started telling people the good news. God gave him a power-filled, effective ministry—a ministry that looked a lot like Jesus'.

His Message
The record of Philip's activities in Acts 8 highlights two significant aspects of his message: the king and the kingdom.

> **Philip went down to a city in Samaria and proclaimed *the Christ* there.** (emphasis added)
>
> *Acts 8:5*

You can bet Philip talked about Jesus as the anointed king, the rejected and crucified savior, and the one God raised from the dead.

> **... he preached the good news of *the kingdom* of God and the name of Jesus Christ....** (emphasis added)
>
> *Acts 8:12*

Remember that Philip's audience was Samaritan—they were all partly of Jewish descent. As we found out from studying the woman at the well (John 4) Samaritans had at least some understanding and expectation of the Messiah and the kingdom to come.

As Philip followed Jesus' pattern of ministry, God began a vibrant, powerful and fruitful work in and through him.

His Ministry
But Philip didn't just preach a message like Jesus; he also actually did ministry and evangelism like Jesus. We also learn in Acts 8 that miraculous signs and wonders accompanied his proclamation of Christ—all in the presence and power of the Holy Spirit. This astounded the crowds.

This ministry sounds a lot like Jesus' ministry doesn't it? Philip didn't just proclaim the kingdom and its king, but he also demonstrated the presence of the kingdom with each demon driven out and each paralytic healed.

Philip was living out the so-called Impossible Promise we talked about from John 14:12. As Philip followed Jesus' pattern of ministry, God began a vibrant, powerful and fruitful work in and through him. He was doing kingdom evangelism. Philip's ministry was already awesome in power and effect, but it turned out that God had another unique assignment for Philip. In this new assignment we learn a little more about the kind of evangelist that Philip was. Let's read the story of Philip and his unusual meeting with the Ethiopian official.

Philip Goes Walking

> **Now an angel of the Lord said to Philip, "Go south to the road—the desert road—that goes down from Jerusalem to Gaza." So he started out, and on his way he met an Ethiopian eunuch, an important official in charge of all the treasury of Candace, queen of the Ethiopians. This man had gone to Jerusalem to worship, and on his way home was sitting in his chariot reading the book of Isaiah the prophet.**
>
> *Acts 8:26–28*

What I want you to notice throughout this narrative of Philip's encounter with the Ethiopian is the divine direction that Philip continually received.

Think for a moment how limited this first divine direction was for Philip. An angel came and basically told Philip to go for a walk—in the desert no less. Here is how I imagine the conversation going:

Then Philip starts walking.

Yes, I am having some fun, but think about it. In the discussion recorded between the angel and Philip, there was absolutely no reason or purpose given for this side trip from Samaria to the desert. If that was all the message you got, would you go? If you heard the still small voice of the Holy Spirit say, "You know the major highway between here and the city? I want you to start walking along it," would you go? I don't think that many of us would.

Consider these important questions:

What would it take for you and me to have a faith like Philip?

What would it take for us to have such a mindset to listen and obey?

God is at work in this world actively extending the kingdom by drawing people to himself.

Now is the time to consider two core kingdom convictions.

Kingdom Conviction #1

God is at work in this world actively extending the kingdom by drawing people to himself. We need to believe deeply that he wants to restore and renew people—to bring the presence of his kingdom into their lives, healing every aspect of who they are. This is one of the key activities of the Spirit of God.

> **"When he [the Holy Spirit] comes, he will convict the world of guilt in regard to sin and righteousness and judgment."**
>
> *John 16:8*

We live in the days of the kingdom when God's declared activity in this world is to bring his kingdom upon Earth as it is in heaven. Do you believe this? Are you living your life in view of it? Are you listening? Philip was.

The second core kingdom conviction is directly related to the first.

Kingdom Conviction #2
He wants to use you. Our Father wants to use you and me as part of his redemptive work, part of advancing his kingdom. This is why Jesus modeled kingdom ministry. This is why the Holy Spirit empowers us and sends us out. For some crazy reason God has chosen to work through sin-stained, hard-of-hearing folks like you and me. He wants to use us so much that he gives us divine direction and divine appointments. The only catch is—are we paying attention? If we want to hear his divine direction, we need to listen. Are you? Do you believe that God wants to use you in this way? Are you living your life for this reason? Philip was.

Availability and Willingness

Living out these two core convictions means being available and willing to witness. When the angel told the evangelist to go for a walk, Philip could have said,

Our Father wants to use you and me as part of his redemptive work, part of advancing his kingdom.

As interesting as that walk in the desert sounds, I have a pretty vibrant ministry going on here in Samaria. I think I should stay put.

I have coffee plans with a guy I just led to the Lord. I really need to disciple him.

But Philip didn't respond that way. His lifestyle was to be available and willing for divine appointments.

I know that this is contrary to our age of day-timers and electronic organizers. But just imagine for a moment if the next time you walked into the grocery store, you prayed something like this—"God, if you are at work here drawing these folks to yourself, and you want to give me a divine appointment with a cashier, or fellow customer, or a neighbor or friend I see—well, I'm listening. I am ready to hear and obey."

Philip Goes Running

Continuing with the story, let's see what happens after Philip went walking:

> **The Spirit told Philip, "Go to that chariot and stay near it." Then Philip ran up to the chariot and heard the man reading Isaiah the prophet. "Do you understand what you are reading?" Philip asked. "How can I," he said, "unless someone explains it to me?"**

So he invited Philip to come up and sit with him. The eunuch was reading this passage of Scripture:

"He was led like a sheep to the slaughter and as a lamb before the shearer is silent, so he did not open his mouth. In his humiliation he was deprived of justice. Who can speak of his descendants? For his life was taken from the earth."

The eunuch asked Philip, "Tell me, please, who is the prophet talking about, himself or someone else?" Then Philip began with that very passage of Scripture and told him the good news about Jesus.

Acts 8:29–35

Did you notice? Philip not only goes walking, he also goes running. Apparently, he was obediently strolling down the desert road when a horse-drawn chariot appeared. In it was a man reading, a high official from Ethiopia. He was probably an African Jew, or convert, who had traveled to Jerusalem to worship. Now he was headed south back to Ethiopia. As the chariot was passing by Philip—still walking along, listening to God—he heard in the quiet voice of the Holy Spirit, *Go to that chariot and stay near it.*

How easy it will be to miss such divine appointments if we are not looking and listening for them!

When I reread this story I kept hearing, "Run, Forest, run!" Or perhaps it was more like, "Follow that car!" In any event, Philip ran. It must have been a pretty comical moment. There was Philip jogging right up next to the moving chariot, wondering what in the world God had in store! And true to form, in the midst of his divine jog, he acted like an evangelist.

Recognizing the opportunity

Jogging along, Philip heard the Ethiopian reading Isaiah 53:7–8 out loud. Philip could have said, "Wow, what a coincidence, he is reading a prophetic passage about Jesus, and I am one of his followers. Hey, God bless you, Ethiopian eunuch." But he didn't. Philip was an evangelist. He recognized this moment for the divine appointment that it was. He ran up and asked the question, *Do you understand what you are reading?*

How easy it will be to miss such divine appointments if we are not looking and listening for them! I believe that I have missed several opportunities that God provided simply because I was not listening. I wasn't attentive to what God wanted to do around me. He has not used those missed appointments to create guilt, but I was convicted to listen better and obey more quickly.

Philip not only modeled how to recognize an opportunity, but he also demonstrated skill in sharing the Gospel.

Communicating the good news

Then Philip began with that very passage of Scripture and told him the good news about Jesus.

Acts 8:35

Philip knew the story of Jesus and his kingdom. He knew what it could mean to all sorts of people, including an Ethiopian government official (a politician!). Philip knew the Scriptures, and modeled what I think was a developed skill in sharing the good news of Jesus' kingdom.

You see, Philip wasn't just available and willing, he was also prepared. He didn't know when or who God was going to lead him to, but he was prepared to cooperate in whatever situation. In Philip's story we've discovered the beauty of spontaneity mixed with preparedness.

Philip Goes Flying

Now, the end of the story:

> **As they traveled along the road, they came to some water and the eunuch said, "Look, here is water. Why shouldn't I be baptized?" And he gave orders to stop the chariot. Then both Philip and the eunuch went down into the water and Philip baptized him. When they came up out of the water, the Spirit of the Lord suddenly took Philip away, and the eunuch did not see him again, but went on his way rejoicing. Philip, however, appeared at Azotus and traveled about, preaching the gospel in all the towns until he reached Caesarea.**
>
> *Acts 8:36-40*

Our Father wants to use you and me as part of his redemptive work, part of advancing his kingdom.

Finally, not only did Philip go for a walk and a run, but he got to go flying! Apparently, the Spirit was so pleased with Philip's availability, recognition of the opportunity and sharing of the gospel, that he became the first teleporting evangelist. Can you imagine the Ethiopian coming up from his baptism, about to give a heartfelt thank you, when suddenly, there he was standing in the water all by himself?

My guess is that the Spirit had another assignment for Philip and didn't want to waste time having him walk everywhere. Do you think the Father has labeled Philip as someone who "got it"—as someone who knew God was at work in the world looking for people to cooperate with him? Did God fondly call Philip a "listener," someone who wouldn't miss the opportunities he had in mind? These may be the characteristics that go along with being labeled an evangelist.

With all this divine direction, somewhere along the line, Philip must have learned to listen and obey. What I think is so neat about Philip is that, in the midst of all this special guidance, we never find a hint of questioning or hesitation. There doesn't seem to be one iota of doubt on Philip's part.

Eddie Doesn't Go Swimming

Even though I have probably missed a lot of divine appointments, I have kept trying to become a better listener. Here is one story from an occasion when I think I got it right. A friend of mine, David, and I were working on discipleship in a Taco Bell (you can tell I am a little bit of a health nut). While we were praying, a Taco Bell employee who was mopping the floor near us asked, "Hey, would you pray for me?" David and I looked up and saw Eddie, a middle-aged Hispanic man with a very sad face. We responded, "Sure, how can we pray for you?" Eddie replied, "I can't talk now because I am working, but just pray because I am always very sad. I really need your prayers, so please just pray for me." And then, he kept on mopping. We told Eddie that we would pray for him right then and we did.

As I was praying for Eddie again afterwards, I had the urge to go back that evening and talk with him some more. It was a *sense*—an urgency in my spirit that compelled me to go. So I returned later and found Eddie taking out the garbage. I told him that I felt led by God to talk with him some more. Eddie said that he would get off in just a few minutes.

When Eddie got off work, he took me to his car. "I want to show something to you, Eric," he said. He popped his hatch and showed me a swimsuit and towel. Explaining, he said, "All day I have been trying to work up the courage to drive to the beach and keep swimming into the ocean until I couldn't swim anymore." Sensing the boldness of the Spirit, I said, "Eddie, God sent me to you today so you wouldn't take your life tonight." And that night Eddie asked Jesus into his life.

It was a *sense*—an urgency in my spirit that compelled me to go.

Ⓡ Reflection—Becoming a Listener Like Philip

Philip's story is a powerful demonstration of listening, obeying and sharing the Gospel. Here are some things that we can do as we seek to become more like Philip.

Pray
Pray for divine direction, for divine appointments. Let God know you are willing and available to be used by him.

Question
Next time you enter the grocery store, a coffee shop, or Taco Bell, ask the question, "Father, how are you at work in this place?"

Listen and Obey
Listen to those around you, but also listen to the Holy Spirit. Commit to stepping into the opportunities that God will bring.

Day 40 | An Inspired Cup of Cold Water

Choose seven who are full of the Spirit and wisdom

There is a simple but beautiful awakening taking place in the North American church today. It is a refreshing emphasis on being the hands and feet of Jesus in very practical ways, both to fellow Christians and to the general community. The focus is on service, on meeting the felt needs of people. Usually this is a physical need of some sort—either due to a traumatic event or ongoing difficult circumstances. This awakening is a wide, eclectic movement, including everything from mending and painting homes in depressed areas, to giving a cup of cold water to vacationers and beachcombers.

The focus is on service, on meeting the felt needs of people.

Movie Buff Moment

This emphasis on meeting felt needs within and without the Christian community has often been called "Random Acts of Kindness." In the movie *Evan Almighty*, the director put a little twist in that phrase. The movie is a humorous, modern retelling of Noah and the ark (with ample editorial license!). This time the main character is Evan, and he is called by God to build an ark. The intent is not to restart the world but to save a neighborhood.

There is a scene where God (played by Morgan Freeman) talks to Evan (played by Steve Carell) and explains the value of acts of kindness. Morgan Freeman takes the word "ark" and makes it into an acronym: **A**cts of **R**andom **K**indness. Pretty clever. Churches were encouraged to lead and participate in this national movement of doing **A**cts of **R**andom **K**indness in their neighborhoods.

Even though I thought this was a great idea, our church didn't carry through on it. Why not? Well, we had already done a test run of Random Acts of Kindness, and there was little interest by our congregation. We had hoped it would become a grass roots movement, but it turned out to have no roots. I talked with another pastor and he too had been disappointed by similar results. In fact, I've heard of a number of churches that have launched different forms of a Random Acts of Kindness campaign, but had less than desired results.

Of course, there are numerous reasons for things not going well for churches. The mistake for many could be going with only a cup of cold water, and not remembering the need to be led and empowered by the Holy Spirit. Have we launched out with this new idea with very little listening prayer? Have we followed only our own inspirations rather than seeking divine inspiration? We might have assumed that meeting physical needs was a straightforward enough purpose and thought we could take the lead on it. After all, we don't need to spiritualize *everything*, right?

Waiting on Tables "in the Spirit"?

In the book of Acts we see an early church experiencing rapid growth. Because the Holy Spirit empowered their ministry, their numbers were multiplied daily. Such rapid growth brought some difficulties. One of the issues was the need for pastoral care, especially related to widows. Back in ancient times most widows were unable to support themselves, so the communities of faith needed to help them. Acts 6 describes the issue:

> One of the issues was the need for pastoral care… so the communities of faith needed to help.

> **In those days when the number of disciples was increasing, the Grecian Jews among them complained against the Hebraic Jews because their widows were being overlooked in the daily distribution of food. So the Twelve gathered all the disciples together and said, "It would not be right for us to neglect the ministry of the word of God in order to wait on tables."**
>
> *Acts 6:1–2*

Before we read further, let's notice a couple of things. At this early point in the church's history, its membership is made up of Jews alone. But there were two groups of Jews. One group was referred to as Grecian Jews, those probably born and raised outside of Israel. Speaking primarily Greek, they had more of a Grecian outlook and perspective. The other group consisted of Hebraic Jews, who primarily spoke Hebrew or Aramaic and were most likely born and/or raised in the Holy Land. There were complaints of inequity regarding the distributions of food and charitable gifts (acts of kindness).

The Twelve referred to are the original twelve apostles (actually eleven plus one, see Acts 1:12–26) appointed by Jesus to lead the church. At this early stage of the life of the church, the Twelve were responsible for every aspect of the church life, not just the ministry of the Word and prayer. At first glance, the remark by the apostles *to wait on tables* seems to devalue the ministry of distribution of charitable gifts and service. Maybe the Twelve were exhausted from all the work and responsibility of leadership. Or perhaps they didn't take criticism very well, but I really don't think either was true.

If we dig a little deeper into the story, we see the apostles actually honoring this ministry of service and, at the same time, making a wise and strategic leadership decision. To me their comment seems based on a perspective of gifts and calling.

They make the point that they had been specifically called and gifted for an apostolic ministry of preaching the Word and prayer. They were seeking to stay focused on their role in the Kingdom of God and the use of their God-given gifts. This makes sense from a leadership position.

What is important about this story are the qualifications the apostles set out for the church to use when choosing others to lead this practical ministry of food distribution. Read the rest of the story.

> **"Brothers, choose seven men from among you who are known to be *full of the Spirit and wisdom.* We will turn this responsibility over to them and will give our attention to prayer and the ministry of the word." This proposal pleased the whole group. They chose Stephen, a man *full of faith and of the Holy Spirit*; also Philip, Procorus, Nicanor, Timon, Parmenas and Nicolas from Antioch, a convert to Judaism. They presented these men to the apostles, who prayed and laid their hands on them. So the word of God spread. The number of disciples in Jerusalem increased rapidly, and a large number of priests became obedient to the faith.** (emphasis added)
>
> *Acts 6:3–7*

Instead of demeaning the ministries of service and meeting of material needs, the apostles honored them.

Why was the whole group pleased with the apostles' decisions and comments? Their wisdom came from a leadership perspective as well as from a desire to put empowered and gifted leaders over this important ministry. They didn't say —

Would you stop your griping and just grab some folks that are behind-the-scenes, service-type folks to do the menial work of meeting physical needs?

No, they wanted disciples appropriately gifted by the Holy Spirit to execute this ministry—men led and empowered by him and characterized by the gifts of wisdom and faith.

Instead of demeaning the ministries of service and meeting of material needs, the apostles honored them. Do we honor these ministries in our churches? Do we look for the same kind of people to lead them? When we seek to help our communities, do we serve as men and women *full of the Spirit and of wisdom*, and *full of faith and of the Holy Spirit*?

The early church didn't just want quality leaders to provide cups of cold water to the poor; their desire was to have gifted leaders provide inspired cups of cold water. I believe that this is the desire of the Father's heart as well. Listen to how he blesses the early church with this kind of empowered ministry of service.

> **So the word of God spread. The number of disciples in Jerusalem increased rapidly, and a large number of priests became obedient to the faith.**
>
> *Acts 6:7*

An Empowered Waiter?

Out of the seven folks identified for this important ministry, you probably recognized Philip. Yes, this was the Philip we read about in Day 39. But another man that is prominent in this list of seven was Stephen. Mentioned first, Stephen was no ordinary servant, or waiter of tables.

It seems as though Stephen didn't simply figure out equitable food distributions and hand out cups of cold water. No, Stephen was described as a man with Holy Spirit power. If I had been a widow in need of material goods—or spiritual counsel, for that matter—Stephen would be the guy I would want to call upon.

In Acts, Luke tells the story of Stephen's stoning in chapter seven. He was the first martyr of the church (except for our Lord Jesus Christ). Luke described the kind of ministry Stephen had in chapter six.

The bigger question is, will we let his Spirit lead and empower us when using the towel and basin?

> **Now Stephen, a man full of God's grace and power, did great wonders and miraculous signs among the people...men began to argue with Stephen, but they could not stand up against his wisdom or the Spirit by whom he spoke.**
>
> *Acts 6:8, 9b–10*

We see a characteristic here of the early church's ministry and outreach. It was plugged in. The early church drew directly on the power source of the Holy Spirit. It was a church in mission, a church listening to and speaking on behalf of the Holy Spirit of God. It was a church that demonstrated the presence and power of the kingdom. As a result, people were saved—made whole physically, spiritually and emotionally. Even Stephen, this ordinary man whose calling and position was *to wait on tables*, operated in the power of the Spirit. And God used him in mighty ways.

(I have sometimes wondered if one of the *miraculous signs among the people* was multiplying fish and loaves of bread for the widows. Or was it turning an ordinary cup of cold water into the sweetest tasting of wines?)

The crucial point is that these people were empowered for mission. Whether it was preaching the word and prayer, or waiting on tables, they lived and ministered in the power and presence of the Holy Spirit—just like Jesus promised they would. After all, remember his explanation about why he left? Holy Spirit would come and they would do the things Jesus did, even greater things! The Impossible Promise!

I believe the Father is stirring in his North American church today to become more responsive to the felt needs and the material needs of the people around us. The question isn't just whether we will pick up the towel and basin in service. The bigger question is, will we let his Spirit lead and empower us when using the towel and basin? He doesn't want us to just hand out a cup of cold water; he wants us to hand out an inspired cup of cold water, a divinely directed cup that touches the soul as well as the body.

Display the Fruit of the Spirit

Ⓡ **Reflection** Meditate on the following Scripture passages. As you do, please think of them in terms of outreach and mission. Think about the kind of impact you would have if you started displaying this kind of fruit, not just to your Christian friends and family, but also to those who don't yet know Jesus Christ.

> **Therefore, as God's chosen people, holy and dearly loved, clothe yourselves with compassion, kindness, humility, gentleness and patience.**
>
> *Colossians 3:12*

> **For this very reason, make every effort to add to your faith goodness; and to goodness, knowledge; and to knowledge, self-control; and to self-control, perseverance; and to perseverance, godliness; and to godliness, brotherly kindness; and to brotherly kindness, love. For if you possess these qualities in increasing measure, they will keep you from being ineffective and unproductive in your knowledge of our Lord Jesus Christ. But if anyone does not have them, he is nearsighted and blind, and has forgotten that he has been cleansed from his past sins.**
>
> *2 Peter 1:5–9*

Think about the kind of impact you would have if you started displaying this kind of fruit, not just to your Christian friends and family, but also to those who don't yet know Jesus Christ.

Note: At your next small group gathering, you will not only study Scripture and pray, you will also go out in the community. Please plan and dress appropriately.

Days 41 & 42 Listen and Act

They tried to enter. . .but the Spirit of Jesus would not allow them to

NOTE: Your small group facilitator will have already prepared a service project for you with an evangelistic emphasis. Days 41-42 are designed as preparation for your service project.

Have you ever wondered how Paul and his companions decided where and when to go on his numerous mission trips?

We have talked about the need for a kingdom emphasis in our evangelistic messages and also about the need for the empowering presence of the Holy Spirit in our daily lives. We have seen this in the early church, and now we will seek to put this dual emphasis into practice. As preparation, let's do a short Bible study about direction and guidance.

In Acts 16 we read Paul's story about his second mission trip. Have you ever wondered how Paul and his companions decided where and when to go on his numerous mission trips? We catch a glimpse of Paul's strategic listening from this chapter in Acts. As you read the following story, keep the issue of discernment and direction in mind.

> **Paul and his companions traveled throughout the region of Phrygia and Galatia, having been kept by the Holy Spirit from preaching the word in the province of Asia. When they came to the border of Mysia, they tried to enter Bithynia, but the Spirit of Jesus would not allow them to. So they passed by Mysia and went down to Troas. During the night Paul had a vision of a man of Macedonia standing and begging him, "Come over to Macedonia and help us." After Paul had seen the vision, we got ready at once to leave for Macedonia, concluding that God had called us to preach the gospel to them.**
>
> *Acts 16:6–10*

Luke didn't stop to define for us just what he meant when he wrote that they were *...kept by the Holy Spirit from preaching…in…Asia*, or that *...the Spirit of Jesus would not allow them to.*

1. **How do you think Paul and his companions might have experienced this kind of direction or "closed door"?**

2. **How would you describe what their decision-making process might have looked like?**

3. **If you were on a mission trip and a member of your team received a vision of a man pleading for you to go to a nearby city, do you think it would register on your radar screen as divine direction? Why or why not?**

Ministry Time—Strategic Listening

What we would like to do now is simply practice some strategic listening prior to our planned service project or evangelistic outreach. As you participate in the exercise of strategic listening, try not to over-think or analyze what you are doing. Just try to keep listening and ask for wisdom and discernment. Remember, like all spiritual disciplines, this is a learning process, something to grow into. This is not an exact science; it is a process of growth through trial and error. Please follow these steps.

...like all spiritual disciplines, this is a learning process, something to grow into.

Listening Prayer Steps

Opening Prayer
The facilitator prays to bind any lies of the enemy or thoughts that obviously don't come from the Holy Spirit.

Listening as Individuals
The group listens as individuals for three minutes. Remember, you are listening in preparation for the service project or evangelistic outreach that you are about to participate in. Listen for: descriptions of people, felt needs of people, an adjustment to the proposed project, and direction for prayer and preparation. Please take the time to write down anything you think you heard or saw.

Comparing Lists
Gather as a group to compare your lists and look especially for similarities. As a whole group offer these leadings to God in prayer. Ask for the filling and direction of the Holy Spirit.

Launching Out
As a group, head to the service project or evangelistic outreach with these leadings in mind. Launch out and seek to minister in the guidance and power of the Spirit. Remember, the Holy Spirit might have a completely different agenda for your team than what you thought. In other words, "the thing might not be the thing."

Sharing Stories
During your small group time, be sure to process your experience. What did you learn about strategic listening? How might you incorporate this in other areas of your life?

Week Seven | The "Not Yet" Kingdom

After that, we who are still alive and are left will be caught up together with them in the clouds to meet the Lord in the air. And so we will be with the Lord forever.

1 Thessalonians 4:17

Day 43 The Return of the King

Behold, I am coming soon

Jesus talks about this time in the future as the renewal of all things.

Wow! We have come a long way, so don't give up now. There is a huge component of the Kingdom of God that we haven't talked much about yet. In fact, the majority of this book shows how the kingdom spills into our present, the *already* aspects of the kingdom. However, much of Scripture talks about the *not yet* features of the kingdom—the things that are yet to come, the last things.

In some circles of the church, there is much discussion about *end times* and the study of the last things. You can find a lot of charts and diagrams and *end times* scenarios. All of those things have their place, but I want to emphasize a different aspect as we talk about the *not yet* kingdom.

What Kind of People Ought You to Be?

In both the Old and New Testaments, passages about end times and the *Day of the Lord* refer to when God will transform the world and our existence as we know it. The Apostle Peter spoke of these things when he wrote,

> **But the day of the Lord will come like a thief. The heavens will disappear with a roar; the elements will be destroyed by fire, and the earth and everything in it will be laid bare. Since everything will be destroyed in this way, what kind of people ought you to be?**
>
> *2 Peter 3:10–11a*

What the apostle is talking about is the climactic end of this world or the end of the world as we know it. Jesus talks about this time in the future as the renewal of all things. There is much information in the New Testament about end times. Yet, we should note that the New Testament authors didn't stress predictions, charts and timing, but rather how we should live today in light of what God has revealed about the future. This was the primary scriptural emphasis in terms of future things. Or, as Peter asked, *what kind of people ought you to be?*

Of course, it is hard to change our lives today when we don't know what Scripture teaches about the future. We need to humbly reflect on what God has revealed about the future coming of the kingdom, as well as acknowledge what he has *not* revealed. We must continue to ask the question, "In light of the future God has revealed, how should I live today?"

The Return of the King

In considering all this, let's start with the future event that towers over all New Testament teaching on future things, the event that is talked about more than any other—the return of the King.

In his first coming, Emmanuel came humbly; he came emptying himself; he came to live and die at the hands of a cruel and sinful world. In his second coming, Jesus will come in power and glory. He will return as the King of all—reigning over all peoples, all nations, for all eternity.

In light of the future God has revealed, how should I live today?

In his first coming Jesus Christ inaugurated the Kingdom of Heaven on Earth. In his second coming he will bring the kingdom in all its wholeness—completed and fully consummated.

The return of the King is what initiates the transition from life as we know it to the eternal life that we will know forever. When the kingdom is consummated, Jesus will completely dispel all of the darkness of this world and will bring the new age, our new reality.

Throughout their writings, the apostles point us to this climactic event. Paul said,

> **May he strengthen your hearts so that you will be blameless and holy in the presence of our God and Father when our Lord Jesus comes with all his holy ones.**
>
> *1 Thessalonians 3:13*

The apostles took their cue from Jesus who spoke repeatedly about his return. At some points he spoke plainly about this event,

> **"At that time they will see the Son of Man coming in a cloud with power and great glory. When these things begin to take place, stand up and lift up your heads, because your redemption is drawing near."**
>
> *Luke 21:27–28*

Jesus also said,

> **"At that time the sign of the Son of Man will appear in the sky, and all the nations of the earth will mourn. They will see the Son of Man coming on the clouds of the sky, with power and great glory."**
>
> *Matthew 24:30*

"He Goes Away" Parables

Jesus not only spoke directly about his return, he spoke indirectly through many parables. These stories point out various aspects of the *not yet* kingdom. I call these the "He Goes Away" parables because someone is always going away and then coming back.

Think of the parable of the **Talents (Matthew 25:14–30)**: A man goes away on a journey and entrusts his money (*talents*) to his workers until he returns. The emphasis is on what happens when the man returns and takes an account of what the servants have done with what he gave them.

Look at the parable of the **Ten Virgins (Matthew 25:1–13)**: Why do the virgins need their lamps and oil? Because they must wait for the bridegroom to come. The point is that you need enough *oil* in your *lamp* to wait it out.

Consider the parable of the **Tenants (Matthew 21:33–46)**: A landowner plants a vineyard and rents it out to some farmers, and then the landowner goes away on a journey. What happens at the end? At harvest time the landowner sends back his servants to collect his share of the fruit because he expects the tenants to have kept their rental agreement.

In these parables Jesus not only pointed to his return, but urged us to live faithfully in the *in-between time*, in-between his first and second coming.

Just before Luke's version of the parable of the *Talents* (Luke 19:12–27) we read,

> **"While they were listening to this, he went on to tell them a parable, because he was near Jerusalem and the people thought that the kingdom of God was going to appear at once."**
>
> *Luke 19:11*

These are all really end times parables, aren't they? They teach us that we need to live today as faithful stewards, as people watchful and prepared, as people who are producing kingdom fruit.

In these parables Jesus not only pointed to his return, but urged us to live faithfully in the *in-between time*, in-between his first and second coming. He wanted us to be ready for this day because it will have huge ramifications for our eternal future. It is on this day that the King will return with a great and awesome purpose—judgment!

Jesus the King, Jesus the Judge

The Apostles' Creed is an ancient summation of our faith. In it we declare: "...He ascended into heaven, and is seated at the right hand of God the Father Almighty; and he will come to judge the living and the dead...."

Movie Buff Moment

You might have seen the movie *A Knight's Tale* with the late Heath Ledger. There are some repeated sentences in this movie that are taken right from Scripture.

Heath Ledger's character is caught lying about his status as a knight and lands in jail. His adversary comes in and roughs him up, saying, "You have been weighed, you have been measured, and you have been found wanting."

Do you recognize these words from anywhere? They are from the book of Daniel, chapter 5, where a disembodied hand appears and writes a judgment against King Belshazzar on the wall. Daniel interpreted one of the words that was written, *Tekel,* to mean, *You have been weighed on the scales and found wanting.* (Daniel 5:27) In this instance, the king's judgment happened before his death. He was weighed, measured, judged and found wanting. That very night he was slain.

This is a picture of what each and every one of us will face at some point in our future. When Christ returns to judge the living and the dead, we will face judgment.

Christ's judgment of mankind begins the transition between this life and the next. This is a tremendously frightful reality for some, but only for those who are unprepared. Again, the biblical emphasis is on preparation. The Apostle John says,

> **...Continue in him, so that when he appears we may be confident and unashamed before him at his coming.**
>
> *1 John 2:28*

What we do today—our actions and attitudes—will matter when we stand before the King.

How we live today will have a profound effect on how that process goes for us. What we do today—our actions and attitudes—will matter when we stand before the King.

Many Christians have a disastrous and fundamental misunderstanding about Christ's return and judgment. We have this sense that if our ticket is punched with Jesus' name on it, then we are good to go. But think back to the end times parables. Jesus doesn't encourage us to be fruitful and productive and then say, "but it really doesn't matter how you live as long as you asked me to be your Lord and Savior." There is no such caveat in Scripture, but many of us Christians live like there is.

There is a tension that we miss. *If you declare with your mouth, "Jesus is Lord," and believe in your heart that God raised him from the dead, you will be saved* (Romans 10:9)—yes, of course. But at the same time the testimony of Scripture is that we will be judged based upon what we have and have not done. Our actions today matter on that Day of Judgment.

And the Books Were Opened

Revelation 20:11–15 describes the amazing scene when all are judged.[18] Pay particular attention to the number of books that are involved in this experience:

> **Then I saw a great white throne and him who was seated on it. Earth and sky fled from his presence, and there was no place for them. And I saw the dead, great and small, standing before the throne, and *books* were opened. Another *book* was opened, which is the *book* of life. The dead were judged according to what they**

18. I realize that many argue that this judgment is limited to those who are not in Christ. However, I do not believe that the text supports this position. But even if you maintain this position, you must still recognize that the primary teaching of the Old and New Testaments are that all will be judged and that our deeds will matter in that judgment.

> **had done as recorded in the *books.* The sea gave up the dead that were in it, and death and Hades gave up the dead that were in them, and each person was judged according to what he had done. Then death and Hades were thrown into the lake of fire. The lake of fire is the second death. If anyone's name was not found written in the *book* of life, he was thrown into the lake of fire.** (emphasis added)
>
> *Revelation 20:11–15*

All right, now a question: Will there be more than one book involved in our judgment? Yes. We know that at least one book is called the Book of Life. This is the *Lamb's book of life.* (Revelation 21:27) It is a register of all the citizens in the kingdom. It is the list of invited and welcomed guests to the wedding banquet in heaven. If your name is in this book, then you are welcomed into the kingdom community.

You may be familiar with this book. But notice that it is not the *only* book present in this picture. There are other books, and it is intriguing to wrestle with their role and purpose in judgment.

The other books are opened, and their significance is repeated twice:

> **...The dead were judged according to what they had done as recorded in the books...and each person was judged according to what they had done.**
>
> *Revelation 20:12, 13*

For this reason, many refer to these books as the Book of Deeds. This implies that there are two books involved in our judgment: The Book of Life and the Book of Deeds.

This idea that our *deeds* or *works* affect how we are judged makes many Christians uncomfortable.

This idea that our *deeds* or *works* affect how we are judged makes many Christians uncomfortable. But this isn't just one random passage in Scripture. The concept of deeds being involved in our judgment is found in a number of places throughout Scripture. Reflect on the following passages:

> **...Surely you [the Lord] will reward each person according to what he has done.**
>
> *Psalm 62:12*

The Apostle Paul quoted this Psalm in Romans 2:6 and then added,

> **To those who by persistence in doing good seek glory, honor and immortality, he will give eternal life.**
>
> *Romans 2:7*

Jeremiah prophesied:

> **"I the Lord search the heart and examine the mind, to reward a man according to his conduct, according to what his deeds deserve."**
>
> *Jeremiah 17:10*

The Apostle Peter noted this teaching as a matter of common knowledge and understanding among believers.

> **Since you call on a Father who judges each man's work impartially, live your lives as strangers here in reverent fear.**
>
> *1 Peter 1:17*

It may have been a commonly held view among the early church, but somehow we have lost it.

Although this is certainly an Old Testament concept, notice how it is affirmed in the New Testament. The covering of Christ does not exempt us from this judgment that involves what we do and do not do.

Keith Green was a tremendous Christian musician and singer in the 1970's and 80's. I still remember hearing his famous rendition of the parable of The Sheep and the Goats. He sings through the parable in his passionate and creative style and at the end he says to the audience, "The only difference between the sheep and the goats, according to this Scripture, is what they did, and didn't do." When I heard that, it grabbed me. It was the first indication that I didn't have a fully developed understanding of the judgment I would face.

"The only difference between the sheep and the goats, according to this Scripture, is what they did, and didn't do."

There is a challenge, of course, about how to maintain the balance between our deeds and our salvation by grace through faith. But I want you to feel the full impact of this idea. Try and put yourself in this future event.

Imagination Station

Use your imagination to visualize that you are standing in the midst of a great multitude of people. You are all gathered and are standing before a great white throne. As you are looking at this picture, you suddenly hear a loud voice call out your name.

You are escorted forward and left to stand by yourself before the throne, and two majestic books are brought forward. One is opened and, in front of everyone, all your deeds are revealed. Not only are your deeds revealed—but every careless word!

> **"But I tell you that men will have to give account on the day of judgment for every careless word they have spoken."**
>
> *Matthew 12:36*

It doesn't stop there. Also revealed in that book are the motives of your heart and the thoughts of your mind.

> **"...He will bring to light what is hidden in darkness and will expose the motives of men's hearts. At that time each will receive his praise from God."**
>
> *1 Corinthians 4:5*

Then, the second book—the Book of Life—is opened. Perhaps it's in alphabetical order, and they begin to skim through the pages looking for your name. *Are you sweating yet?*

Are you ready? Ready not just for the second book, the *Book of Life,* but also for the first, the *Book of Deeds*? Are you living today in light of what your future holds? Too many of us have failed to realize the existence of more than one book. How do you need to change in light of your impending judgment?

Ministry Time

"Dear Father, I do not want to fear this climactic day as the world should, with trembling and dread. But my desire is to live in godly fear, in awe and reverence of you. My desire is that on that Day of Judgment, after my life is revealed, that I would hear the words, '*. . . Well done, good and faithful servant. . . Come, you who are blessed by my father; take your inheritance, the kingdom prepared for you since the creation of the world.*' (Matthew 25:21, 23, 34)

"And Lord, I also want to share in the prophet Habakkuk's prayer, 'LORD, I have heard of your fame; I stand in awe of your deeds, O LORD. Renew them in our day, in our time make them known; in wrath remember mercy.' (Habakkuk 3:2)"

Are you living today in light of what your future holds?

Day 44 So, What Happens Now?

Jesus, remember me when you come into your kingdom

Death can certainly be an incredibly frightening event for us. At one point or another, most people struggle with feelings about the inevitability and finality of death. When someone dies, we who are left behind mourn because of our loss, because of the absence of our loved one, and because of the changes that death brings.

When someone dies, we who are left behind mourn because of our loss, because of the absence of our loved one, and because of the changes that death brings.

For those and other reasons, many people have a great fear of death. Part of that fear comes from the unknown, the mystery that surrounds death.

A little while ago, the son of some dear members of our community of faith passed away. I arrived at the home and found the mother tenderly kissing and hugging her beloved son that she had lost. We prayed together, and there were many members of their small group seeking to extend comfort and empathy. After the prayer, one member of the small group interjected, "Pastor Eric, she (the mother) has an important question for you." And so the mother rose up from the body of her son and asked, "So what happens now… I mean, I know that this body is not my son." Certainly this was a thoughtful question at a sensitive time.

What do we believe then about the end times? What happens when we die? We have important questions about the afterlife, about heaven and hell, about eternity. Since these are questions regarding things yet to come, and because of the mystery of the future, there is a lot of confusion and concern. Even the great Apostle Paul quotes Isaiah in 1 Corinthians 2:9, saying, *"…No eye has seen, no ear has heard, no mind has conceived what God has prepared for those who love him."* Then Paul goes on to say,

> **"…but God has revealed it to us by his Spirit." The Spirit searches all things, even the deep things of God.**
>
> *1 Corinthians 2:10*

So, in spite of these deep and puzzling questions about life and death, we as Christians can humbly learn and understand what God has chosen to reveal by his Spirit.

Although we do have this revelation, there seems to be tremendous ignorance and confusion within the Christian church. One way to clear up some of the confusion is to set aside the charts, diagrams, and predictions for a moment. If we focus on the foundational events of the end time revelation, we can dispel some of the ignorance, as well as build anticipation for Christ's return. Our goal is not predictions or calculations, but life change.

The way the New Testament talks about the end times motivates us to use our knowledge about the future to affect how we live in the present. The study of end times is not simply about gaining knowledge and taking positions (amillenial, postmillenial, premillenial, realized, etc.), but is especially about comfort, clarity and righteousness.

So, how *does* the Kingdom of God come in fullness? What are the primary events that will take place that God has revealed to us?

The way the New Testament talks about the end times motivates us to use our knowledge about the future to affect how we live in the present.

Don't Want You to Be Ignorant

In his first letter to the Thessalonians, Paul addresses numerous issues within the Thessalonian church. One of these issues is what happens in the end.

Apparently, the Christians there were concerned that those who died prior to the return of King Jesus would miss out. They had questions about what happens. Paul encourages them with these words:

> **Brothers, we do not want you to be ignorant about those who fall asleep, or to grieve like the rest of men, who have no hope. We believe that Jesus died and rose again and so we believe that God will bring with Jesus those who have fallen asleep in him. According to the Lord's own word, we tell you that we who are still alive, who are left till the coming of the Lord, will certainly not precede those who have fallen asleep. For the Lord himself will come down from heaven, with a loud command, with the voice of the archangel and with the trumpet call of God, and the dead in Christ will rise first. After that, we who are still alive and are left will be caught up together with them in the clouds to meet the Lord in the air. And so we will be with the Lord forever. Therefore encourage each other with these words.**
>
> **Now, brothers, about times and dates we do not need to write to you, for you know very well that the day of the Lord will come like a thief in the night.**
>
> *1 Thessalonians 4:13–5:2*

Paul reminds them of the basic facts he had already taught about what will take place, e.g., Jesus died and rose again (resurrection) and Jesus is coming back (second coming). Paul gives a very general flow of main events. But notice in this passage that Paul says, Jesus will not come back alone.

He Comes Again, but Not Alone

Clearly, Paul is communicating that those who have gone before us will return with Christ on that great and awesome day.

Randy Alcorn recently published an excellent and thorough book simply titled *Heaven,* and explains: "When we die, believers in Christ will not go to the heaven where we'll live forever. Instead, we'll go to an intermediate heaven. In that heaven—where those who died covered by Christ's blood are now—we'll await the time of Christ's return to the Earth, our bodily resurrection, the final judgment, and the creation of the New Heavens and New Earth. If we fail to grasp this truth, we will fail to understand the biblical doctrine of Heaven." (p. 42)

It is important to note that Alcorn, from a biblical perspective, is distinguishing between what we can call the "eternal heaven" (the heaven that will be) and that of the "intermediate" or present heaven (the heaven that is now). The intermediate heaven is where our loved ones are now (who are dead in Christ) and it is from there that they will return with Christ at his second coming.

"When we die, believers in Christ will not go to the heaven where we'll live forever."

Think about what Paul said:

> **I am torn between the two: I desire to depart and be with Christ, which is better by far; but it is more necessary for you that I remain in the body.**
>
> *Philippians 1:23-24*

Paul understood clearly that when he died, he (and others in Christ) would be immediately with Christ, and then accompany him upon his return.

Think of the thief on the cross. He said, *"Jesus, remember me when you come into your kingdom."* Jesus answered him, *"I tell you the truth, today you will be with me in paradise."* (Luke 23:42–43) The thief would be with Christ in paradise until they returned to the Earth at Jesus' second coming.

To the grieving mother who had questions about her son, I could communicate with confidence that her son was with King Jesus now, in his presence. However, he was in the intermediate heaven. Though his present body was not "her son" so to speak, he would one day come to reclaim his new body.

Coming Down and Rising Up

Now I want to call your attention to an interesting dynamic about this Thessalonians passage. I would call it a direction question.

We learned in the 1Thessalonians 4:13–5:2 passage that when Christ comes from heaven down to Earth he is not alone, but those who have fallen asleep in Christ (living now in his presence in the intermediate heaven) come with him from heaven. They *come down* from heaven. Then Paul says in verse 16 that the dead in Christ will *rise* first. So which is it? Do the dead in Christ come down or do they rise up?

This is pointing us to another important truth. In our intermediate state, the physical body has died, but that is not the end of life. As Christians, we believe that we are with the Lord in a *soul* or *spirit* existence; the New Testament uses both terms. Anthony Hoekema talks of this existence as "… provisional, temporary, and incomplete. Because man is not totally man apart from the body." (*The Bible and the Future,* p. 95)

Those who are with Christ in spirit in the intermediate heaven will come down with Christ, then their bodies are gathered up and experience resurrection. At that point, we who are still alive will experience a similar transformation or glorification. Or, as Paul says, we will be *caught up* with Christ as we experience this transformation.

Getting Caught Up and Changed

> **Listen, I tell you a mystery: We will not all sleep, but we will all be changed—in a flash, in the twinkling of an eye, at the last trumpet. For the trumpet will sound, the dead will be raised imperishable, and we will be changed.**
>
> *1 Corinthians 15:51–52*

To the grieving mother… I could communicate… that her son was with King Jesus now….

Here is what we can't miss: When Scripture talks about resurrection or this *change*, it is saying that we reclaim our physicality. Our promised eternal life is not in a non-physical *spirit* or *soul* experience. It is in a NEW BODY.

Again, Alcorn helps us with this clarifying word: "Of Americans who believe in a resurrection of the dead, two-thirds believe they will not have bodies after the resurrection. But this is self-contradictory. A non-physical resurrection is like a sunless sunrise. There's no such thing." (*Heaven,* p. 112)

N.T. Wright says it like this: "Resurrection … was a way of talking about a new bodily life *after* whatever state of existence one might enter immediately upon death. It was, in other words, life *after* life after death." (*Surprised by Hope*, p. 151)

What Scripture teaches, and what these scholars point out, is a crucial part of God's revelation. Though vital, many Christians do not understand this teaching and therefore fail to properly anticipate the end times. Let's look again to Paul.

Our *New Body* Promise

> **So will it be with the resurrection of the dead. The body that is sown is perishable, it is raised imperishable; it is sown in dishonor, it is raised in glory; it is sown in weakness, it is raised in power; it is sown a natural body, it is raised a spiritual body.**
>
> *1 Corinthians 15:42–44*

Some have misinterpreted Paul's terminology here. When he contrasts *natural* with *spiritual*, he is not talking about *physical* as opposed to *non-physical.* He is talking about a weak, fragile and *of the earth* body, versus a new, strong, immortal and *of heaven* body.

This teaching really does lead to all sorts of interesting questions about life in heaven. For instance, how similar will our new bodies be to our old ones? What age will we be? Will we experience people at different ages? These are all great questions. Many of them are not answered specifically in Scripture, so we are left with conjecture. We have been given some clues, however.

After one Sunday service, Miles approached me. He was no more than ten or eleven years old. He was always coming up with great questions. "Pastor Eric," he asked, "what are we going to be like in heaven? You know, when we are resurrected." (I think Miles is going to be a pastor someday.)

"Always look to Jesus, Miles," I responded. We should not just look to Christ in the life that he lived in his mortal body, but also to life in his immortal body. The Apostle John said,

> **Dear friends, now we are children of God, and what we will be has not yet been made known. But we know that when he appears, we shall be like him, for we shall see him as he is.**
>
> *1 John 3:2*

...how similar will our new bodies be to our old ones?

In other words, we don't know all the details, but we do know that Christ was resurrected, and he is our model. Do you recall the descriptions of the resurrected Jesus?

He could suddenly disappear, as well as appear. Luke 24:31, 36

He could also eat and digest food and drink. Luke 24:41–42

At one time he said to the disciples,

> **"Look at my hands and my feet. It is I myself! Touch me and see; a ghost does not have flesh and bones, as you see I have."**
>
> *Luke 24:39*

Movie Buff Moment If you are any kind of a fantasy literature fan then you have read the books, or at least seen the movies, *The Lord of the Rings* trilogy. At the end of the first movie, we saw the fellowship of friends lose Gandalf the Grey. He fell from a cliff in front of their eyes and died.

But in the second movie he returned as Gandalf the White. He spoke about his experience of death, "Darkness took me and I strayed out of thought and time ... but it was not the end. I felt life in me again. I have been sent back until my task is done."

I really get excited when movies illustrate biblical concepts or teachings. It seems to me that Tolkien (a strong Catholic) may have modeled Gandalf's return after the resurrection.

In the 1 Thessalonians 4 passage we are left with the picture of those *dead in Christ* coming down and rising up with resurrection bodies. Those *who are still alive* are caught up with him and it seems like we are left hanging out in the air. But I don't think that we will be just floating around from cloud to cloud with our new resurrected bodies.

We know that the main point of the passage is that we get to be with Christ Jesus forever. But the question remains as to where we are with the Lord. We will get to that in Day 45, but before we do, we need to remember the important question we've asked before: *What kind of people ought we to be?*

I realize that this picture of eternal life is different than many of us have understood, so we need to keep meditating upon the Scriptures, upon these ideas. Remember our emphasis is on how we live today in light of what we know about our future. These revelations have several implications that lead us to understand how God is calling us to be a different kind of people.

A People Who Grieve Differently

Paul told us this up front: We are not a people without hope—we believe in the awesome promises that God has revealed to us. After reminding us of the great hope we have in Christ whether *awake or asleep* (1 Thessalonians 5:10), Paul finished with this statement: *Therefore encourage one another and build each other up, just as in fact you are doing.* (v.11)

To the grieving mother… I could communicate… that her son was with King Jesus now….

We need to talk about these things, remind one another of them, and take great courage and comfort from this hope.

I wish I had more clearly understood these things when my own father passed away. I remember the cold winter day when we lingered by the graveside and I saw them lower my father's casket into the cold, hard earth. I watched as they shoveled the dark, dark dirt all over the casket.

I wish I had had a greater conviction and hope that my father's essential self, his soul and spirit were not and are not just dead. He *is* truly with Jesus now, with our heavenly Father. And my dad will come with Jesus when he returns. Even my dad's body—I haven't seen the last of it! I will see him again someday, and we will *both* be changed, renewed, resurrected. Hallelujah! I will live with him in eternity.

This understanding of Scripture has become such a significant part of the hope in which I live now. I want to live my life in the present with this eternal hope in the forefront of my mind.

Ⓡ **Reflection** Do we grieve death as Christians? Of course. We grieve the loss and the change it brings. But we also celebrate. And we don't just celebrate lives that have been well-lived. But we celebrate and claim these incredible revelations and promises. For too long we have celebrated only a portion of God's good news.

Pray this prayer with me: "Lord, keep the hope of this great truth front and center in my life. '*Then will … they see the Son of Man coming on the clouds of the sky, with power and great glory. And he will send his angels with a loud trumpet call, and they will gather his elect from the four winds, from one end of the heavens to the other.*' (Matthew 24:30b–31)"

Day 45 | Seeing the New Heavens and the New Earth

Blessed are the meek, for they will inherit the earth

Have you ever noticed the portrayal of heaven on television and in movie land? It's really just a broad-stroke sketch of a happy place, with clouds and harps and angels. The unfortunate problem is, that even for many mature Christians, the concept of heaven is derived from these vehicles of popular culture, rather than from Scripture itself.

...how similar will our new bodies be to our old ones?

For many of us the Kingdom of Heaven idea is some kind of ethereal or misty existence as spirits. Maybe we get wings like angels? Maybe we don't?

The teaching in Day 44 about a physical resurrection may have been very new to some of us and challenged our preconceived notions of what the promise of resurrection means. Today might be even more shocking for you. We are going to look at a scriptural perspective of God's eternal kingdom, and it doesn't look a whole lot like clouds and harps. I will make a statement that might throw you, but allow yourself some time to unpack it in your mind before rejecting it altogether. Here is the statement:

Heaven is not your final home!

Well, at least not the heaven that we normally think about—an ethereal, non-physical place, a somewhere-off-in-space heaven. This off-in-space heaven is *not* where we will live for eternity.

Before you think that I've completely lost it, ponder Revelation 21:1-7:

> **Then I saw a new heaven and a new earth, for the first heaven and the first earth had passed away, and there was no longer any sea. I saw the Holy City, the new Jerusalem, coming down out of heaven from God, prepared as a bride beautifully dressed for her husband. And I heard a loud voice from the throne saying, "Now the dwelling of God is with men, and he will live with them. They will be his people, and God himself will be with them and be their God. He will wipe every tear from their eyes.**

There will be no more death or mourning or crying or pain, for the old order of things has passed away."

He who was seated on the throne said, "I am making everything new!" Then he said, "Write this down, for these words are trustworthy and true."

He said to me: "It is done. I am the Alpha and the Omega, the Beginning and the End. To him who is thirsty I will give to drink without cost from the spring of the water of life. He who overcomes will inherit all this, and I will be his God and he will be my son…."

This is the biblical depiction of our final home, our promised inheritance—the consummated Kingdom of God.

Kingdom Questions As you consider these verses, keep this question before you, "What does this picture say about my life in eternity?" Let's investigate.

Since God comes down to dwell on Earth, we have a merging of heaven and Earth.

Question 1. **Where are *we* in this picture? Are we in heaven?**

Answer: No, we are not in heaven but on Earth. The New Jerusalem (the Holy City) comes down from heaven to Earth, to be the center of our lives in eternity.

Question 2. **Where is *God* in this picture?**

Answer: He is living with us on this New Earth.

How incredible is that? This is an amazing picture of intimacy with God restored. It certainly has elements of the Garden of Eden. God does not bring us up to heaven to live *with him*, but he actually promises to come down to Earth to live *with us*. This is a very different idea than many of us have had about our eternal life.

By the way, here's my definition of heaven: *where God dwells*. Since God comes down to dwell on Earth, we have a merging of heaven and Earth.

Question 3. **What is life like on this New Earth in the presence of God?**

Answer: This is a multi-pronged answer, because we need to examine three very significant aspects of our lives in his eternal kingdom.

Intimacy with God (Revelation 21:3)—Fulfillment of God's Promise

In the Revelation 21 passage there is an overarching promise: *They will be his people and God himself will be with them…* (21:3) *"… I will be his God and he will be my son"* (21:7). This promise echoes throughout the Old and New Testaments. When the kingdom is fully restored, we will realize God's promise to restore our intimacy with him has been fulfilled.

The Curse Removed (Revelation 21:4)—The Garden Recovered

All the pain and sorrow in this world will finally be wiped away. The struggle, loss and difficulties in our lives will be removed and redeemed. All that was lost in the Fall will be recovered. All the angst that was introduced to creation because of that fateful decision by our parents, Adam and Eve, will be finally and completely dissolved. What a beautiful picture of our heavenly Father tenderly wiping away our tears! Hallelujah!

All Things Made New (Revelation 21:5)—Restoration of All Things

This Earth and everything in it may be burned or tested by fire. It may be shaken to its very core in the transition from the present age to the next, but it will not be destroyed. Earth will not be left a formless mass as it was in the beginning. It will not be annihilated completely for eternity, but will be renewed and restored.

The Earth will finally attain its original mandate from the time of its creation; it will become the eternal home for those of us who have followed God.

The Earth will finally attain its original mandate from the time of its creation; it will become the eternal home for those of us who have followed God.

New Bodies Made for a New Earth

Consider how all of this connects with the previous teaching about our new bodies. Alcorn, in his book *Heaven*, quotes Anthony Hoekema: "Resurrected bodies are not intended just to float in space, or to flit from cloud to cloud. They call for a new earth on which to live and to work, glorifying God. The doctrine of the resurrection of the body, in fact, makes no sense whatever apart from the doctrine of the new earth." (p. 113)

Isn't this a different picture than most of us have been led to believe? This is far from being disembodied spirits, living an ethereal existence somewhere off in space. Instead, we will experience a physical resurrection and live on a physical Earth.

Instead of going to be with God in an ethereal heaven as only eternal spirits, we will live in our glorified bodies with God on the New Earth for eternity! Our heavenly Father himself will come and live among us. He will make his home on Earth. He will reclaim Eden for us, but in a new and better way.

It is important to realize that this concept of living eternally on a restored Earth in the presence of God does not originate in the last few chapters of Scripture. We can actually trace it back to the very beginning of God's plan for us.

Foundations of Hope

The foundations of the New Earth promise are found throughout the Old Testament.

Adam and Eve, the Original Mandate:

> **Then God said, "Let us make man in our image, in our likeness, and let them rule ... over all the earth, and over all the creatures that move along the ground."**
>
> *Genesis 1:26*

God purposed at the beginning that humankind would be the rulers, the stewards, of the Earth, over all creation. The Earth was created to be our home, and we were created to rule it.

Abraham, the New Promise: Our human relationship with the Earth got messed up with the Fall, because our original mandate to be stewards was broken, shattered. Consequently, God chose Abraham and made a covenant with him, giving him the promises in Genesis 12:1-3.

> **The LORD had said to Abram....**
>
> **"I will make you into a great nation and I will bless you; I will make your name great, and you will be a blessing.**
>
> **"I will bless those who bless you, and whoever curses you I will curse; and all peoples on earth will be blessed through you."**

This is part of the promised shalom of God—to live on the Earth in peace.

God purposed that through Abraham and his offspring he would work out the destiny of the whole world. God said that through Abraham *all peoples on earth will be blessed.*

In the New Testament, the apostle Paul talked about Abraham:

> **It was not through law that Abraham and his offspring received the promise that he would be heir of the world, but through the righteousness that comes by faith.**
>
> *Romans 4:13*

Implicit in this promise is that humankind (through Abraham and his offspring) would be heirs of this world or, specifically, of creation. Man's original mandate from God to rule and be stewards of the Earth would be restored. Psalm 37:11: *But the meek will inherit the land and enjoy great peace.* This is part of the promised shalom of God—to live on the Earth in peace.

Isaiah, a Glimpse of the Future: This Old Testament prophet often warned against disobedience and proclaimed God's punishment. The book of Isaiah is filled with frightful warnings, but it is also a book of great hope. It beautifully points us to when Jesus Christ, the Messiah, the suffering servant, would come to Earth to save us. But it does not end there. It also points us to a new life in the eternal Kingdom of God.

> **"Behold, I will create new heavens and a new earth. The former things will not be remembered nor will they come to mind."**
>
> *Isaiah 65:17*

The remaining verses of Isaiah 65 depict that life on the New Earth. Also through Isaiah, God says,

> **"As the new heavens and the new earth that I make will endure before me...so will your name and descendants endure."**
>
> *Isaiah 66:22*

You see, the Revelation of John is intimately tied to these promises of the Old Testament prophets. The New Heavens and the New Earth are not brand new ideas, but ancient ones.

Peter, Promises Remembered: The Apostle Peter, in the New Testament, spoke about Jesus and the end when he said,

> **"He must remain in heaven until the time comes for God to restore everything, as he promised long ago through his holy prophets."**
>
> *Acts 3:21*

Peter was referring to these *long ago* promises that we just read from Genesis and Isaiah.

"Blessed are the meek, for they will inherit the earth."

The absolutely amazing thing that I want you to remember above all is this: The restoration of the Earth—this idea of our eternal home being on the New Earth with God—was God's plan from the beginning. It is a recovery of Eden, the renewal of our intimate lives with God here on Earth, the ultimate fulfillment of the Lord's original design. God never gave up on his plan for the Earth because of the sinfulness and rebelliousness of humankind, but will restore the plan to its original intent. He will never bail on his kingdom plans, but will patiently restore his rule and reign, restore his creation, and restore his people.

This concept is crucial because it changes how we interpret what we hear and see in Jesus' message and ministry.

Jesus' Message and Ministry

His Message: *"Blessed are the meek, for they will inherit the earth."* (Matthew 5:5)

Does the perspective of the New Earth deepen and bring clarity to this beatitude? I confess that I never understood this beatitude before. I always thought the Earth was ultimately going to be burned up and destroyed. Why would I want to inherit something that would soon be gone?

His Ministry: Jesus brought recovery and healing, renewal and restoration to every person that he ministered to. What was he doing? Let's bring this New Earth understanding into the Lord's Prayer:

> **This, then, is how you should pray: "Our Father in heaven, hallowed be your name, your kingdom come, your will be done on earth as it is in heaven."**
>
> *Matthew 6:9–10*

Do you see this prayer in a different light now? Jesus was bringing heaven to Earth. He was bringing the realities of the future New Earth (when the Curse is removed) to our present reality. He was instructing his disciples, as well as you and me, to do the same.

The Revelation 21 passage talked about the beauty of our life on the New Earth. Now let's consider some of Jesus' words about our inheritance in the consummated Kingdom of God:

> **..."I tell you the truth, at the renewal of all things, when the Son of Man sits on his glorious throne ... everyone who has left houses or brothers or sisters or father or mother or children or fields for my sake will receive a hundred times as much and will inherit eternal life."**
>
> *Matthew 19:28–29*

Do you understand that differently now? Do you realize that the inheritance Jesus is talking about is received at the renewal of all things, received on the Earth that has been made new?

As children of the light, he is calling us to join the family business.

These are awesome truths about our future, but what effect should they have on our present? We need to remember to ask the Apostle Peter's question:

> **What kind of people ought you to be...as you look forward to the day of God?**
>
> *2 Peter 3:11b–12a*

Joining the *Family Business*

In light of our revealed future, I believe God has a call on our lives. As children of the light, he is calling us to join the family business.

By family I am talking about the family of God. What is God's family business? His business is what we have been talking about throughout our entire study of the kingdom. God's vision—his plan from the beginning—was the restoration of all things. This is the family of God's business.

In light of family business, here are Jesus' words:

> **"I no longer call you servants, because a servant does not know his master's business. Instead, I have called you friends, for everything that I learned from my Father I have made known to you."**
>
> *John 15:15*

Do we know our Father's business? If you have been paying attention, you can say an emphatic, "Yes!" He is in the business of reconciliation, renewal and restoration.

Imagination Station

I want you to think of it like this. Imagine that you're the son or daughter of Henry Ford. What was Henry Ford's business? Well, of course it was automobiles.

His vision was of an automobile that was inexpensive and available to the common man, so that we would all have motorized horseless carriages.

If you were a son or daughter of Henry Ford, you would have to decide whether or not to join in your father's vision, your father's business. Would you make a career in your father's business? Would you use your skills, gifts and abilities such as sales, accounting, or management to work directly for the Ford Company? Or, might you work on the outside but still be on the board of directors? All these are questions that you would need to answer as a son or a daughter of such a famous and successful man.

All of us as Christians need to ask these questions in response to knowing *our* Father's vision for his kingdom. Will we use the gifts, talents and abilities that God has given us for his kingdom or not? Will we serve as sons and daughters of the King in the family business, or will we opt out?

He has made his purposes of restoration and reconciliation known to us. Will you make a life out of this vision of restoration? Jesus certainly did. Do you hear his invitation to be imitators of him?

He has made his purposes of restoration and reconciliation known to us. Will you make a life out of this vision of restoration?

Lives of Restoration and Reconciliation

The Apostle Paul summed up God's call on our lives:

> **All this is from God, who reconciled us to himself through Christ and gave us the ministry of reconciliation: that God was reconciling the world to himself in Christ, not counting men's sins against them. And he has committed to us the message of reconciliation.**
>
> *2 Corinthians 5:18-19*

Paul's message is that we have been given the family business—this ministry of reconciliation, renewal and restoration.

How should you pray in response to this sacred ministry and message entrusted to you?

Day 46 | New Bodies, New Earth

Creation itself will be liberated from its bondage to decay

Have you ever put together a jigsaw puzzle? Most of us have, or at least we have tried to fit in a few pieces.

Scripture clearly teaches that God's ultimate plan is to restore or renew the Earth itself.

Imagination Station

Now imagine for a moment that I gave you a thousand-piece puzzle to put together. You lay out all the pieces, then you prop up the cover so you can see a picture of what you are striving for, the picture of the end result. This picture guides you. It helps when you look at the individual pieces and consider how they might fit together. Many people begin with the corners and straight-edged pieces. They build the outer frame and then work their way toward the middle.

Just suppose that I decided to be funny, and deliberately put a different set of pieces in the puzzle box. It might be a similar picture in color and motif, but half way through you would discover that you have pieces that just don't fit the picture on the box.

Our view of eternal life and the consummated kingdom has been like that. Many of us have been trying to fit pieces into the puzzle that just don't belong. The true picture of the consummated kingdom centers on the two important scriptural teachings that we have been learning.

1. **The New Earth**: Most of us have pictured our final home in some distant, ethereal, non-physical place off in space that we called heaven—a picture of harps, wings and clouds. But in fact, Scripture clearly teaches that God's ultimate plan is to restore or renew the Earth itself. The New Heaven will come to and merge with this New Earth and we will live eternally right here on Earth.

2. **The Physical Resurrection:** Most of us have believed in some kind of a resurrection but saw it as a non-physical, eternal life of the spirit or soul. We did not include physical bodies; we did not see the physicality of the resurrection. Scripture, however, plainly teaches that we will be like Christ. This includes our bodies. Our present earthly bodies that are weak and perishable will be raised imperishable, strong and full of glory.

With these two important truths framing our picture, we can now fill in some of the detail pieces of our view of eternal life, the consummated kingdom. Once when I preached a series of sermons on the topic "When Heaven Comes to Earth," I received some great questions as feedback: "What will our new bodies be like? I hope we get to choose!" "Will we have clothes on or will we be like Adam and Eve?" "What will the New Earth be like? What about eating and drinking?" "What about culture and the arts? What about work and athletics?" Good questions!

Many of these very specific questions are beyond our scope to answer here. We haven't yet been given the pieces to fill in these spaces in the puzzle. My hope is that we will begin to put in the pieces we already have so that our jigsaw puzzle view of eternal life can take shape and make sense in line with Scripture.

God has given us some crucial pieces of this puzzle of our future. On this side of heaven, we will never finish the puzzle, but we *can* keep adding pieces from Scripture and working toward the complete picture.

God has given us some crucial pieces of this puzzle of our future.

He Is Still Jesus, So You Will Still Be You

There is not a lot of scriptural material on what our resurrected bodies will be like but there are Scriptures that point us in the right direction.

Paul tells us *our* resurrected bodies will be like *Jesus'* resurrected body.

> **But our citizenship is in heaven. And we eagerly await a Savior from there, the Lord Jesus Christ, who, by the power that enables him to bring everything under his control, will transform our lowly bodies so that they will be like his glorious body.**
>
> *Philippians 3:20–21 (see also 1 John 3:2 and Romans 6:5)*

If Jesus' resurrected body is our model, then what was his body like? Let's see what we can learn from Luke 24:36–49.

> **While they were still talking about this, Jesus himself stood among them and said to them, "Peace be with you."**
>
> **They were startled and frightened, thinking they saw a ghost. He said to them, "Why are you troubled, and why do doubts rise in your minds? Look at my hands and my feet. It is I myself! Touch me and see; a ghost does not have flesh and bones, as you see I have."**
>
> **When he had said this, he showed them his hands and feet. And while they still did not believe it because of joy and amazement, he asked them, "Do you have anything here to eat?" They gave him a piece of broiled fish, and he took it and ate it in their presence.**
>
> **He said to them, "This is what I told you while I was still with you: Everything must be fulfilled that is written about me in the Law of Moses, the Prophets and the Psalms."**

> **Then he opened their minds so they could understand the Scriptures. He told them, "This is what is written: The Christ will suffer and rise from the dead on the third day, and repentance and forgiveness of sins will be preached in his name to all nations, beginning at Jerusalem. You are witnesses of these things. I am going to send you what my Father has promised; but stay in the city until you have been clothed with power from on high."**

The first thing to notice from this passage is that Jesus was still Jesus. When Jesus' disciples saw him for the first time after the resurrection, he said to them, *It is I myself!* Jesus still maintained his personality and distinguishing traits. Jesus had been resurrected and glorified, but he was still Jesus.

Not only was he still Jesus, but he remembered all his life and personal history. He related with people like Thomas, Mary, and Peter in very personal ways, clearly drawing on his previous experience with them.

Jesus had been resurrected and glorified, but he was still Jesus.

Think of Peter in his famous reinstatement at the end of the Gospel of John.

> **Peter was hurt because Jesus asked him the third time, "Do you love me?"**
> *John 21:17*

Why was he hurt? It was a reminder of Peter's denial of Jesus during the trial and crucifixion. Jesus' memory of his life and relationships with people had not been erased.

Because Jesus was still Jesus after the resurrection, we can project that *you* will still be *you* after your resurrection. Death does not destroy the *self*—the individuality of the people God created. The self is not absorbed into a universal "oneness," but continues.

We will not lose the personal identity that God endowed us with when we were born. Just as Moses and Elijah did not cease being themselves when they appeared in the transfiguration (Mark 9:4), so we will not cease being ourselves when we are glorified.

Some questions that people usually ask about the afterlife are, "Will I remember my life on Earth?" or "Will I recognize people that I knew in my life?" Because Jesus is our model, we can answer those questions in the affirmative.

By now I hope you are getting the idea of how we can use these pieces of our puzzle to help us develop a biblical picture of our lives in God's consummated kingdom, deducing it from the perspectives that God gives us in Scripture.

Renewed Bodies and the Renewed Earth

In talking about eternal life, the Apostle Paul makes an amazing link between human beings and the Earth. Listen to this fascinating connection:

> **I consider that our present sufferings are not worth comparing with the glory that will be revealed in us. The creation waits in eager expectation for the sons of God to be revealed. For the creation was**

> **subjected to frustration, not by its own choice, but by the will of the one who subjected it, in hope that the creation itself will be liberated from its bondage to decay and brought into the glorious freedom of the children of God.**
>
> **We know that the whole creation has been groaning as in the pains of childbirth right up to the present time. Not only so, but we ourselves, who have the first fruits of the Spirit, groan inwardly as we wait eagerly for our adoption as sons, the redemption of our bodies.**
>
> *Romans 8:18–23*

In this Scripture, Paul connects our redemption with creation's liberation from decay. The creation waits alongside us with *eager expectation* for the sons of God—you and me—to be renewed. Why? Because *our* renewal signals the renewal and restoration of *all* things. When we are freed, creation is freed. Our judgment and resurrection is the dawning of the new age of the Kingdom of God. So creation groans, we groan, everything groans in expectation of our adoption and redemption.

The creation waits alongside us with eager expectation for the sons of God—you and me—to be renewed.

Many theologians have noted that our bodies will be restored to function appropriately on the New Earth. This raises many intriguing questions. One question frequently asked is, "Will we have our five senses?" In Jesus' appearance to the disciples, he went out of his way to demonstrate that his resurrection was a physical one. His resurrected body could engage with the world in a way similar to the way it did before the crucifixion. He said, *Touch me*, and *Do you have anything here to eat?* I don't think the piece of broiled fish Jesus ate in front of the disciples was tasteless or odorless to him. Now apply this to our understanding of the New Earth. Why would the Father give Jesus his five senses, if he couldn't use them? Therefore, why would the Father resurrect our physical bodies if he weren't planning a physical place—the New Earth—for us to live?

Think of when Jesus said to his disciples during the last supper,

> **"...I will not drink of this fruit of the vine from now on until that day when I drink it anew with you in my Father's kingdom."**
>
> *Matthew 26:29*

The same Jesus (though resurrected) will drink wine with the same disciples (though resurrected) in the consummated kingdom on the New Earth. Will this wine be tasteless? I don't think so. In fact I bet it will be the best wine the disciples ever tasted.

The Earth will be *laid bare*, as Peter says in 2 Peter 3:10, but also renewed as he says in 2 Peter 3:13. Just as we will still be ourselves, so the Earth will still be the Earth. It will still be a physical place where we live. However, the Earth will be different in two important ways.

Paradise Lost, Paradise Regained

We don't have a lot of biblical information about the New Heavens and the New Earth, but we can fill in a few crucial pieces of the puzzle from Scripture. For example, every part of our lives that is associated with the Fall will pass away.

As we think about the New Heavens and New Earth, we must think of the beautiful passage that we keep returning to:

> **Then I saw a new heaven and a new earth...He will wipe every tear from their eyes. There will be no more death or mourning or crying or pain, for the old order of things has passed away.**
>
> *Revelation 21:1, 4*

Anything in this creation that causes pain, injury, death; anything that is part of the Fall; anything that was introduced to our creation because of sin—all will be removed. Think of disease and death, *big* things. Think of mosquito bites and minor aches and pains, *small* things. The new world will be liberated from *all* decay.

Let's begin to see the world through this new lens, with this new piece of the puzzle in place. Think of it for a moment. The relational strife between two brothers—that won't be a part of the New Earth, will it? Racism and prejudice—those won't be a part of the New Earth. Loss, disillusionment, divorce and pain—these won't be a part of the new world. Hallelujah!

Loss, disillusionment, divorce and pain—these won't be a part of the new world.

Are you beginning to groan for that new world? Are you beginning to eagerly await the inheritance that has been promised to you? But our inheritance isn't just about what is removed; it is also about what is added. This is an important puzzle piece to put in place. It's God's bonus, the extras, everything that's added.

What God *Renews* He *Improves*

Scripture points us not only to the Father's glorious promise that all the effects of the Fall will be removed, but also to his original plans and purposes that will be perfected. It will be a world not only *set free* from decay, but *gloriously* set free.

Yes, the Garden of Eden was our beautiful beginning, but compare it with our glorious end. The last two chapters of Scripture (Revelation 21–22) reveal themes of beauty, joy, glory, and the presence of God. Visualize the renewed Holy City of Jerusalem as described in Revelation.

> **It shone with the glory of God, and its brilliance was like that of a very precious jewel, like a jasper, clear as crystal....The wall was made of jasper, and the city of pure gold, as pure as glass. The foundations of the city walls were decorated with every kind of precious stone.**
>
> *Revelation 21:11, 18–19*

Whatever God renews he makes better than the original.

Perhaps the most thrilling part of the New Earth is the incredible presence of our God.

> **The city does not need the sun or the moon to shine on it, for the glory of God gives it light, and the Lamb is its lamp.**
>
> *Revelation 21:23*

Possibly it will be more glorious to us because, in contrast, we have known what it is like to live separated from the Father. And surely it will be more glorious because we will be there among all the generations of people who have loved God and now are fully loved.

We Receive an Upgrade

We just saw in Revelation how the New Earth is enhanced beyond God's original design. This is true of our bodies as well. Since neither the curse nor the Fall will affect our bodies, we will live vigorous lives, flourishing in ways we have never experienced before. What a great piece to add to the picture we're developing in the puzzle!

During our "When Heaven Comes to Earth" series, one of the members of the congregation commented to me, "I hope we get to choose our new bodies." This wonderful saint was implying that she wasn't too happy with her present body, so she was hoping to have some say in the next. After reflecting on her words, I pondered that we probably won't be able to choose; but not to worry, I'm sure we won't be disappointed. Our bodies will still be *our* bodies, but they will be made new in a glorious way.

Let us not sell the gospel short by understanding only a part of our promised inheritance—by not seeing the hope of new life and new bodies as God intended from the beginning.

A vibrant evangelical Christian, Joni Eareckson Tada has a significant ministry that reflects deeply on her life as a quadriplegic. She wrote a book entitled *Heaven: Your Real Home*. In it she writes: "I still can hardly believe it. I, with shriveled, bent fingers, atrophied muscles, gnarled knees, and no feeling from the shoulders down, will one day have a new body, light, bright, and clothed in righteousness – powerful and dazzling. Can you imagine the hope this gives someone spinal-cord injured like me? Or someone who is cerebral palsied, brain-injured, or who has multiple sclerosis? Imagine the hope this gives someone who is bipolar. No other religion, no other philosophy promises new bodies, hearts, and minds. Only in the Gospel of Christ do hurting people find such incredible hope." (p. 48–49)

Do we have a grand hope, or what? Let us not sell the gospel short by understanding only a part of our promised inheritance—by not seeing the hope of new life and new bodies as God intended from the beginning. And let us not sell the gospel of the kingdom short by missing the new body *and* New Earth promises. These are part of our glorious hope!

Picture Puzzle People

We are the people in the puzzle's picture. We are Christ's body, his Church. Imagine a Church that sought to bring the future to the present. Imagine a movement that was about restoring people—spirit, soul and body. Imagine a committed core of disciples that were about restoring creation for the glory of God. Imagine people living as kingdom disciples who are proclaiming the kingdom, bringing the kingdom, and making more kingdom disciples. Imagine a community of faith living in the presence of the future.

Anthony Hoekema reflects on some of the implications of these biblical truths in his comments: "As citizens of God's kingdom, we may not just write off the present earth as a total loss, or rejoice in its deterioration. We must indeed be working for a better world now. Our efforts to bring the kingdom of Christ into fuller manifestation are of eternal significance.... As we live on this earth, we are preparing for life on God's new earth. Through our kingdom service the building materials for that new earth are now being gathered. Bibles are being translated, peoples are being evangelized, believers are being renewed, and cultures are being transformed. Only eternity will reveal the full significance of what has been done for Christ here." (*The Bible and the Future*, p. 289)

Ministry Time

Live the Prayer

Consider the first part of the Lord's Prayer in light of the New Earth and new body perspectives.

> **"...Our Father in heaven, hallowed be your name, your kingdom come, your will be done on earth as it is in heaven..."**
>
> *Matthew 6:9–10*

"As we live on this earth, we are preparing for life on God's new earth."

Let's stop right there to ask some questions:

Where is his kingdom in full operation right now?

What does Jesus want us to pray for (and live for) so that the kingdom will come in ever-increasing measure?

In the future, where will his kingdom come in its fullness?

Now, pray the Lord's Prayer from a new perspective.

Enjoy the picture forming in the puzzle, even though it isn't yet complete. We have the frame and now we recognize many of the pieces.

DAY 47 | FINDING YOUR PLACE AT THE TABLE

For the wedding of the Lamb has come

During this final week of the *not yet* kingdom, we have wrestled with some astounding truths from Scripture. We have many questions regarding the end of all time, but at least we have some of the detail pieces and the framework of the puzzle from which to build.

The centurion humbly believed in a long-distance miracle.

I am sure you have heard the saying, "saving the best for last." Our emphasis in Day 47 is the end times or "when heaven comes to Earth." If we were to miss this Day we might as well have missed the whole week. It is definitely a topic we don't want to overlook!

Would you like me to tell you what is the most important thing to know and to meditate on about the end times? What *is* this most crucial of truths? It's ... well, I can't just *tell* you! That wouldn't be any fun at all. Don't you remember a truth better if you discover it on your own—with just a little help?

A Journey

Let's go on a little journey through Scripture, tracing one particular concept and see where it leads.

Look at the story of the Roman centurion in Matthew 8 whose servant is sick at home. Jesus agrees to go to his home and heal his servant, but the centurion says, "*I don't deserve to have you come under my roof. But just say the word, and I know my servant will be healed.*" The centurion humbly believed in a long-distance miracle. This is one of the few places that Jesus is "astonished" by someone's faith. Let's pick up the story:

> **When Jesus heard this, he was astonished and said to those following him, "I tell you the truth, I have not found anyone in Israel with such great faith. I say to you that many will come from the east and the west, and will take their places at the feast with Abraham, Isaac and Jacob in the kingdom of heaven.**

But the subjects of the kingdom will be thrown outside, into the darkness, where there will be weeping and gnashing of teeth." (emphasis added)

Matthew 8:10–12

Impressed by this Gentile's faith, Jesus used the opportunity to speak of a belief held by many Jews of his time that may be new to us. The belief centers on a great feast in heaven.

A Feast in the Kingdom of Heaven

This great feast in heaven was a developed concept in Jesus' day. It was believed to be a feast that all the children of God are called to take part in. To begin to understand this belief, I will ask you a few questions about the story we just read. (This is your self-discovery part!)

It was believed to be a feast that all the children of God are called to take part in.

Question 1. **Where is this feast?** Try to answer from the Matthew 8 passage above before you read further.

Answer: In the consummated kingdom, when heaven comes to the New Earth.

Please notice that Jesus was not speaking in a parable or figuratively. From this straight forward teaching, we can assume that Jesus is talking about a literal feast that he expected to happen in the new world.

Imagination Station

Now you use your imagination. Imagine a long table, perhaps a table made of richly carved wood. On this table there are hundreds, maybe even thousands, of gold place settings, made up of gold cups and plates and the most elegant silverware you have ever seen. Imagine that the table is covered with platters of some of the best food known to humankind, a literal smorgasbord of the finest foods—and don't forget the wine, good wine! Now a few more questions from the text.

Question 2. **Who is sitting at the table?** Again, please try to answer on your own before you continue to read.

Answer: From the text we know that at least Abraham, Isaac and Jacob (the patriarchs of the faith) are present. Also, it is implied that those who walked with God while they lived on this old Earth will be present. Jesus tells us that people will come *from the east and the west* (used to represent all four directions—east, west, north and south). Do you think the centurion has a place at the table? YES. But remember, he was not a Jew.

When Jesus said the *subjects of the kingdom will be thrown outside,* he was changing the current belief in those days about who was to have a place at the table. By this statement, he was challenging the traditional viewpoint.

Continue with the scene in your imagination. Picture all the saints you can think of from Scripture—Abraham, Moses, David, Paul and a host of others—all sitting at the table.

Many of the religious leaders and people of Jesus' day assumed that having a place at the table was about heritage; if you were born a Jew you were good to go. But Jesus was saying, no, it is not about heritage, it is about faith. The amazing faith of the non-Jewish centurion had earned him a spot at the banquet table of heaven. This was a radical departure from the thinking of the time.

Our next question needs to be a personal one. It is one that I can't answer for you.

Question 3. Do you have a place at the table?

Answer: Please enter once again into the scene you have been imagining. Take a moment to look down the table at all the people sitting there. You begin to feel a deep sadness because you don't see an open place for yourself.

I don't know about you, but when I think about taking a place at this kingdom feast, I get a little intimidated. I mean, it's hard to imagine pulling up a chair next to Abraham or any of the great men and women of the faith. Would there even be a place at the children's table for me? (Did you ever have those kids' tables for Thanksgiving or Christmas dinners? I was an older cousin, so I couldn't wait to get to the adult table.)

I think I could be happy being a doorkeeper if it meant living on the New Earth with the greats of the faith.

Or perhaps you and I could just be servants at this feast in the kingdom. We could wait on others at the table who seem far more important than we are. I am guessing that we would be pretty happy just serving tables or even working in the kitchen in the Kingdom of God.

It was David that said,

> **Better is one day in your courts than a thousand elsewhere; I would rather be a doorkeeper in the house of my God than dwell in the tents of the wicked.**
>
> *Psalm 84:10*

I think I could be happy being a doorkeeper if it meant living on the New Earth with the greats of the faith.

Got the Right Clothes?

Hold onto these thoughts, and let's go to another passage on this theme of a kingdom feast. In Matthew 22 Jesus told a parable that illustrates what the Kingdom of God is like.

> **"The kingdom of heaven is like a king who prepared a wedding banquet for his son. He sent his servants to those who had been invited to the banquet to tell them to come, but they refused to come."**
>
> *Matthew 22:2–3*

The servants ran out to tell all who were invited that the wedding banquet was ready, but … some paid no attention and went about their business … they don't have a place at the table. Some even seize the servants and mistreat them. Finally the king says, fine, if they won't come, invite others. Let's read on.

> **So the servants went out into the streets and gathered all the people they could find, both good and bad, and the wedding hall was filled with guests. But when the king came in to see the guests, he noticed a man there who was not wearing wedding clothes. "Friend," he asked, "how did you get in here without wedding clothes?" The man was speechless. Then the king told the attendants, "Tie him hand and foot, and throw him outside, into the darkness, where there will be weeping and gnashing of teeth." For many are invited, but few are chosen.**
>
> *Matthew 22:10–14*

Do you think that Jesus had a particular feast in mind when he was telling this parable?

Again, let's ask some questions of the text.

Question 1. What kind of feast is it? Please try and answer the question before you read the answer provided.

Answer: It is a wedding banquet for the son of the king.

Do you think that Jesus had a particular feast in mind when he was telling this parable? Of course, it is a parable illustrating the kingdom. He is talking about the feast in the Kingdom of Heaven, just like we have been reading about.

Now he throws a twist into the story. We are told that many people are invited, both *good and bad.* When the king comes across someone that doesn't seem to fit, he gets upset. Next question.

Question 2. What was the man lacking?

Answer: He doesn't have any wedding clothes! He has the wrong clothes on and it does not go well for him, does it? True, he accepted the invitation. But he comes to the banquet unprepared.

He doesn't get to stay at the wedding banquet, he doesn't belong. He has the wrong clothes.

Jesus is telling this about the end times, the feast in the Kingdom of Heaven. This parable leads us to a very significant question.

Question 3. Do *you* have your wedding clothes ready?

Here is the problem with this question. Not only can I not answer it for you, but we aren't exactly sure what the wedding clothes represent. They are figurative, of course, but if we don't know what they represent, we don't know if we have the right clothes or not.

We'd better find out though! In order to answer this question, we will look at the last book of the Bible, Revelation.

A Feast in the Throne Room

This is a glimpse of the throne room of heaven that has been given to John the Apostle.

> **Then a voice came from the throne, saying: "Praise our God, all you his servants, you who fear him, both small and great!" Then I heard what sounded like a great multitude, like the roar of rushing waters and like loud peals of thunder, shouting: "Hallelujah! For our Lord God Almighty reigns. Let us rejoice and be glad and give him glory! For the wedding of the Lamb has come, and his bride has made herself ready. Fine linen, bright and clean, was given her to wear." (Fine linen stands for the righteous acts of the saints.) Then the angel said to me, "Write: 'Blessed are those who are invited to the wedding supper of the Lamb!'" And he added, "These are the true words of God."**
>
> *Revelation 19:5–9*

Her works have been empowered by the Spirit, and she has spent her life on Earth sewing her wedding dress for the day when she will be joined to her beloved Bridegroom.

There is a very special invitation contained in this passage. Again, let's ask some questions.

Question 1. **Whose wedding is it?**

Answer: The Lamb, the Son (We already knew this, didn't we?)

Question 2. **Who is the bride?** Keep trying to answer for yourself before you continue reading.

Answer: You and I are, the true Church, the saints.

Now here is the climactic question we are looking for:

Question 3. **What is her (our) wedding dress made of?** (Did you see it in the text? Look again.)

Answer: *The righteous acts of the saints.* Isn't it great when Scripture directly answers our questions?

Randy Alcorn speaks about this: "It's only because of the Bridegroom's work that the chosen princess, the church, can enter the presence of her Lord. Yet her wedding dress is woven through her many acts of faithfulness while away from her Bridegroom on the fallen Earth. The picture is compelling. Each prayer, each gift, each hour of fasting, each kindness to the needy, all of these are the threads that have been woven together into this wedding dress. Her works have been empowered by the Spirit, and she has spent her life on Earth sewing her wedding dress for the day when she will be joined to her beloved Bridegroom." (*Heaven*, p. 199–200)

Is that not a compelling picture? When we think about the wedding feast in the Kingdom of God, don't you want to have faith like the centurion? Doesn't it make you want to live such a life that you are weaving your wedding clothes together with every act of kindness, with every word of truth spoken, with every loss suffered for Christ Jesus?

Actually, you can also answer Question 3 from Matthew 21:43,

> **"Therefore I tell you that the kingdom of God will be taken away from you and given to a people who will produce its fruit."**

Producing the fruit of the kingdom is how we weave the wedding clothes.

Imagination Station

> *We* get to sit next to Jesus! *We* are the Bride of Christ, the Church.

Return in your mind to that long table. Return to the finest of foods, with all the saints sitting at their places. Do you remember? There wasn't an open chair for you. But, before you begin to worry, let me ask you this, where does the bride sit at a wedding banquet? Next to the groom. *We* get to sit next to Jesus! *We* are the Bride of Christ, the Church.

He is calling to us; he has saved this place for us. He is not calling you to be a servant, a doorkeeper, a waiter, a cook. The place he has saved isn't at the children's table. It's right next to him—to be close to him, to eat with him, to drink with him, to see his face, to love him and be loved by him.

What kind of extravagant love is this? This is the whole point of eternity. This is God's plan. In his great love story, he redeems us, heals us, draws us in close and celebrates us as his beloved. If we neglect this, we miss the whole point of when heaven comes to Earth.

The Main Point of "*with*"

In Revelation 21:3 we read:

> **..."Now the dwelling of God is *with* men, and he will live *with* them. They will be his people, and God himself will be *with* them and be their God."** (emphasis added)

Think of how amazing this is: The God of the Universe, the Creator of all things, wants to be *with* you and me. He speaks such thrilling words—"I am not just going to bring *you* into *my* presence. I love you so much that *I myself will come* and make your home my home. I will do this so we can be together forever. Why? Because I love you that much." (paraphrase mine) It is the ultimate love story.

What Kind of People Ought You to Be?

Let Jesus answer the question:

> **"Be dressed ready for service and keep your lamps burning, like men waiting for their master to return from a wedding banquet, so that when he comes and knocks they can immediately open the door for him. It will be good for those servants whose master finds them watching when he comes. I tell you the truth, he will dress himself to serve, will have them recline at the table and will come and wait on them."**
>
> *Luke 12:35–37*

First of all, did anything catch your attention about this parable? Jesus uses the wedding banquet metaphor but switches it around—here *we* are waiting for our master to come from the banquet. And if we are dressed for service (connection to Revelation 19:8) what does the master do? Incredibly, *he* actually serves *us*! Think of a groom standing up and gently saying to his bride, "Can I get anything for you, my beloved?"

From these passages we realize that in this fallen world, we are called to weave our wedding clothes together with service, acts of righteousness and kindness, with works of the kingdom. Yes, we are called to serve just like our savior, our groom, serves. We are to be like him.

> …we are called to weave our wedding clothes together with service, acts of righteousness and kindness….

Ⓡ Reflection—Prepare for *Your* Wedding

Brides put a lot into preparing for the big day to come. In light of our big day, what does that preparation look like for you right now? How is our servant-bridegroom calling *us* to acts of service, righteousness and kindness? Now meditate on this verse:

> **"… whoever wants to become great among you must be your servant … just as the Son of Man did not come to be served, but to serve, and to give his life as a ransom for many."**
>
> *Matthew 20:26, 28*

Days 48 & 49 | The Impossible Promise

He will do even greater things than these

For our final small group together, I want to end where we started. In the Introduction, we began with some words from Jesus about how his disciples could carry on his mission. Read these words again. Remember, they are also his words to you and me.

> "I tell you the truth, anyone who has faith in me will do what I have been doing. He will do even greater things than these, because I am going to the Father."

The Impossible Promise:

> **"…The words I say to you are not just my own. Rather, it is the Father, living in me, who is doing his work. Believe me when I say that I am in the Father and the Father is in me; or at least believe on the evidence of the miracles themselves. *I tell you the truth, anyone who has faith in me will do what I have been doing. He will do even greater things than these, because I am going to the Father.* And I will do whatever you ask in my name, so that the Son may bring glory to the Father. You may ask me for anything in my name, and I will do it. If you love me, you will obey what I command. And I will ask the Father, and he will give you another Counselor to be with you forever – the Spirit of truth…."** (emphasis added)
>
> *John 14:10–17*

If you recall from the Introduction, we called this the *Impossible Promise.* As we thought about who said these words, and all that he said and did when he lived here physically on the Earth, we noted that this promise seemed ridiculously impossible. But it is my hope that from your exploring Jesus' big idea and living in these days of the kingdom, you will now see the Impossible Promise in a different light. Let's ask a few questions of each part of the promise (see verse 12 in italics in the passage above):

1. **In John 14:12, Jesus was speaking specifically to the 12 disciples. Do you think that the promises emphasized above were meant just for them?**

2. **When Jesus said …*will do what I have been doing*…, what are some of the things you think he had in mind?**

3. **Jesus said that we would ...*do even greater things than these*.... If Jesus was the greatest human being to ever live, how in the world could he say we would do even greater things than he did?**

4. **Jesus ends this promise with the phrase ...*because I am going to the Father*. Relating to this promise, what is so significant about him going to the Father?**

5. **In the Introduction, I propose that Jesus did not intend the words above to be the *impossible* promise. It was to be the *guiding principle* for his disciples to follow. Has studying Jesus' big idea and living in these days of the kingdom helped you understand this?**

6. **How do you think Jesus' promise connects with the Kingdom of God? See Matthew 12:28.**

The Lesser-Known *Great Commission*

In the context of your life—what does it look like for you to live in the kingdom?

I would now like to commission you for the work of the kingdom according to the lesser-known version of the Great Commission found in the final words of the Gospel of Mark:

> **He said to them, "Go into all the world and preach the good news to all creation. Whoever believes and is baptized will be saved, but whoever does not believe will be condemned. And these signs will accompany those who believe: In my name they will drive out demons; they will speak in new tongues; they will pick up snakes with their hands; and when they drink deadly poison, it will not hurt them at all; they will place their hands on sick people, and they will get well."**
>
> **After the Lord Jesus had spoken to them, he was taken up into heaven and he sat at the right hand of God. Then the disciples went out and preached everywhere, and the Lord worked with them and confirmed his word by the signs that accompanied it.**
>
> *Mark 16:15–20*

In the context of your life—in your family, in your work place, in your school, in your church—what does it look like for you to live in the kingdom?

What are the next steps for you as you continue to obey the lifelong command of Jesus? "...*Seek first his kingdom and his righteousness*...." (Matthew 6:33)

Ministry Time

In light of the answers shared to the questions above, please take the remaining time to pray for one another.

Bonus Questions: Why does this study contain 50 days? Does the number 50 have a connection with the ministry of the kingdom?

Day 50 | The Year of Jubilee

It shall be a jubilee for you

Congratulations! You made it. I commend you for wrestling through the concepts and challenges of the last 50 days. I trust that you have not only wrestled conceptually, but also experientially. My hope is that you have taken some risks, in terms of sharing and praying for others, and that the Lord has blessed you in those kingdom activities.

The number 50 is connected to an ancient concept found in the Old Testament.

While living and working through the last 49 days of the kingdom, have you ever asked the question, "Why *fifty* days? Why not 40 or 60?" Fifty is not a random number that I chose for our study of Jesus' big idea. It actually has profound significance as it relates to Jesus' ministry and message. So this is a bonus day, no extra charge.

The number 50 is connected to an ancient concept found in the Old Testament. Many scholars believe that it served as the foundation of Jesus' teaching and preaching of the Kingdom of God and the restoration of all things.

In fact, this ancient concept was a significant part of the history of the Jewish people. Even though the concept has been lost to many, it has also served a role in our own history here in the United States.

Perhaps one of the primary reasons that this profound idea is not familiar to many of us is because it is buried deep within the Old Testament, in a book where many of us rarely tread, in the book of Leviticus.

The Year of Jubilee

For our final day, we will look at the concept of *Jubilee*. It appeared in the early stages of the nation of Israel, when God was in the process of forming the desert wanderers into a nation, a kingdom. He established laws and a judicial system. He instituted the rituals and the practices of faith. He created the feasts and the agricultural calendar. Then right in the middle of these directives, he introduced this unprecedented and surprising idea to his people, the *Year of Jubilee*.

> **Count off seven sabbaths of years—seven times seven years—so that the seven sabbaths of years amount to a period of forty-nine years. Then have the trumpet sounded everywhere on the tenth day of the seventh month; on the Day of Atonement sound the trumpet throughout your land. Consecrate the fiftieth year and proclaim liberty throughout the land to all its inhabitants. It shall be a jubilee for you; each one of you is to return to his family property and each to his own clan. The fiftieth year shall be a jubilee for you; do not sow and do not reap what grows of itself or harvest the untended vines. For it is a jubilee and is to be holy for you; eat only what is taken directly from the fields.**
>
> *Leviticus 25:8–12*

Now, some have called this a *Super Sabbath* because it is related to the Sabbath year—the seventh year, the resting year. They were supposed to take a break, agriculturally, every seventh year (Leviticus 25:1–7). After seven of these seven-year cycles, in the 50th year, they were to blow the trumpet and declare liberty and freedom throughout the land for everybody, a kind of *Super Sabbath*.

…in the 50th year, they were to blow the trumpet and declare liberty and freedom throughout the land for everybody, a kind of *Super Sabbath*.

Leviticus 25 goes on to explain the details of Jubilee, and I want you to understand three of its overarching concepts:

Restoration / Liberation from Debt:

> **"If one of your countrymen becomes poor and is unable to support himself among you, help him…."**
>
> *Leviticus 25:35*

At the year of Jubilee all debts were to be cancelled, tossed out, forgotten and forgiven. Not a bad concept. Think about this for today: If 2012 were the year of Jubilee, then all our credit card debts, all our mortgages, car loans, and medical bills would be forgiven. We would be restored to complete financial health. Doesn't it make you want to call your credit card company and make a suggestion? The next concept is very similar.

Redemption of Land:

> **"Throughout the country that you hold as a possession, you must provide for the redemption of the land."**
>
> *Leviticus 25:24*

You see, when the Jewish people entered the promised land, God apportioned it out. Every tribe and family had its own section. If they experienced hard times and had to sell off the land to make ends meet, God said this was not to be permanent. Why? Because it was really *his* land. The people were just leasing it from him. He had given it out as he had chosen. When the trumpet was slated to blow on the Day of Atonement in the 50th year, it was to be the time of restoration. God's plan was that the poor impoverished soul, who had lost his family inheritance, was to be given a second chance. The family could redeem or retake the land that God had given them in the beginning. Imagine that!

Release from Slavery:

> **"Then he [the slave] and his children are to be released, and he will go back to his own clan and to the property of his forefathers."**
>
> *Leviticus 25:41*

Closely related to debt was slavery. In ancient times if people became really desperate they would sell themselves (and family members) as slaves. God said that when such a thing happened, no one should treat these people as slaves; rather, they should be treated as hired hands. But when the trumpet blew on the Day of Atonement in the fiftieth year, they and their children were to be released, set free. It was to be the glorious *Year of Jubilee.*

 **Imagination Station** Imagine yourself as an Israelite. Due to misfortune like famine, or your own poor economic decisions, you can't seem to make ends meet. You begin to accrue debt and finally reach a point that in order to survive you have to start selling off portions of your land, the land given to your family by God. In spite of selling your land, things get worse. You are forced to sell yourself and even your family to the service of others just for survival. In essence, you have become an indentured servant. All is lost, even your children are now bound with the shackles of poverty and slavery. Five—ten—fifteen years go by. Your family still labors under this bondage.

He knew that we would need release and restoration....

Now imagine another day. It is not an ordinary day. Not only is it the *Day of Atonement*—a day when your sins are wiped away and your relationship with God is restored—it is the *tenth day of the seventh month...of the fiftieth year...* (Leviticus 25:9–10). You hear the trumpet blast and realize that this is the sound that heralds liberty in the land, restoration of what has been lost, freedom from the oppression of poverty and slavery! Oh, how that music resounds in your ears!

Perhaps another poor soul not too far away from you starts running and yelling words of release: *Liberty – Restoration – Redemption – Freedom*! All your shackles of poverty are thrown off. The land that your forefathers received but lost long ago is redeemed. The cycle of sin and poverty has been broken, and with that your dignity and sense of worth are restored. Your hope and purpose are recovered anew. What a day! What a concept! It's the *Day of Jubilee.*

The Heart of God

Now consider what this idea of the Jubilee tells us about the heart of God. This ancient concept reveals the God we worship—who he is and what he desires for his people.

Even before his people entered the Promised Land, even before they had really become a kingdom of priests or a holy nation, our Heavenly Father knew that people like you and me would inevitably fall into places of need. He knew that we would need release and restoration, that we would need redemption in all its many forms.

So from his immensely gracious heart, he built into the seasonal rhythms of life for his people this special year of liberation and redemption, this Year of Jubilee. God's heart is to heal, renew and redeem his people from everything that would bind or rob them of all he desires. ***Hallelujah***!

The Jubilee Influence

Whether we realize it or not, this incredible concept of Jubilee has had a significant influence on several different areas of our lives.

Jubilee and the United States. If you think about the concepts contained in the Jubilee, especially liberty and freedom, you realize that as a nation, we have been profoundly influenced.

What would you say are the two most famous symbols of liberty in our nation? Right away don't we think of the Statue of Liberty and the Liberty Bell?

Did you know that the Liberty Bell has a passage of Scripture inscribed across it? Do you know which passage? We read it a little earlier...*proclaim liberty throughout all the land unto all the inhabitants thereof.* (Leviticus 25:10, KJV)

God's heart is to heal, renew and redeem his people from everything that would bind or rob them of all he desires.

Hanging in Philadelphia, the bell has been rung at some of the most crucial times in our nation's history. Tradition holds that it was rung at the first public reading of the Declaration of Independence.

The Liberty Bell, with the Jubilee passage of Scripture inscribed on it, has become a symbol of our nation, the land of the free. Throughout our history, people have come seeking liberty and freedom—religious, political and economic. All of these freedoms are symbolized by the Liberty Bell.

The Liberty Bell grew in prominence and recognition when it was adopted as the symbol of the abolitionist movement to fight slavery and oppression. These concepts were also significant for the modern civil rights movement, as people of color cried out for justice and freedom.

Similar to the Old Testament prophets who challenged people to live out God's provision of release, recovery and redemption, so Martin Luther King Jr. called our nation to put these divine provisions into practice. Now we have an even greater understanding of Dr. King's "I Have a Dream" speech. In it he calls out, "Let freedom ring! Let freedom ring!"

Jubilee and Jesus. At the very beginning of Jesus' public ministry, Luke records for us how he was handed a scroll of the prophet Isaiah. As Jesus read from the famous words of Isaiah 61, it was as if he was not only announcing the beginning of his ministry, but also the beginning of a new day, a new time in history.

> **"The Spirit of the Lord is on me, because he has anointed me to preach good news to the poor. He has sent me to proclaim freedom for the prisoners and recovery of sight for the blind, to release the oppressed, to proclaim the year of the Lord's favor."**
>
> *Luke 4:18–19*

Did you catch the elements of Jubilee? Some have called this pronouncement a "Jubilean Manifesto."[19] When Jesus announced the *year of the Lord's favor,* the Israelites of his time would have been reminded of the Year of Jubilee—the Jubilee time of release, recovery and freedom. This is the essence of his message and ministry. This is the good news of the kingdom.

Jesus often took truths and concepts from the Old Testament and perfected and expanded them. If we look at his ministry and how he fulfilled such proclamations, we realize that he wasn't only talking about economics and poverty, about civil liberties and freedoms. He was applying the Jubilee to the deepest places of the human heart, the spiritual and eternal needs of restoration and redemption.

You may have achieved financial freedom in your life—even becoming rich—but if you are still struggling under the indebtedness of sin, then you are truly poor.

You may be living free from prejudice or injustice today, but if you are still held captive by the enemy of our souls, then you have not truly been released and set free.

This is the essence of his message and ministry. This is the good news of the kingdom.

You may be a citizen of this amazing nation, living in the "land of the free", but if you have not invited Jesus Christ into the center of your life and received his spiritual forgiveness and redemption, then you are not a citizen of the Kingdom of God. You are not truly free.

In an amazing way, Jesus takes these incredible ancient concepts, and expands them to all of life. He sees us as we truly are—broken people in desperate need of liberation—people bound by sin in need of forgiveness—people separated from God and in need of restoration—people broken by the Fall, with broken souls, broken relationships, broken emotions, broken bodies and in desperate need of healing. Jesus proclaimed "*the time has come, …the Kingdom of God is near…*" (Mark 1:15) and—the year of Jubilee has arrived.

Our Jubilee is not meant to be a calendar year like in the Old Testament; it is intended to be an age, this age. The Jubilee is meant to be the kingdom coming; an age of the Church joining in the Jubilean mission of God. It is a mission of liberation and release, a mission of reconciliation and redemption, a mission of the restoration of all things. This is why Paul quoted from Isaiah 49:8:

"I tell you, now is the time of God's favor, now is the day of salvation."
2 Corinthians 6:2

I tell you today, we are still in that time; we are still living in this day of God's favor. Have you recognized it yet?

19. Michael Schluter and John Ashcroft, *Jubilee Manifesto: A framework, agenda and strategy for Christian social reform.* Downers Grove, IL: InterVarsity Press, 2005.

Living in the Days of the Kingdom

Our 50-day spiritual journey isn't just about understanding Jesus' vision, but about adopting *his* vision as *our* vision. Only from such a perspective can we make sense of what Jesus says in Luke 12:32:

> **"Do not be afraid, little flock, for your Father has been pleased to give you the kingdom."**

And then again in Luke 22:29:

> **"And I confer on you a kingdom, just as my Father conferred one on me."**

He calls us to understand the kingdom, but he does not end there. He also calls us to receive the kingdom, to enter the kingdom, to live the kingdom and ultimately to bring the kingdom to others. That is the only way that the *impossible* promise that we began our journey with can become *possible.*

May his kingdom come and his will be done, on Earth as it is in heaven.

Remember the promise:

> **"I tell you the truth, anyone who has faith in me will do what I have been doing. He will do even greater things than these, because I am going to the Father."**
>
> *John 14:12*

Jesus doesn't want us just to *understand* how he brings the true Jubilee—how in each person's life he brings restoration, redemption and release. He wants us to *join* him in bringing it. This is the essence of being a disciple of Jesus, a kingdom disciple.

He is calling you right now to declare the *time of God's favor* (2 Corinthians 6:2b) and, by the power of the Holy Spirit, to bring God's favor into people's lives. That is why Jesus went to the Father—so we might know God's power and cooperate with him in bringing his kingdom to Earth.

The Ultimate Jubilee

Personally, it has been an incredible experience to study, pray, write and teach about Jesus' big idea—the Kingdom of God. I know that my life and ministry will never be the same because of this experience. My hope and prayer are that these 50 days will be just the beginning for you.

You see, someday, the kingdom tension of the *already but not yet* will be resolved. Someday, this age of *coming* will become the age of *arrived.* Someday a final trumpet will sound and the age of *restoring* will become the age of the *restored.* Someday, Jesus will come back, and what we see in part now we will then fully see.

But until that day comes, he calls us to live in the days of the *in process of coming* kingdom—to seek, to look, to yearn, to fight, to pray. May we live out our calling as sons and daughters of the kingdom. May his kingdom come and his will be done, on Earth as it is in heaven.

Bibliography

The Alpha Course Manual, Alpha North America, NY, 1995.

Alcorn, Randy C. *Heaven*. Wheaton, IL: Tyndale House, 2004.

Banister, Doug. *The Word & Power Church*. Grand Rapids, MI: Zondervan Pub., 1999.

Boyd, Gregory A. *God at War: the Bible & Spiritual Conflict*. Downers Grove, IL: InterVarsity Press, 1997.

Colson, Charles W. *Born Again*. Grand Rapids, MI: Chosen Books, 2008.

Deere, Jack. *Surprised by the Power of the Spirit: Discovering How God Speaks and Heals Today*. Grand Rapids, MI: Zondervan Pub., 1993.

——. *Surprised by the Voice of God: How God Speaks Today through Prophecies, Dreams, and Visions*. Grand Rapids, MI: Zondervan Pub., 1996.

France, Richard T. *New Bible Commentary: 21st Century Edition,* section on *Matthew*. Leicester, England: InterVarsity Press, 1994.

Grudem, Wayne. *Systematic Theology: An Introduction to Biblical Doctrine*. Grand Rapids, MI: Zondervan Pub., 2004.

Hiebert, Paul G. *The Missiological Implications of Epistemological Shifts: Affirming Truth in a Modern/Postmodern World*. Harrisburg, PA: Trinity Press International, 1999.

Hoekema, Anthony A. *The Bible and the Future*. Grand Rapids, MI: Wm. B. Eerdmans Publishing Company, 1994.

Jackson, Bill. *The Quest for the Radical Middle: A History of the Vineyard*. Cape Town: Vineyard International Pub., 1999.

Johnson, Bill. *When Heaven Invades Earth: A Practical Guide to a Life of Miracles*. Shippensburg, PA: Treasure House, 2003.

Kallman, Ted, and Isaiah Kallman. *Stark Raving Obedience*. Grand Rapids, MI: EMET, 2006.

Ladd, George Eldon. *The Gospel of the Kingdom: Scriptural Studies in the Kingdom of God*. Grand Rapids, MI: Wm. B. Eerdmans Publishing Company, 1959.

——. *The Presence of the Future: The Eschatology of Biblical Realism*. Grand Rapids, MI: Wm. B. Eerdmans Publishing Company, 1974.

Little, Paul. *How to Give Away Your Faith*, 2nd edition. Downers Grove, IL: InterVarsity Press, 1988.

MacNutt, Francis. *Healing*. Notre Dame, IN: Ave Maria, 1974.

Morneau, Bishop Robert F. "God in Our Midst: The Beatitudes' Promises", *Every Day Catholic* newsletter. URL: http://www.americancatholic.org/Newsletters/EDC/ag0102.asp, January 2002.

Munroe, Myles. *Rediscovering the Kingdom: Ancient Hope for Our 21st Century World*. Shippensburg, PA: Destiny Image, 2004.

Raysbrook, Randy D. *One Verse Evangelism: How to Share Christ's Love Conversationally and Visually*. Colorado Springs, CO: NavPress, 2000.

Richardson, Rick. *Reimagining Evangelism: Inviting Friends on a Spiritual Journey*. Downers Grove, IL: InterVarsity, 2006.

Sapp, Roger. *Performing Miracles and Healing: A Biblical Guide to Developing a Christ-like Supernatural Ministry*. Southlake, TX: All Nations Publications, 2000.

Schluter, Michael and John Ashcroft. *Jubilee Manifesto: a framework, agenda and strategy for Christian social reform*. Leicester, England: InterVarsity Press, 2005.

Stott, John R.W. *The Spirit, the Church, and the World: The Message of Acts*. Downers Grove, IL: InterVarsity Press, 1990.

Stott, John R.W. *The Message of Ephesians: God's New Society*. Downers Grove, IL: InterVarsity Press, 1986.

Tada, Joni Eareckson. *Heaven: Your Real Home*. Grand Rapid, MI: Zondervan Pub., 1996.

Wagner, Peter C. *How to Have a Healing Ministry Without Making Your Church Sick*. Ventura, CA: Regal Books, 1988.

Walker, Paul. "Holy Spirit Gifts and Power." *Spirit-Filled Life Study Bible*. Nelson, Nashville, 1991.

Weible, Wayne. *Medjugorje: the Message*. 25th Anniversary Edition ed. Brewster, MA: Paraclete, 2006.

Willard, Dallas. *Hearing God: Developing a Conversational Relationship with God*. Downers Grove, IL: InterVarsity Press, 1999.

Wimber, John with Kevin Springer. *Power Evangelism*, San Francisco: Harper & Row, 1986.

——. *Power Healing*, San Francisco: Harper & Row, 1987.

Wright, Henry. *A More Excellent Way; Pathways of Wholeness Spiritual Roots of Disease*. New Kensington, PA: Whitaker House, 2009.

Wright, N. T. *Surprised by Hope: Rethinking Heaven, the Resurrection, and the Mission of the Church*. First ed. New York: HarperOne, 2008.